Things Hold Together

"Parler's portrait of Yoder's understanding of Christ and culture reveals the gross distortions of many previous portrayals. However, this informative book does much more: it shows Yoder to be offering the Christian community a way into the future that embodies love and service while providing a clear witness to the gospel."
—Mark Thiessen Nation, author of *John Howard Yoder: Mennonite Patience, Evangelical Witness, Catholic Convictions*

"Since Yoder read widely, mined gems from multiple traditions, and incorporated them into his project, it often takes thinkers beyond his tradition to see themes in his work that resonate deeply with their own."
—John Nugent, professor of Old Testament, Great Lakes Christian College

"By reading Yoder's body of work as a whole, Parler reorients our attention to the strong trinitarian logic that grounds his understanding of Christian pacifism. We are in his debt."
—Chris K. Huebner, associate professor of theology and philosophy, Canadian Mennonite University

Things Hold Together

John Howard Yoder's Trinitarian Theology of Culture

Branson L. Parler

Foreword by Richard J. Mouw

Herald Press
Harrisonburg, Virginia
Waterloo, Ontario

Library of Congress Cataloging-in-Publication Data
Parler, Branson L., 1980-
    Things hold together : John Howard Yoder's Trinitarian theology of
culture / Branson L. Parler.
        p. cm.
    Includes bibliographical references and index.
    ISBN 978-0-8361-9618-4 (pbk. : alk. paper) 1. Christianity and
culture. 2. Yoder, John Howard. 3. Trinity—History of doctrines—20th
century. 4. Christian sociology. I. Title.
  BR115.C8P3255 2012
  232—dc23
                                                    2012025294

Scripture from *The Holy Bible, New International Version*®, NIV®
Copyright © 1973, 1978, 1984, 2011 by Biblica, Inc.™ Used by permission. All rights reserved worldwide.

THINGS HOLD TOGETHER
Copyright © 2012 by Herald Press, Harrisonburg, Virginia 22802
    Released simultaneously in Canada by Herald Press,
    Waterloo, Ontario N2L 6H7. All rights reserved.
Library of Congress Control Number: 2012025294
International Standard Book Number: 978-0-8361-9618-4
Printed in United States of America
Cover design and photo by Merrill Miller
Design by Joshua Byler

To order or request information, please call 1-800-245-7894 in the U.S.
or 1-800-631-6535 in Canada. Or visit www.heraldpress.com.

16 15 14 13 12   10 9 8 7 6 5 4 3 2 1

For Sarah

Contents

Foreword

John Howard Yoder started writing important books in the early 1960s. For many of us, however, he really appeared on the theological scene in 1972, with his *The Politics of Jesus*. For me, reading that book began to cure me of many of my misconceptions about Anabaptist life and thought.

I say that reading Yoder's book was the *beginning* of a cure, because my curative process has taken a long time—indeed, as I discovered in reading this very fine study of Yoder's theology of culture, it is still going on.

John Yoder and I engaged in many exchanges, both in written form and in face-to-face public settings. One of my favorite stories of those exchanges is about a response that Yoder gave to a question from an audience at a Mennonite campus. After he and I had gone back and forth about "Christ and culture," someone asked Yoder what he saw as the most basic matter on which he and I disagreed. His answer was memorable: "Mouw wants to say, 'Fallen, but *created*,' and I want to say, 'Created, but *fallen*.'"

The important point to be learned from that formulation is that the real difference between, say, a Kuyperian kind of Calvinist view of culture and the perspective set forth by Yoder is not that one side thinks primarily about the continuing goodness of creation while the other focuses almost exclusively on fallenness. Each of the perspectives is trying to find the right way of construing the relationship between God's creating purposes and the tragic consequences of human sin.

In my own wrestlings with Yoder's thought, I have thought of myself as trying, more than most Calvinists do in depicting Anabaptist life and thought, to give Yoder credit for having developed a complex theology of culture. Now Branson Parler's detailed study of Yoder on culture has convinced me that things are even more complex than I had been acknowledging.

As Branson reports in his own introduction to this study, I was one of the official evaluators for the doctoral dissertation that served as the basis for this published version. I gave that dissertation very high marks and, needless to say, I do the same for this book. It is a wonderful exploration of the highly original contribution that John Howard Yoder made to the study of the foundations of Christian discipleship as we prepared to enter the 21st century. I am greatly indebted to Yoder for all that he taught me. And now I am also indebted to Branson Parler for making it clear to me that the learning process still continues.

—*Richard J. Mouw, president,*
Fuller Theological Seminary
June, 2012

Preface

John Howard Yoder's most well-known work remains *The Politics of Jesus*. The Jesus-centered focus this title implies causes some non-Mennonites to slot Yoder into their preconceived notions of Mennonites and others in the Anabaptist theological stream. Anabaptists, they feel, focus on Jesus and ignore the Old Testament, creation, nature, or natural law. Anabaptists focus on being faithful to Jesus and reject culture. Anabaptists reject the sword and participation in the state, which means that they see power as bad. What is worse, because the state is grounded in creation, Anabaptists reject the goodness of God's original creation and posit a sharp divide between God as Creator (Father) and God as Redeemer (Son). Given these assumptions, the knee-jerk responses to Yoder's Christological pacifism are many: critics accuse Yoder of having a problematic Christology, of denying the Trinity by focusing only on Jesus, of having a sharp disjunction between nature and grace, or creation and redemption, and of rejecting the goodness of creation.

As someone who has been educated in evangelical and Reformed institutions and who works from within the Reformed tradition, I have both seen these responses in scholarly publications and heard them in casual conversations. And it is not only outsiders to the Mennonite tradition who agree with this way of reading Yoder, because some Mennonites have leveled similar charges against Yoder. In short, this way of reading Yoder sees things falling apart: Father and Son are set against each other, creation and redemption are divorced from each other, and nature and grace become opposites rather than proper interrelated partners.

This book is my attempt to spell out why I see this way of reading Yoder as wrong. This way of reading Yoder depends on many factors, especially when employed by those outside the Mennonite tradition: the typical criticisms of Anabaptists that date back to the sixteenth century, the pervasive influence of H. Richard Niebuhr's *Christ and Culture*, and certain theological traditions such as Lutheran two kingdoms, Roman Catholic natural law, and Reformed views of the state and warfare. This interpretation of Yoder also depends on reading bits and pieces of Yoder, and then drawing broad conclusions about him.

In contrast, this book argues for reading Yoder wholly and holistically. Many authors will engage Yoder, but only rely on one or two sources to do so (perhaps *The Politics of Jesus* or *The Christian Witness to the State*). Now, anyone who knows Yoder knows that these works might be a place to begin, but to summarize Yoder's thought (even on Jesus or church and state) will require attention to far more sources. Yoder himself complicates matters because of his apparent lack of interest in making his thought easily accessible to others. Nevertheless, Yoder needs to be read more wholly, that is more comprehensively. This concern has motivated John Nugent, Jason Vance, and me to begin working on a John Howard Yoder Index (www.yoderindex.com) that will allow both scholars and more casual readers to search Yoder's works in order to locate where he discusses specific topics, texts, and figures.

Perhaps even more importantly, this book contends that Yoder needs to be read more holistically. Some see Yoder's view as mutually exclusive with creedally orthodox Christianity. For example, some cast Yoder's Jesus as incompatible with the Jesus of Nicea or Chalcedon. For others, Yoder's emphasis on the political or social nature of Christianity is mutually exclusive with a view that emphasizes the spiritual or sacramental nature of Christianity. For these interpreters, again, things fall apart: Yoder accepts the dichotomies and dualisms generated by Constantinian social ethics and by modernity. Then, he opts for one side. By interpreting Yoder as a reductionist, it is thought that Yoder divorces what should be held together. In response, this book outlines the case for reading Yoder holistically, as a voice that endeavors to hold together what modernity, skeptical biblical criticism, and many Christian theologians and ethicists have split apart—namely, Christ and creation, as well as Father, Son, and Holy Spirit. In arguing that things hold together in Yoder's theology, my ultimate goal is not simply to focus on Yoder's thought as an end in itself but to look at the way it points to the one in whom, as the author of Colossians puts it, "all things hold together" (Col 1:17).

The first task of theological analysis is to read well and listen well. Yoder himself underscores the value of patient listening in order to better understand what one's conversation partners are saying. So I write this book as one who is outside the Mennonite tradition, hoping that this book will help those inside and outside the Mennonite tradition to better understand Yoder and, in the process, to further the dialogue between Christian traditions. In my experience, Yoder speaks not just to Mennonite questions or issues but to matters that all Christian traditions care about.

Acknowledgments

Things Hold Together grew out of my graduate work at the Institute for Christian Studies and my dissertation at Calvin Theological Seminary. I am thankful for the careful and critical feedback given to the original manuscript by my dissertation supervisor, Ronald Feenstra. I am also grateful for the helpful wisdom given by my dissertation committee, which included John Bolt, James K. A. Smith, and Richard Mouw. While at ICS, Nik Ansell provided helpful guidance that laid the foundation for future work. I am also thankful to Paul Doerksen and Mark Thiessen Nation, who provided helpful feedback on the manuscript. Mark's encouragement has been a great gift. Byron Rempel-Burkholder's editorial work has been very valuable in crafting this book as well. My thanks also go to Andrew Zwart and Melissa Martin for helping me to write more clearly, as well as for Melissa's help with the index. I am especially thankful to John Nugent. John's wide and deep knowledge of Yoder's works and our innumerable conversations over the course of the last seven years have been invaluable in helping me to be a better reader of Yoder. John's feedback and editorial comments have also been an immense help to me. Finally, my inexpressible thanks go to my wife, Sarah, and our two daughters, Eliana and Ruby. This book is dedicated especially to Sarah, whose love and support has been a continual source of encouragement and strength. Without her, none of this would be possible.

A note on previously published material

Chapter 5 develops material originally published in "John Howard Yoder and the Politics of Creation," in *Power and Practices: Engaging the Work of John Howard Yoder*, eds. Jeremy M. Bergen and Anthony G. Siegrist (Scottdale, PA: Herald Press, 2009).

Chapter 7 contains material originally published in *The Forest and the Trees: Engaging Paul Martens'* The Heterodox Yoder (Englewood Review of Books, 2012), ebook.

"Turning and turning in the widening gyre
The falcon cannot hear the falconer;
Things fall apart; the centre cannot hold . . . "
                    —W. B. Yeats, "The Second Coming"

"The Son is the image of the invisible God, the firstborn over all creation. For in him all things were created: things in heaven and on earth, visible and invisible, whether thrones or powers or rulers or authorities; all things have been created through him and for him. He is before all things, and in him all things hold together."
                    —Colossians 1:15

"Suffering love is not right because it 'works' in any calculable short-run way (although it often does). It is right because it goes with the grain of the universe, and that is why *in the long run* nothing else will work."
        —John Howard Yoder, "The Political Meaning of Hope"

"The newness of Jesus is a new culture. A new society . . .
This is not defeatism, or withdrawal. This is the triumphant declaration of independence from the models of a fallen world culture in the name of God's original purpose. There are some theological traditions which try to help us interpret this conflict as a conflict between redemption and creation . . . [But Jesus is] talking about what God really wanted and nothing else. He's talking about the meaning of the created order restored in Him in a fallen world."
        — John Howard Yoder, "The Price of Discipleship"

1

Introduction:
Christ, Creation, and Culture

John Howard Yoder lamented that creation and redemption
had been improperly divorced in modern theology and ethics.[1]
Because of this divorce, theologians construct theologies of culture
by taking one of two broad approaches: either Christ or creation
serve as foundation.[2] Various traditions begin with a focus on creation. Roman Catholic thinkers emphasize natural law, and some
Protestants have embraced this position in recent years. Abraham
Kuyper and his neo-Calvinist heirs emphasize creation orders and
sphere sovereignty. Lutherans appeal to a two kingdoms model,
grounding the civil kingdom or state in creation. This position
begins with the reality of God as creator and the nature and destiny of humanity in God's created order, whether articulated as
general revelation, a doctrine of creation orders, natural law, the

---

1. Yoder explicitly and repeatedly emphasizes the continuity and
connection between creation and redemption. For example, see John
Howard Yoder, "Creation and Gospel," 8–10; "How H. Richard Niebuhr
Reasoned: A Critique of Christ and Culture," 61–62; "Reformed versus
Anabaptist Social Strategies," 5–6; and "That Household We Are,"8.

2. The term "culture" is notoriously difficult to define. I intend it to
have a broad frame of reference, such as that indicated by H. Richard
Niebuhr, who defined it as language, habits, ideas, beliefs, customs, social
organization, inherited artifacts, technical processes, and values. *Christ
and Culture*, 32.

first act in the biblical drama, or theological anthropology.[3] This approach outlines the meaning of humanity and God's intentions for human life on the good earth, and then it relates both Christ and culture back to that foundational framework of creation. This approach often argues that God's revelation in the book of nature enables us to know both God and God's will for human culture and ethics. Although sin is taken seriously, sinful humans can still, to some extent, know and do what God desires.

This view has strengths: it begins with creation, which is the starting point of Scripture; it takes seriously the enduring goodness of God's creation, despite the entrance of sin and death into the created order; and it roots its theology of culture in a robust theological view of what it means to be human.[4] With respect to our ability to know God's will, this position emphasizes creation rather than fall. Although the fall affects what we can know, the emphasis lies on those things revealed in creation, both external and internal to humanity. In addition, advocates of a creation-centered approach often give a complex account of the variety of institutions and orders that are ordained by God for the flourishing of human life. For example, the Roman Catholic emphasis on natural law and the neo-Calvinist emphasis on sphere sovereignty have both proved fruitful in accounting for the complex nature of human social life.

But this approach also has weaknesses. The emphasis on creation risks downplaying the way that the fall affects both the will and the mind. Because of this, the effects of human sin are not taken as seriously as they should be. More crucially, some thinkers see creation and redemption as not just different or complementary,

---

3. For example, see Brunner, *The Divine Imperative*, 208; Brunner, "Nature and Grace," 15–64 (page citations are to the reprint edition); Budziszewski, *Written on the Heart*; Budziszewski, *What We Can't Not Know*; Charles, "Protestants and Natural Law," 33–38; Charles, *Retrieving the Natural Law*; Dooyeweerd, *Roots of Western Culture*, 40–60; Haas, "Creational Ethics Is Public Ethics," 13; Kuyper, *Lectures on Calvinism*, iii, 53, 70–71, 78; Mouw, *Politics and the Biblical Drama*, 21–36; Walsh and Middleton, *The Transforming Vision*, 43–60; Wolters, *Creation Regained*, 13–15.

4. Wolters, "Creation Order," 33–48.

but as contradictory.[5] For example, the Swiss theologian Emil Brunner states, "As Creator, God requires us to recognize and adjust ourselves to the orders he has created, as our first duty; as Redeemer, as our second duty, He bids us ignore the existing orders, and inaugurate a new line of action in view of the coming kingdom of God."[6] For Brunner, the natural orders include five "forms of community" that are derived from creation: marriage and family, economic life, the state, culture, and the church. To set creation and redemption against each other is theologically dangerous because it rejects the coherent purpose of God throughout redemptive history and rejects the unity of Father, Son, and Spirit in carrying out God's purposes of redemption.

In addition, a creation-centered approach does not always clearly relate creation and culture to Christ. Since creation reveals what we ought to do and be in culture, Christ may be seen as performing the task of restoration, but not revelation. For example, Albert M. Wolters focuses on the healing worked by Jesus, thus affirming the goodness of the body and Jesus' restoration of the ability to contribute to culture and society.[7] However, it appears that Jesus brings nothing new to our understanding of culture and society. Although he shows us the nature and character of God, he does not reveal anything that we did not already know about what it means to be a human creature of God. As Richard J. Mouw puts it, this view treats the New Testament's witness to Jesus as "little more than a 're-publishing' of the politics of creation."[8] Because of this overemphasis on creation and underemphasis on redemption, a creation-centered approach may lead to problems in the doctrine of the Trinity, problems that suggest the Father, Son, and Spirit are divided or competing with one another, rather than cohering in the work of creation and redemption.[9] At their worst,

---

5. Brunner, *Divine Imperative*, 330–33.

6. Ibid., 208.

7. Wolters, *Creation Regained*, 61–64.

8. Mouw, "Creational Politics," 191.

9. See the criticisms offered by Begbie, "Creation, Christ, and Culture in Dutch Neo-Calvinism," 123–27; van der Kooi, "A Theology of Culture," 99–100; and Mouw, "Abandoning the Typology," 9.

some who begin with creation emphasize a static order embedded in creation, making Christianity a religion of the status quo that does not take seriously the earth-shaking advent of God's kingdom in Jesus Christ.[10] In the end, this view often fails to provide a good account of how Christ and creation are related and how both inform our theology of culture. Without coherence, our theology of culture is not properly biblical or trinitarian.

A second broad approach to Christ, creation, and culture emphasizes Christ and the new creation.[11] The eminent theologian of the twentieth century, Karl Barth, renewed a Christocentric approach to theology. Anabaptists and Baptists emphasize the importance of witness and following Jesus for the Christian life. Nineteenth-century liberal humanists and twenty-first century evangelicals take their cues (not to mention their bracelet acronyms) from the question: What would Jesus do? For this broad approach, Christ rather than creation is the primary source of norms for human life and culture. As true God and true human, Jesus is the central and authoritative revelation of both God and humanity, such that he reveals how we ought to live in this world. He does not just teach us about the relationship between God and individual humans, but he also reveals to us what God desires in the social-cultural realm. The focus of this Christ-centered approach, therefore, is kingdom ethics, not creational ethics. Consequently, those who hold this view look to Jesus for their view of culture and social ethics.

Whereas the previous approach emphasizes creation and downplays the fall, this view emphasizes the fall and downplays creation. Human sin is so severe that we can only know God and

---

10. de Gruchy, *The Church Struggle in South Africa*, 202.

11. For example, Barth, *Christ and Adam*, 44–45; Barth, "The Christian Community and the Civil Community," 153, 165; Barth, *Church Dogmatics* III/1, 1–44; Bonhoeffer, *Ethics*, 43–44; Carter, *Rethinking Christ and Culture*, 94–108; Finger, *A Contemporary Anabaptist Theology*; Hauerwas, *The Peaceable Kingdom*; McClendon, *Systematic Theology*, Vols. 1–3; Moltmann, "Creation and Redemption," 120; Moltmann, *The Future of Creation*, 164; Moltmann, "Religion, Revolution, and the Future," 22; Stassen and Gushee, *Kingdom Ethics*; and Volf, "Creation, Eschaton, and Social Ethics," 135.

God's will for human cultural life insofar as we look to Jesus. Often, general revelation is seen as functionally worthless. As Helmut Thielicke asks, "Where and how can I recognize this order of creation? From what authoritative source is it to be deduced? Is it to be read off from the world as it was originally, before the fall—for it was undoubtedly present there, present and intact—or is it to be read off from *this aeon*, in which, to put it mildly, it has undergone some disruption? Is it really so plain and accessible in this aeon? And if it is, can we from this general order casuistically deduce directives for specific situations here and now?"[12] Although it may be true that creation is the starting point of Scripture, this position argues that Christ is its central point. For some, this merely relativizes whatever might be said about creation apart from Christ. For others in this camp, any attempt to articulate truth about the nature of reality, creation, or culture apart from Christ amounts to a sub-Christian natural theology that opens the door to anything from a health and wealth gospel to Nazism.

This approach also has its strengths: it takes sin seriously and avoids modern optimism about human nature. It takes Jesus seriously by echoing the New Testament call to be conformed to the image of Christ. This approach focuses on the humanity and historical-cultural context of Jesus. It makes the claim that how Jesus lived within his own context sheds light on how we ought to live in ours.

This approach also has weaknesses. Often, there is little or no account of how Christ relates to creation, to the original good order that God established, and to the creation mandate of Genesis 1.[13] In addition, some in this camp risk portraying Jesus as not merely different from or complementary to God's will in creation, but at odds with it. Discontinuity is thus emphasized over continuity, and Jesus, or the new creation, is emphasized over creation. Biblically and theologically, this approach falls short because it fails to make clear the connections between creation and Christ. In the end, it needs a better account of how creation is related to Christ and culture.

----

12. Thielicke, *Theological Ethics*, 1:393.

13. For example, though it may be outside their scope, Stassen and Gushee do not make clear how, if at all, the "kingdom ethics" of Jesus are related to creational ethics.

All Christians ought to be concerned that creation and Christ cohere in our theology of culture. Our theology of culture must affirm and then explain how God's purposes in redemption connect to God's purposes in creation.[14] If we pit creation and redemption against each other, it is we, not the biblical narrative, who have become incoherent and dualistically put asunder what God has joined together—creation and redemption. Even worse, this dualism between creation and redemption would be not only an ethical dualism, but a theological dualism, dividing the persons of the Trinity against one another. Jesus is not only the Son but the Word by whom the Father creates. Despite the temptation to emphasize Christ at the expense of creation, or creation at the expense of Christ, a careful and consistent theology will articulate the relationship between these two and show how they—taken together with the Spirit's work in redemption—inform a truly trinitarian theology of culture.

Radical trinitarianism and a theology of culture

The New Testament makes the startling claim, in the first century and in ours, that in Jesus "all things" hold together—including the created order, spiritual powers, and human destiny (Col 1:17). This truth grounds Christians but also generates questions, questions that relate directly to John Howard Yoder's theological project. How do we articulate theologically the coherence and continuity between God's work in creation and redemption? What impact does this continuity (or lack thereof) have on the way we understand the continuity between Father, Son, and Holy Spirit? And how do these things affect our theology of culture?

For John Howard Yoder, these are not abstract theological questions but vitally connected to the church's life and witness, not least to the church's peace witness. If the Father, maker of heaven and earth, is a warrior who gives us a natural law but the Son is a pacifist, then it may be legitimate for Christians to hold differing and contradictory positions on various questions of culture, including war and peace. If, however, Jesus is not only redeemer but also agent of creation, and the one who truly reveals the Father, then

---

14. See O'Donovan, *Resurrection and Moral Order*, 15.

our approach to all facets of culture will have to account for continuity in the overarching biblical drama of creation and redemption. Since Augustine, trinitarian thinkers have affirmed that the external acts of the Trinity are undivided. In other words, Father, Son, and Holy Spirit do not act in a way that is contradictory (or even separate from) one another. Furthermore, as Joe Jones articulately argues, radical trinitarian orthodoxy is needed to sustain the kind of radical discipleship that Yoder calls for.[15] The answers we give to questions about the interrelationship of Christ, creation, and culture are directly connected to the answers we give to questions about the trinitarian God.

Jesus, John Howard Yoder, and culture

Given the persistent focus on Jesus in his writings, John Howard Yoder is often accused of dualistically separating Christ and creation rather than holistically integrating them. This mistake is said to expose his problematic views of the Trinity, creation, and culture. Yoder himself sometimes contributes to the perception of dualism by criticizing certain theological uses and abuses of terms such as *creation, creation orders, natural law,* and *nature.*[16] This makes it easy for non-Mennonites to slot Yoder into their preconceived notions of Anabaptists. There are several Mennonite scholars who criticize Yoder along these lines as well. Across the ecumenical spectrum, scholars such as J. Budziszewski, J. Daryl Charles, Guenther

15. Jones, "Yoder and Stone-Campbellites," 107–128.

16. For example, see Yoder, *Body Politics* (page references are to the 2001 reprint), vii–viii, 26, 76; "Christ, the Light of the World," in *The Royal Priesthood,* 183–84; *Christian Attitudes to War, Peace, and Revolution,* 66–68, 235; "The Hermeneutics of Peoplehood," in *The Priestly Kingdom,* 41, 43–44; "The Kingdom as Social Ethic," in *Priestly Kingdom,* 84; "The New Humanity as Pulpit and Paradigm," in *For the Nations,* 45; "The Otherness of the Church," in *Royal Priesthood,* 60; *The Politics of Jesus* (page references are to the 1994 edition), 99, 100, 144, 190, 193, 226; *Preface to Theology,* 359; "Primitivism in the Radical Reformation," 84, 89; "Sacrament as Social Process: Christ the Transformer of Culture," in *Royal Priesthood,* 371; "Why Ecclesiology is Social Ethics," in *Royal Priesthood,* 110, 113–14, 123. Notably, these references almost always come in passing remarks rather than in a sustained treatment of the issue.

Haas, James Reimer, Gerald Schlabach, and Nigel Goring Wright all argue in one way or another that Yoder has a deficient doctrine of creation.[17] Several critics connect Yoder's supposedly deficient doctrine of creation to Yoder's Christ-centered pacifism. Because the sword and the state are thought to be grounded in creation, critics accuse Yoder of rejecting the creation order placed by God in God's world. Even worse, Yoder ends up echoing (or so it is thought) the early heretic Marcion, who set the God of the Old Testament and Jesus against each other.[18]

If correct, these scholars are right to see a deficiency in Yoder's theology that needs to be taken seriously. A theology without a biblical doctrine of creation and the Trinity is deficient. These critics, however, are mistaken. Moreover, there are good reasons to raise preliminary questions about these criticisms. Just as Yoder often refers briefly and in passing to creation and its connection to Christ and culture, so Yoder's critics offer brief and passing criticisms. None of them offer a sustained treatment of his whole theology with a view toward his doctrine of creation or theology of culture and how both relate to his view of the Trinity. Yoder himself affirmed that theology necessarily and inevitably gives "attention to coherence, system, and organization," as well as the "inter-relations" of thought patterns.[19]

---

17. For charges that Yoder has a deficient doctrine of creation, see Budziszewski, "Four Shapers of Evangelical Political Thought"; Charles, "Protestants and Natural Law," 33–38; Charles, *Retrieving the Natural Law*, 137–41; Haas, "Effects of the Fall on Creational Social Structures," 108–29; Reimer, "A Positive Theology of Law and Civil Institutions," in *A Mind Patient and Untamed*, 245–73; Schlabach, "The Christian Witness in the Earthly City," in *A Mind Patient and Untamed*, 221–44; and Wright, *Disavowing Constantine*, 163–66.

18. For charges that Yoder is Marcionitic and insufficiently trinitarian, see Miller, "In the Footsteps of Marcion," 82–92; Reimer, "A Positive Theology of Law and Civil Institutions," in *A Mind Patient and Untamed*, 249–51; Reimer, "Mennonites, Christ, and Culture," 12. Reimer also notes Yoder's apparent ambivalence toward trinitarian orthodoxy in "Biblical and Systematic Theology," in *Mennonites and Classical Theology*, 253–56. J. Denny Weaver approvingly cites Yoder's "relativizing" of the creeds in *The Nonviolent Atonement*, 92–96; and "The United States Shape of Mennonite Theologizing," 639–40.

19. Yoder, *Preface to Theology*, 230.

Far from lacking a doctrine of creation or Trinity, Yoder's trinitarian theology of culture upholds the continuity and coherence between God's work in creation and redemption.[20] The coherence between creation and redemption is directly related to the coherence and unity of the persons and work of the Father, Son, and Spirit. Unlike those who pit creation against redemption or conflate creation and fall, Yoder's theology of culture adequately accounts for the unity of the Trinity.

Jesus Christ is the center of Yoder's theology of culture. If either Christ's divine or human nature is denied, or if the union of those two natures in the one person of the Son is denied, Yoder's theology of culture ceases to make sense. Jesus' humanity directly connects Christ and culture. Humanity's social, cultural, and political life has its norm in Jesus, who is the true image of God. According to Yoder, Jesus, as the second Adam, reveals the nature of true cultural power: it is for service, not for domination. In Jesus' divinity, Christ and creation are immediately related. The Word who became flesh is the Word by whom all things were created in the beginning. The God at work in creation is the same God at work in redemption. A basic theological and ethical rule, then, is that what God desires of humanity's cultural life in creation does not contradict what God desires of humanity's cultural life in redemption and reconciliation.

Moreover, the God of creation and redemption is the God who is guiding the church and all creation to its appointed destiny. Yoder sees the church's life as a sacramental presence and power. As sacramental presence, the church is both a sign and seal of where God is taking the whole creation. The church is empowered by the Spirit and therefore rooted in both a creational and a new creational way of being cultural. In its life together, the church participates in the true power granted to humanity as *imago Dei*. It does so by following Jesus in the power of the Spirit. Yoder's Spirit-empowered ecclesiology underscores the need for careful discernment about existing cultural practices and the need to pioneer new cultural practices. Yoder highlights five sacraments that do just that, and his work on the sacraments breaks down any strict dichotomy between public and private life, between culture

---

20. See footnote 1 of this chapter.

and religion, and between creation and Christ.[21] Yoder's theology of culture thus reflects the unity of the Trinity: the Father who creates and reveals himself by the Son, the Son who does the will of the Father, and the Spirit who leads the church along the way of Jesus to the glory of the Father. Taken together, these form the indivisible unity of his trinitarian theology of culture. So the Word that ordered the creation is the same enfleshed Word that provides the shape our lives ought to take in and with creation. The Spirit that hovered over the waters at creation hovers over the life of the new creation, shaping Christ's body to live with the grain of the universe so that we might hear the pronouncement, "It is very good."

Yoder and systematic theology

What lens should we use to evaluate Yoder's own thought? Yoder wrote occasionally rather than systematically. That is, he wrote primarily in short essays that dealt with one issue at a time. Even his most well-known work, *The Politics of Jesus*, is a collection of related essays, not a systematic theology textbook. The occasional nature of Yoder's work complicates the task of evaluating his thought. Despite his occasional method of writing, I examine various facets of Yoder's thought through a systematic lens to see whether and how various themes and doctrines are connected. Some may object to systematizing Yoder's thought, noting that he was averse to systematic theology. Thus, before undertaking this approach, we must see why this more systematic approach is justified on Yoderian grounds, beginning, as Yoder often does, by clarifying the pertinent terms and what is meant by them, especially the term "systematic theology."

For Yoder, specific types of systematic theology are especially problematic. One type assumes that we can isolate an "unchanging body of timeless propositions"[22] and then use those propositions to construct "a system that ideally would be rationalistic, stable, and closed."[23] Both conservative and liberal theologians

---

21. I address the practices in chapter 7 below. See also my "Spinning the Liturgical Turn," in *Radical Ecumenicity*, 173–92.

22. Yoder, "The Use of the Bible in Theology," in *To Hear the Word*, 86.

23. Ibid., 88.

in this systematic vein problematically assume that before theology can speak about Jesus it must lay a rational foundation that enables it to speak to other Christians or to the world.[24] This rationalistic foundation then filters Scripture through its own preconceived lens rather than allowing Scripture to determine both the form and content of theology. Yoder vehemently resists this type of systematic theology, not only by speaking directly against it, but by *doing* theology in a way that is distinct. He writes in occasional, scattered essays and never brings his thought together into a comprehensive systematic tome. This is not accidental, for he thinks that theology's *form* is as important as its *content*. The medium and message go together.

Given Yoder's criticism of this bad type of systematic theology, it is understandable why some would say we should not analyze his thought in a systematic way. For example, Harry Huebner asserts that "just as Yoder rejects the notion of a fundamental starting point derived from the work of abstract reasoning, so he rejects the ultimate unification of all knowledge."[25] In Huebner's view, Yoder repudiates any system and affirms fragmentary knowledge and paradox.[26] Huebner is exactly right that Yoder rejected the idea of some kind of abstract principle from which all further theology could simply be deduced. Yoder also speaks strongly against "methodologism," the idea that one particular method of doing theology or ethics should be privileged over other ways of doing theology or ethics.[27]

Yet, Yoder himself argues for a good type of systematic theology. He outlines this especially in "The Use of the Bible in Theology" and *Preface to Theology*. This type of theology does not proceed with the rationalistic or foundationalist underpinnings

---

24. As examples, Yoder lists Gordon Clark, Cornelius Van Til, Emil Brunner, Gordon Kaufman, and David Tracy. Yoder, "The Use of the Bible in Theology," in *To Hear the Word*, 88.

25. Huebner, "The Christian Life as Gift and Patience," in *A Mind Patient and Untamed*, 27.

26. See also Huebner, "Globalization, Theory, and Dialogical Vulnerability," 49–62, esp. 53–55.

27. For example, see Yoder, "Walk and Word," in *Theology Without Foundations*, 77–90.

noted above. Rather, this form of good systematic theology recognizes that the Bible contains numerous modes of theological discourse, including narrative and hortatory genres.[28] Rather than see these genres as creating problems to be solved by our systems, we should recognize that they are irreducible to a system that would preclude needing to return to the Bible. In other words, Yoder does not want us to "figure it out" such that we never have to look to the Bible. Drawing on Paul Minear, he contends that "the points at which we will most likely learn will therefore not be those already previously reduced to rational system [sic] but the odd, forgotten, or systematically erratic blocks within the literature."[29] The Bible is not a hermeneutical puzzle to be solved, but a foundational narrative to which we must ever return. Yoder is fond of referencing John Robinson's statement to the effect that "the Lord hath yet more truth to break forth from his holy word." Good systematic theology must affirm rather than deny this point.

For Yoder, good systematic theology also recognizes that it is not an end in itself; it is meant to serve the church.[30] Importantly, he clarifies, "I do not argue that the reflexes of abstraction and generalization have no function at all."[31] Instead, these reflexes must recognize a valid pluralism of methods in theological discourse, not only because we must be modest about our fallible efforts at constructive theology, but also because the Bible itself models a variety of modes of theological discourse. For Yoder, God chose to reveal himself "through a multiplicity of literary forms that are mostly narrative in framework and doxological in tone," thus revealing not only the *content* of theology but the proper pluralistic *forms* of theology as well.[32] Good systematic theology does not lord it over other modes of theological discourse, but sees itself as a servant. But how exactly does it serve the church?

Yoder outlines several services that good systematic theology has to offer. First, he sees the need for clarity, order, logic, unity,

---

28. Yoder, "The Use of the Bible in Theology," in *To Hear the Word*, 88.

29. Ibid., 85.

30. Ibid., 87.

31. Ibid., 88.

32. Ibid.

and coherence in theology. In *Preface to Theology*, he affirms the importance of "attention to coherence, system, and organization," as well as the "inter-relations" of thought patterns.[33] This, I submit, sets a proper task for good systematic theology. As a result, Yoder contends that the test of a doctrine is "its adequacy in inter-relating and synthesizing the exegetical material into an intellectually graspable whole."[34] Importantly, Yoder notes that this good type of systematic theology is going on already in the pages of Scripture. In *Preface to Theology*, he labels Paul, John, and the author of Hebrews as "theologians" of the New Testament. Why does he label them as such? Because they are especially attuned both to what Yoder calls the test of coherence (what we might call systematic theology) and the test of communication (what we might call occasional or contextual theology).[35] In their emphasis on coherence, these writers go deeper than other New Testament writings in that they develop implications and assumptions that have previously gone unstated. They say things that have not been said before. They "bring logic to bear" and "rise to a higher level of generalization in the affirmations they make" to make explicit what is implicit in the church's proclamation about Jesus.[36] Yoder assumes this is a legitimate task of the theologian. These same authors also emphasize contextual communication. All of them write to a particular audience, a fact that shapes, in part, the great differences between writings of Paul, John, and the book of Hebrews. These writings are occasional in that the authors "make statements about how [specific truths] are to be understood in a new context, by a new audience, as answering some new question."[37] For Yoder, good theology always must pass *both* tests—the test of coherence and the test of communication. Because the very text of Scripture is both occasional (in that it addresses particular concerns) and systematic (in that it is concerned with connecting previously unconnected theological dots), Christians may not prohibit

---

33. Yoder, *Preface*, 230.

34. Ibid., 313.

35. Ibid., 92–93.

36. Ibid., 93.

37. Ibid.

either of these modes of theology, for that would undermine both good systematic theology and the Bible itself.[38]

In addition to extolling coherence, Yoder notes that theology serves catechetical and corrective functions, both of which call for some type of systematizing.[39] The church inevitably must teach or catechize new members about what it means to be a Christian. The church must therefore prioritize what should be taught and in what order it will be taught. In this sense, catechesis requires some type of system with some kind of rationale based in part upon the church's particular place and time, as well as the surrounding culture from which new converts come. Yoder notes that biblical materials like the book of Matthew might originally have served a catechetical function in the sense that the author selectively systematizes and arranges specific materials for inclusion based on both the record of Jesus and the particular needs of the audience. Thus, precisely because teaching always involves some level of systematizing, we dare not write off all systematizing, for to do so would be to abandon context-sensitive and learner-sensitive instruction.

Good systematic theology also serves a corrective function. That is, when Christians disagree, they appeal to some common authority. Though the appeal is typically made to Scripture, the form the argument takes must proceed logically and trace coherence between various topics. If the argument is "inchoate" and "impressionistic" rather than a clear and reasoned appeal to Scripture, then the very contours of the argument will cease to carry logical force and the dialogue will cease. Although Yoder does not allude to specific texts, we should note that many texts of Scripture serve this corrective function by drawing logical connections and inferences. Often, biblical writers argue as follows: "If you say doctrine X, then Y follows, and saying Y is a problem because it conflicts with doctrine Z, which you must hold if you are to hold fast to the gospel. Therefore, you must not hold to doctrine X." For example, if the church in Corinth had not needed correction on the issue of resurrection, we would not get

---

38. On this point, see also Yoder, "That Household We Are."

39. The following is a summary of Yoder, "The Use of the Bible in Theology," in *To Hear the Word*, 77–82.

Paul's logical and Christological exposition of the resurrection in 1 Corinthians 15. If John's audience had not been tempted to deny that Jesus had a fully human body, we would not have his emphasis on Jesus' humanity in 1 John 1:1-4 or John 1:14. Thus we see that good systematic theology is necessary in part to refute problematic views of certain topics. We also see that occasional, contextual concerns and good systematic thinking are not opposites but two sides of the same coin.

It is helpful to see that Yoder not only talked about the importance of coherence and consistency, he exemplified coherence and consistency in his theological work, a fact noted by scholars across the spectrum, including those who generally agree with him and those who do not.[40] Although the rest of this book offers a sustained example of Yoder's systematic thinking, it is helpful at this juncture to briefly allude to a couple of examples from his work. One example of Yoder's concern for good systematic thinking can be seen in *Preface to Theology*, where he assesses several thinkers and schools of thought in the church's first centuries. Yoder notes that the Bible demands that theologians faithfully talk about several matters at once, including the preexistence of the Son, the distinctness of Father and Son, and monotheism.[41] He then analyzes Monarchianism, Tertullian, Origen, Sabellius, and Arius based on their ability to coherently connect these key doctrines, noting that most of them give unsatisfactory answers.[42] Yoder does not say, "Well, all knowledge is fragmentary, so we should not expect these theologians to connect the dots in a consistent way." Nor does he say, "Since one cannot theologize from scratch on the basis of some sort of

---

40. For affirmations of consistency and coherence, see Craig A. Carter, *Politics of the Cross*, 18, 225–226; Cartwright, "Radical Reform, Radical Catholicity," in *Royal Priesthood*, 3; Finger, "Did Yoder Reduce Theology to Ethics?" in *A Mind Patient and Untamed*, 320; Hauerwas, "Lingering with Yoder's Wild Work," in *A Mind Patient and Untamed*, 13; Nation, *John Howard Yoder*, 189; Reimer, "Theological Orthodoxy and Jewish Christianity," in *Wisdom of the Cross*, 432; Zimmerman, *Practicing the Politics of Jesus*, 178.

41. Yoder, *Preface*, 191.

42. Ibid., 187–97.

indubitable foundation, one should give up on internal consistency altogether." On the contrary, Yoder says, for example, that Monarchianism, Sabellianism, and Arianism cannot be made to cohere with what Scripture teaches. Thus, Yoder's way of theological reasoning demonstrates that connecting various doctrines coherently and systematically is possible and desirable.

This is further seen in the way that Yoder utilizes a systematic lens both to assess other thinkers and to argue his own case. That is, he recognizes that every statement of doctrine is entwined with other doctrinal statements. Yoder's work is rife with examples of this type of systematic reasoning. He criticizes H. Richard Niebuhr because Niebuhr's use of the term *Trinity* was inconsistent with both Scripture and Nicea. He raises questions about how Reformed views of human depravity and God's sovereignty fit (or not) with Reformed political theory. He argues that Constantinianism operates with an implicit eschatology, even if that eschatology is not explicitly stated or foregrounded. He argues that Christian pacifism, properly understood, is systematically connected with Christology, such that removing Christ would also undermine his view of pacifism. He contends that Christian ethics flows from a proper doctrine of the ascension and the Holy Spirit. Indeed, Yoder has ecumenical appeal because he often shows that his views do not simply spring from Anabaptist quirks or peculiarities (which other traditions might then conveniently ignore), but from doctrines that nearly all Christians hold very dear.

Some still might object, however, that theologians ought to avoid systematically setting out how doctrines are related or connected. Is not the Bible itself largely composed of occasional documents, such as letters, that respond to specific circumstances? Did not Yoder himself only do theology in an occasional mode because of this?[43] If he did not bring his thoughts together to show how they systematically relate, why should we? For starters, the task of interrogating Yoder in a systematic mode is ecumenically necessary and healthy. Yoder often does not receive a fair hearing from more systematically-inclined theologians in part because he never did for them what he did for others, namely, strategically package

---

43. Yoder, "The Use of the Bible in Theology," in *To Hear the Word*, 86–90.

his thought for the purposes of dialogue without assuming that one particular packaging is the only or best way to do theology. There is, thus, a good Yoderian reason why I am justified in assessing his thought systematically—to further the dialogue among systematic theologians—so long as I avoid the presumption that systematic theology is the best or the only way to do theology. Yoder's work is a gift to the whole church (not just Mennonites). But it is also a gift that may not be received by the whole church if scholars attempt to regulate Yoder's legacy in a way that forbids translation by more systematically-inclined traditions or by those more systematically-inclined within the Mennonite tradition.

There is an irony here: if one were to prohibit a more systematic approach to Yoder's theology, it would entail the type of methodologism that Yoder spoke against. To say "you may not examine this from a more systematic angle" would be to argue that a certain method—say, an occasional approach—is inherently superior to other types of theology—say, a systematic approach—by virtue of the method it employs.[44] I would argue, however, that theology in a Yoderian vein would recognize that systematic theology is always also occasional and that, conversely, occasional theology is always also systematic. Yoder's *Preface* makes clear that biblical authors and later theologians *must* think more systematically precisely because of occasional concerns—questions asked and issues raised in their particular contexts. Conversely, occasional theology always contains statements that are inherently and systematically connected to other doctrines. So, for example, a thinker like Arius must be examined with attention to contextual details. He is addressing concerns particular to his audience and we can even say that his concerns or motivations are understandable, given his place in history. However, once Arius's occasional statements are teased out in terms of their logical implications—the test of coherence mentioned above—he is weighed in the balance and found wanting.[45]

---

44. Yoder himself sometimes comes close to turning nonmethodologism into a methodology, as in his caricature of scholasticism. For more on Yoder, scholasticism, and method, see Kaethler, "The Practice of Reading the Other," in *Power and Practices*, 47–64.

45. Yoder, *Preface*, 195–97.

So how do we go forward in theology? The same way the biblical theologians did, recognizing that we are always called to speak in new and different contexts and that, in those new occasions, we must be committed to logical and theological coherence. My engagement with Yoder is not meant to be systematic in a bad sense, that is, an attempt to turn Yoder's theology into a rationalistic, enclosed system that thereby closes down any further theological discussion. Instead, I seek to engage Yoder in a threefold way that is connected with the proper services that good systematic theology may render and that will serve to further good theological dialogue. First, I ask about the consistency and coherence in Yoder's thought. Does it cohere with the Bible? And is what he says about various topics logically consistent with what he says elsewhere about other topics? Second, I approach Yoder with a catechetical, or instructive, lens. If I want to present Yoder's thought to someone, I have to start somewhere, and I have to pick and choose certain elements that I see as important and connected. Given that I am interested in Yoder's theology of culture, this book addresses the doctrinal issues that intersect with his theology of culture. Third, I approach Yoder with a corrective function. That is, good systematic theology validly asks, "Is this right? Does it fit with Scripture?" I have seen many Yoder interlocutors (especially non-Mennonites) prematurely make negative judgments about Yoder's theology. I want to join that conversation in order to ask whether, when one reads Yoder deeply and widely, that judgment can be sustained. I do not suggest that Yoder has no theological faults but, in an ecumenical context, I think it is first important to be clear about what Yoder actually says. I thus approach Yoder and other conversation partners with the assumption that good systematic theology wants to stop us from saying and believing things that should not be said and believed and that it wants to help us learn what we should say and should believe. As Yoder repeatedly emphasizes, faithfulness and unfaithfulness are real possibilities, and the good theologian is therefore ever testing, never resting, in an attempt to better understand and clarify what we say and what we mean, both for the glory of God and for the sake of the church.

Chapter survey

Yoder's theology cannot be understood apart from the conversations in which he was engaged. Reinhold Niebuhr and H. Richard Niebuhr were essential conversation partners for Yoder because they set the intellectual framework for mid-twentieth century North American ethics and theology, convincing Mennonites and non-Mennonites alike that Anabaptists could claim faithfulness to the way of Jesus but that they had to thereby admit their irresponsibility, ineffectiveness, and irrelevance in relation to the wider culture, society, and politics. Yoder spent his life explaining why the dilemma between faithfulness and effectiveness was a false one. Chapter 2 argues that the Niebuhrs' theologies of culture and social ethics are integrally linked with other key doctrinal issues, such as their explanation of creation, fall, and redemption; their doctrine of the Trinity; and their Christology. These doctrinal positions are not accidental but essential to their social ethics and theology of culture. As a result, Yoder is at odds with both the Niebuhrs, not just on ethical issues, but theological issues as well.

Whereas the Niebuhrs use trinitarian language without the substance of true trinitarian orthodoxy, Yoder's thought has the substance of true trinitarianism. This claim may be counterintuitive, since scholars sometimes think Yoder is indifferent to the creeds, if not downright hostile to them. If he is, the claim that he presents a trinitarian theology of culture would be highly suspect. Chapter 3 argues that Yoder's thought is compatible with the early ecumenical creeds of Nicea and Chalcedon. To do so, Yoder's view of the creeds must be understood in the context of Yoder's broader theology, including his view of the nature of theological language and the authority of tradition.

Chapter 4 sets forth Yoder's biblically-grounded Christology. Yoder argues that Jesus, in his humanity and his divinity, not only relates directly to culture, but also serves as the linchpin for creation and redemption's coherence. Yoder's exegesis helpfully shows how—as a fully human Jewish person—Jesus directly addresses culture, politics, economics, and other questions of social ethics. Yoder also rightly argues that the fully divine Jesus creates, sustains, and directs all things and, in him, all things hold together.

Many scholars accuse Yoder of lacking a sound doctrine of creation and thereby of having a deficient theology of culture. These thinkers rightly note that any biblical theology of culture must have a robust doctrine of creation. Chapter 5 argues that, for Yoder, the power of Jesus reestablishes the politics of creation. Yoder's account of creation, fall, and redemption reveals that humans were created to exercise peaceful, Christlike power, and the Powers were created to be flourishing and dynamic servants of peace. Far from neglecting creation, careful attention to Yoder's theology reveals a doctrine of creation that coheres with redemption.

To some, Yoder's denial that the state is rooted in creation is evidence that he has a deficient doctrine of creation, which in turn reveals problematic views of redemption and the Trinity. If the state is evil but is part of the orders of creation, then Yoder's doctrine of creation seems to conflate creation and fall. If the state is part of God's original intentions for creation but is not redeemed, then Yoder appears to concede some realm of creation to sin and the fall, thus limiting the scope of Christ's redemptive activity. Chapter 6 follows Yoder's argument that the sword-bearing state is not rooted in God's prefall creation order but in God's postfall preservation of the world. God providentially allows for the sword, but this should not be confused with God's creative and redemptive will.

When Yoder rejects the sword, however, his concern is to disavow *fallen* culture, not culture as God intends it. In fact, Yoder wants to make clear that he is not against but *for* the nations. To that end, in the last decade of his life, Yoder more intentionally connected his account of the social processes of the Christian community with his view of the sacraments and the doctrine of the Holy Spirit, and he showed how all the above have direct relevance to a theology of culture. Chapter 7 argues that, for Yoder, the transformation of culture depends on the pioneering work of the Spirit and the in-breaking of God's kingdom. When the power of creation and the politics of Jesus are unleashed by the person of the Spirit, the public practices of the church cannot help but overflow and exert a transformative effect, not only in the church, but in all of human culture.

Readers who wish to dig into Yoder's thought without first comparing it to the Niebuhrs may skip chapter 2. Although this chapter sets the context for Yoder's thought by looking at the Niebuhrs, readers who move straight to chapter 3 will still be able to follow the overall argument of this book.

2

The Niebuhrs on Christ, Creation, and Culture

Although Reinhold[1] and H. Richard Niebuhr[2] greatly influ-enced twentieth-century North American theology and ethics, John Howard Yoder routinely criticizes them. Reinhold and

---

1. To avoid confusion, I refer to the Niebuhrs by Reinhold or H. Richard. Reinhold Niebuhr, *Moral Man and Immoral Society*; *An Interpretation of Christian Ethics*; *The Nature and Destiny of Man*; "Why the Christian Church Is Not Pacifist," in *The Essential Reinhold Niebuhr*, 102–22. For recent and excellent engagement with Reinhold's thought, see the collection of essays in Rice, *Reinhold Niebuhr Revisited*.

2. H. Richard Niebuhr, *Christ and Culture*; "The Doctrine of the Trinity and the Unity of the Church" was originally published in *Theology Today* 3, no. 3 (1946): 371–84. It was republished as "Theological Unitarianisms," *Theology Today* 40, no. 2 (1983): 150–57. My references are to the original publication. Other significant works include *Radical Monotheism and Western Culture* and *The Responsible Self: An Essay in Christian Moral Philosophy*. For commentary on H. Richard's thought, see Carter, "The Legacy of an Inadequate Christology," 387–401; Carter, *Rethinking Christ and Culture*; Long, *The Goodness of God*; Long, *Theology and Culture*; Marsden, "Christianity and Cultures," in *Insights: The Faculty Journal of Austin Seminary* (Fall 1999): 4–15, accessed online at http://www.religion-online.org/showarticle.asp?title=517, June 20, 2008; Stassen, "Concrete Christological Norms for Transformation," in *Authentic Transformation*, 127–90; Wittmer, "Analysis and Critique of 'Christ the Transformer of Culture;'" and Yoder, "How H. Richard Niebuhr Reasoned," in *Authentic Transformation*, 30–91.

H. Richard differ on many aspects of their theology and social ethics. Yet Yoder argues that certain aspects of both Niebuhrs' thought are skewed because of some basic theological differences with both Scripture and classical orthodoxy, including doctrines of the Trinity, Christology, the Holy Spirit, creation, resurrection, and regeneration.[3] These theological positions are not incidental but essential to their social ethics and theology of culture. Although the Niebuhrs certainly offered helpful and astute commentary on a wide range of theological and ethical topics, they did have their weaknesses—weaknesses that Yoder rightly argued should be a stumbling block for those whose theology of culture seeks to correspond with a proper biblical view of the doctrines listed above.

Yoder's theology and ethics are a response to Reinhold Niebuhr's charge that, as Gerald Schlabach puts it, "Christians who embrace the nonviolent ethic of Jesus get Jesus right, but they at the same time render themselves politically irrelevant and socially irresponsible."[4] As Schlabach notes, Yoder's engagement with Reinhold and his heirs "run[s] like a thread throughout his career."[5] Yoder worked relentlessly for forty years to dismantle how both Reinhold and H. Richard's thought influenced Mennonites and non-Mennonites alike. In doing so, Yoder did not merely try to make Mennonites more respectable in ecumenical circles, but he argued that his alternative to the Niebuhrs' theology and ethics was actually more ecumenical insofar as it appealed to both Scripture and orthodox Christian teaching for its conclusions.

In particular, Yoder and the Niebuhrs differ on how to understand the biblical and theological distinctions between creation, fall, and redemption.[6] The Niebuhrs use these terms as dialectic,

---

3. For example, see Yoder, "How H. Richard Niebuhr Reasoned," in *Authentic Transformation*, 58–65; and *Reinhold Niebuhr and Christian Pacifism*, 20–22.

4. Schlabach, "John H. Yoder as Augustinian Interlocutor," in *A Mind Patient and Untamed*, 228.

5. Schlabach, "The Christian Witness in the Earthly City," 239, n. 24.

6. This lens is utilized by several Reformed authors, including Bartholomew and Goheen, *The Drama of Scripture*; Plantinga, *Engaging God's World*; Walsh and Middleton, *The Transforming Vision*; Wittmer, *Heaven Is a Place on Earth*; Wolters, *Creation Regained*.

existential categories, with a primary focus on how those terms explain the present spiritual condition of humanity. Many will concur and follow them in doing so. Yet other thinkers still take the categories of creation, fall, and redemption to have some kind of ontological and historical component. That is, the theological language we use not only describes the present spiritual condition of humanity but references the past events of salvation history. For those who take this approach, there may be reason to have doubts about whether one can naively appropriate the Niebuhrs' thought in a theology of culture.

Reinhold Niebuhr: The fall into creation

Reinhold's interpretation of creation, fall, and redemption are shaped by his views of the nature of biblical and theological language. For Reinhold, biblical symbols ought to be taken seriously, but not literally.[7] By biblical symbols, Reinhold means things such as creation, fall, incarnation, atonement, resurrection, and eschaton. He contends that when taken literally, these symbols destroy the dialectic, or tension, between history and eternity, which he regards as the mistake of orthodoxy. But if the symbols are not taken seriously, Reinhold argues, the concept of an eternity that fulfills rather than destroys history is lost, which he regards as the mistake of modern liberal Christianity. Reinhold sees himself as charting a middle way between these two: biblical language is true when taken symbolically and false when taken literally.

What should we make of Reinhold's view? As Langdon Gilkey points out, Reinhold is neoorthodox. He sounds orthodox because he uses the same central words as the classical biblical, Pauline, Augustinian, Reformation tradition, words such as *creation, fall, revelation, incarnation/atonement*, and *grace*. Reinhold does not set these symbols aside in favor of something else (as with much liberal theology), but sees these symbols as mediating something true about God's transcendent activity in relation to human reality. Because he insisted on retrieving and utilizing biblical and

---

7. Niebuhr, *Nature and Destiny*, 2:50. Further references to this work in this chapter will be noted parenthetically and include volume and page number. Other works of Niebuhr will be cited with footnotes.

theological language, many liberal theologians and secularists alike disdained his theology.[8] Because Reinhold uses the words of Scripture and classical theology, he is neo*orthodox*.

With respect to the meaning of those words, however, Reinhold differs with classical theology. Gilkey notes that modernity affected Reinhold such that the secular materials present in his thought "transmute the traditional theological doctrines from their frequently literalistic and objectivistic meanings into a modern symbolic and existential understanding."[9] Because Reinhold gives different content to the language of Scripture and classical theology, he is *neo*orthodox. Gilkey brings further clarity to this point, noting that for the writers of Scripture and most theologians, events such as creation, the fall, and Jesus' resurrection were taken as "representing *both* particular historical events *and* events of transcendent significance for the rest of history, and in that sense they are theologically symbolic."[10] Reinhold, along with many modern theologians, rejects the former but attempts to embrace the latter.[11] Many will concur and follow this pattern of thinking. Yet, for those who hold the traditionally orthodox position that the events in the Bible are both particular historical events and events of transcendent significance (as Gilkey notes above), this raises grave doubts about whether one can naively appropriate the Niebuhrs' thought in a theology of culture.

Reinhold's pattern of interpretation is seen in *The Nature and Destiny of Man*.[12] Here Reinhold employs the anthropological lens through which he reads Christ, creation, and culture.

The fall into creation

Expressed in mythical or suprarational terms, God is Creator. For Reinhold, the Bible retains primitive myths of God shaping the

---

8. Gilkey, *On Niebuhr*, 226.

9. Ibid., 79.

10. Ibid., 135.

11. Ibid., 135–36.

12. I focus on this work because Reinhold provides a thorough and systematic overview of his theological anthropology, which is intimately connected to his views on a variety of other subjects.

world because these myths contain within them the reality of God's transcendence and freedom, as well as his relation to the good creation and history (1:133). Although creation is other than God, it is not evil by virtue of its otherness (1:127, 133–34). Because God is Creator, the world as a whole reveals God's majesty and power (1:132). The nature of humanity, however, reveals a dark side to Reinhold's Creator God. Rather than seeing the sin and fall as a perversion or corruption of humanity's nature, Reinhold explains creation and fall in such a way that humanity is inevitably sinful because of what we are as nature and spirit (1:182, 2:73).[13] As Gilkey points out, Reinhold seems unaware that this view portrays sin as an "ontological necessity" in which "the results of the fall are the consequences of creation."[14] *Ontology* simply means the nature of reality, or what is. So to refer to sin as an ontological necessity means that sin is an essential component of being human rather than an unnecessary add-on.

As Reinhold never tires of reiterating, there are two basic facets that comprise the nature of humanity (1:78, 145, 163). On the one hand, we are children of nature, finite and limited by the reality of our organic life. As such, we are subject to the vagaries of history and the necessities of our bodily impulses. On the other hand, we are spirits who transcend both nature and our own life and reason (1:3). As spirit, the human is self-transcendent. We can see beyond our natural limits and perceive that our essence is free self-determination (1:16). The human condition is defined by the fact that humanity "stands at the juncture of nature and spirit" (1:17).

Reinhold sees Genesis 1–3 as a description of the individual's moral life, not a description (historical, mythical, or otherwise) of how humanity got into the predicament of sin. Original sin, for Reinhold, refers to the paradox that sin is inevitable but that we are also responsible for our sin (1:262). If original sin is thought to be an inherited, second nature (as in the Western theological tradition), he does not see how each individual can truly be

---

13. Reinhold distinguishes between sinning "inevitably" and sinning "necessarily." He affirms the former but not the latter. Niebuhr, *Nature and Destiny*, 1:250–51.

14. Gilkey, *On Niebuhr*, 133 n. 7.

held responsible for their sin. Therefore, he seeks to avoid this conundrum by avoiding the "literalistic errors" that plague this interpretation of Scripture. As a result, he denies that the perfection from which humanity fell can be located prior to the fall (1:268). On his read, humanity never was, in actuality, in right relation to God, other humans, and the rest of the created order. So, original righteousness is not located in humanity's original, uncorrupted nature before the fall, but in each individual (1:277). According to Reinhold, in our ability to transcend ourselves and pass judgment on our own actions, the consciousness of "original perfection" arises. That is, "original perfection" (or original righteousness) entails the realization that the self is capable of "free self-determination," which is the essence of humanity (1:16). So the "memory" of original perfection is a way to talk about the perpetual need to judge and criticize one's past and future self. To say "original righteousness" is to say "I always could have done better" as I judge my particular actions. Thus, on Reinhold's interpretation, original righteousness is relevant not as a *past* description of something lost or something to be restored in the *future* but as a *present* description of the moral self.

So, for Reinhold, the fall is not an event in history but "a symbol of an aspect of every historical moment in the life of man" (1:269). Thus, "perfection before the Fall is, in other words, perfection before the act" (1:278). To act in history and creation is to fall. Adam's "sinlessness . . . preceded his first significant action and his sinfulness came to light in that action. This is a symbol for the whole of human history. The original righteousness of man stands, as it were, outside of history" (1:280). Although we ought to accept our finitude—the fact that we have limits—we are unable to do so because our freedom and ability to transcend ourselves produces an anxiety that leads to sin.

Anxiety explains the origin of sin. Sin is occasioned by the paradox of being human. Because we are both nature and spirit, our anxiety works in a twofold manner (1:178–80).[15] On the one hand, we are free (as spirit) to determine ourselves. We know that

---

15. Niebuhr's concept of anxiety follows Kierkegaard. Niebuhr points to Søren Kierkegaard as having "the most profound analysis of the relation of sin and anxiety in Christian thought" (1:182, n. 2).

we have great potential and we are compelled to be creative in maximizing that potential. Anxiety can be positive in this way. On the other hand, this same anxiety causes us to delude ourselves into thinking that we can overcome our contingency, the fact that we are *not* the unlimited Absolute. We perpetually grasp after godlikeness, and perpetually fall. For Reinhold, the creative and destructive aspects of anxiety cannot be untangled (1:186). The conditions for the possibility of a great and glorious end are simultaneously the conditions for the possibility of an ignominious and inglorious demise. These two possibilities become actual in every human being. The state of anxiety thus leads inevitably to sin (2:73).

Reinhold's view on original sin indicates two things: sin is inevitable and we are responsible. As self-transcending humans, we are culpable for our failure to be what we ought to be (1:254). Reinhold repudiates Augustine and Calvin's historical and overly literal view of original sin, arguing instead that original sin is a dialectical, existential truth that points to the inevitability of humanity's self-love and self-centeredness (1:260). Because the freedom of the self stands "outside all relations," the real essence of sin is the soul's relation to God, not in any social relations (1:257). Original sin is thus primarily a psychological description of the individual's relation to God and an account of why each individual inevitably, but not necessarily, sins (1:251). The reality of original sin "is true in every moment of history, but it has no history."[16]

Reinhold's view of humanity, or anthropology, conflates creation and fall in the sense that the fall into sin is the inevitable consequence of how humanity was created, not its perversion or corruption. The fall and sin are no longer contingent. Instead, the fall and sin become essential to humanity because sin is the natural outworking of what we are. Reinhold's declaration that neither he nor the Christian tradition confuses finitude with fallenness sounds very orthodox (1:137), but that is because human nature is generally identified as finite, whereas for Reinhold, that is but one aspect of human nature. He argues that as spirit, we *transcend* our selves, nature, time, and history, and stand in direct relation to eternity. So although *finitude* does not lead inevitably to

---

16. Niebuhr, *Interpretation of Christian Ethics*, 86.

sin in Reinhold's account, *being human* does. Against the biblical view that all things were "very good" in the beginning, Reinhold's view of humanity makes sin a structural necessity of creation. The distinction between creation and fall refers simply to "qualities of existence" that are always true in the life of each individual.[17] Unlike Augustine and the Western tradition following him, there is no historical, contingent entry of sin into human history in the fall. But if sin is not historical and contingent, it appears to be ontological and necessary.[18] Reinhold's fall is not a fall *from* creation but a fall *into*, a fall *inherent in* the creation of humanity. Therefore, his view of humanity is simultaneously a response to the problem of evil. But his solution to the problem of evil goes too far, because it appears to explain sin by making it simply a product of the nature of humanity.[19]

Reinhold's conflation of creation and fall affects his view of sanctification (spiritual growth) and eschatological glorification (when we will be made like Christ at the fulfillment of history).[20] He criticizes both Augustine and John Calvin for their views on sanctification. The central issue, he declares, is whether humanity's "historical existence" is such that a person can ever have an easy conscience.[21] If someone can have an easy conscience, "it means that it is possible for a will centered in an individual ego to be brought into essential conformity with the will and power which governs all things" (2:141).[22] But this, thinks Reinhold, is an impossible possibility—something to shoot for, but something that can never in fact happen. We may pray, "Thy will be done,"

---

17. Niebuhr, *Interpretation of Christian Ethics*, 86.

18. Cf. Gilkey, *On Niebuhr*, 133, n. 7.

19. Cf. Minnema, *The Social Ethics of Reinhold Niebuhr*, 114.

20. As Gilkey notes, if sin has a historical cause, it leaves open the possibility of redemption. If, however, sin is inevitable given the ontological constitution of humanity, it will inevitably affect how one conceives of redemption. Gilkey, *On Niebuhr*, 133, n. 7.

21. The pastoral difference between Niebuhr and Luther on the doctrine of justification by faith should be noted. Whereas for Luther justification by faith is a doctrine that brings comfort because we rest in Christ, for Niebuhr justification by faith is a doctrine that perpetually unsettles us.

22. Niebuhr, *Nature and Destiny*, 141.

but we know we will never do it. Why? He does not say because of humanity's *sinful* existence, but because of humanity's *historical* existence. The problem is ontological, in the very nature of things. Sanctification is an impossible possibility in Reinhold's theology because his view of humanity does not permit it. Just as Reinhold cannot acknowledge an original righteousness in time and space, he cannot imagine the possibility of growing in grace and truth as the Christian life progresses. We fall short not because we are sinful, but because we are not God.

Reinhold's conflation of creation and fall also presents problems for his notion of glorification. Reinhold criticizes Martin Luther for agreeing with the Christian tradition that human life before the fall was free of anxiety. Reinhold thinks this is a nice ideal, but it misses the point that "a life totally without anxiety would lack freedom and not require faith" (1:183, n. 3). Since anxiety is an essential part of who we are as nature and spirit, overcoming anxiety does not mean union with Christ, but a loss of one's humanness. The implications for future glorification are profound. Reinhold has defined the essence of humanity as "free self-determination." But that freedom inevitably generates anxiety that, when it has conceived, inescapably brings forth sin. Because he defines freedom as autonomy, or self-determination, the perfect conformity of our will to God's will would be a *loss* of freedom and self-determination. Rather than defining true human freedom as the free will that cannot will evil (as Augustine does)[23] or as true covenant faithfulness (as Barth does),[24] Reinhold can only see future glorification as the erasure of humanity, the overcoming and absorption of humanity's anxious freedom into God's will. For Reinhold, anxiety, freedom, and sin are thus permanently woven into the fabric of human nature. To leave any of those behind is to cease to be human. This view of humanity significantly affects Reinhold's Christology.

---

23. Augustine, *The Enchiridion on Faith, Hope, and Love*, 28.105; and *The City of God against the Pagans*, 22.30.

24. Barth, *The Humanity of God*, 77.

The ideal Jesus

The ethic of Jesus is, for Reinhold, the ethic of absolute love. In its unconcern for calculation and practical compromises, it is contrasted to both naturalistic and prudential ethics. According to Reinhold, "the ethic of Jesus does not deal at all with the immediate moral problem of every human life—the problem of arranging some kind of armistice between various contending factions and forces."[25] The ethic of Jesus therefore has nothing to say to the horizontal realities of politics and economics; it is focused solely on the vertical relationship between the will of God and the will of the individual. For Reinhold, Jesus has to do with purely religious matters, not sociomoral concerns.[26] But Reinhold also argues that since love is the essence of God, it is also the moral ideal. That ideal is, by definition, an "impossible possibility" and "historically unrealizable" in actual human life.[27] The ethic of Jesus serves a primarily negative function: it presents an ideal that we never attain and thus forces us to acknowledge our sin and limitation. Against liberal optimism, Reinhold emphasizes that the kingdom of God is "always coming but never here."[28]

This point is reiterated through Reinhold's focus on the cross and neglect of resurrection. The meaning of the cross of Christ is part of a larger question about the meaning of history, according to Reinhold. To speak of a "Christ" is to say that history is meaningful but in need of fulfillment from beyond itself (2:5). To declare that the Christ must suffer is to make vicarious suffering the meaning of history (2:45). The suffering of the Messiah for human sin reveals that humanity cannot solve our sin problem; only the eternal and divine can do so. But the eternal does not destroy history. Rather, God's mercy makes itself known in history so that humanity may become aware of both guilt and the possibility of redemption (2:46).

---

25. Niebuhr, *Interpretation of Christian Ethics*, 45.

26. Ibid., 50.

27. For the first term, see Niebuhr, *Interpretation of Christian Ethics*, 36, 50, 60, 97, 106, 109, 111, and 120. For the second, see Niebuhr, *Interpretation of Christian Ethics*, 18, 37, 59, and 101.

28. Niebuhr, *Interpretation of Christian Ethics*, 60.

According to Reinhold, the cross therefore reveals the limits and possibilities of history. Because he defines historical existence and society as the realm where individuals and groups seek their own interests at the expense of others, the sacrificial love of the cross is a "tangent towards 'eternity'" that appears within history (2:69). But, on Reinhold's read, there is no real possibility of mutual love in history. The ultimate freedom and "perfect disinterestedness" of the divine love can appear in history only in a life that ends tragically because it refuses to participate in the selfish conflict of interests that characterizes human history (2:78). By nature, divine love cannot maintain itself in historical society or be involved in any exercise of power because any involvement in history and society necessarily means the assertion of one interested ego against another. Thus, for Reinhold, the divine can symbolize disinterested love only by a refusal to participate in those rivalries. True love can appear in history only to be negated and crossed out.

For Reinhold, the cross is therefore simply another way to represent the paradoxical human condition: as spirit we are free to love as we ought, and as nature we are limited and driven by the necessities of biophysical life. This interpretation of the cross of Christ can also be confirmed by "the fruit of natural experience and a natural (rational) analysis of experience" (2:96). The cross is thus another way to symbolize Reinhold's view of humanity as nature and spirit.

Human nature is inevitably fallen and sin always manifests itself in social and cultural life, according to Reinhold. So, in order for Jesus to point to God, he must point away from all culture, social life, economics, and politics. Humanity's social-cultural life cannot be considered inherently good but distorted; rather, the creation/fall dialectic characterizes culture, such that society and culture are necessary for human life but also necessarily fallen. The ethic of Jesus therefore has "only a vertical dimension between the loving will of God and the will of man," with no point of contact between any political or social ethic.[29] Furthermore, Reinhold ensures that the disinterested ethic of Jesus stands on the "edge of history" and never becomes a divine possibility in history by his tacit denial of the resurrection of Jesus (1:298).

---

29. Ibid., 45.

Notably, Reinhold's discussion of the work and person of Christ in *The Nature and Destiny of Man* terminates with the cross. Rachel King asks of Reinhold, "What is the sequel to the crucifixion in the career of Jesus of Nazareth?"[30] As she points out, there is none—no discussion of the resurrection, the ascension, or the pouring out of the Holy Spirit.[31] But as King argues, if Jesus points to God but God does not actually raise Jesus from the dead, we have a theological conundrum. The resurrection validates Jesus' life, teaching, and truth in pointing to the Father. If the Father is the omnipotent loving Father that Jesus thinks he is, he will not abandon Jesus. But if God did not raise Jesus, "then Jesus was simply mistaken in his understanding of the character of God. And so the ethic that he preached is foundationless, for the type of life he counsels men to live is advised on the presupposition that it is permanently supported by the all powerful Heavenly Father."[32]

But for Reinhold, the cross of Christ—not the resurrection or the ascension—is the ultimate interpretive principle that makes clear the truth that humanity is self-transcendent spirit and history-embedded nature (2:97). In other words, Reinhold interprets the cross as the prime example of the view of humanity he had already developed on other grounds. The resurrection cannot fit that schema, for it is the kingdom coming *in actuality* and *in history*. Therefore, his omission of the resurrection is not merely an accidental oversight or matter of emphasis but is essential to his thought. There can by definition be no true mutual love in human culture and community. The doctrines that would support that mutuality—resurrection, the love of God poured out in our hearts through the Holy Spirit (Rom 5:5), regeneration, a robust ecclesiology—are left out of the picture.

This lack of mutuality and presence of strife in human life has profound effects on the relations of the Godhead. Because he sees mutual love as an ontological impossibility for humanity, Reinhold

---

30. King, *The Omission of the Holy Spirit from Reinhold Niebuhr's Theology*, 129.

31. King, *Omission of the Holy Spirit*, 129. Cf. Yoder, *Reinhold Niebuhr and Christian Pacifism*, 20–22; and Song, *Christianity and Liberal Society*, 77–78.

32. King, *Omission of the Holy Spirit*, 138.

cannot affirm that the Father raises the Son but leaves him in the ground. Rather than allowing the perfect mutual love between the Father and Son to overflow into human communion with God and one another, Reinhold gives the fallenness of humanity such sway that it pulls the very relation of the Father and Son into its orbit. Conceptually, human sin is so powerful that it not only puts Christ on the cross, but also leaves him in the grave. Although Reinhold sees Jesus as providing the moral ideal, the sum total of his Christology is less than ideal.

The absent Spirit

In Reinhold's thought, those loci generally classified under the third article of the Apostles' Creed, in particular the Holy Spirit and salvation, are underemphasized and weak.[33] His view of justification and sanctification follows from how he has conceptualized creation and fall. The point of justification, for Reinhold, is that all we can ever do is repeatedly see that we fall short. We must recognize that sin is inevitable, given that we are nature and spirit, and trust that God forgives us. Justification is simply another way to restate the paradoxical nature of humanity that Reinhold repeatedly emphasizes in *Nature and Destiny*. In a bit of Protestant bravado, Reinhold declares that "the full gospel was never fully known or explicitly stated in the church until the Reformation" (2:148). By this, he means that the Reformation renounces the effort to complete life and history, *with* or *without* divine grace, thereby understanding the "tragic aspect" of history better than any preceding classical or Catholic view. Justification by faith is therefore just as much about how to interpret history as it is about soteriology.

Sanctification is in one sense a repetition of justification, the recognition of our continually falling short. According to Reinhold, neither Calvin nor Augustine truly sees this. Reinhold chastises Calvin for being too positive about sanctification because Calvin argues that in sanctification, our carnal desires are increasingly mortified, and our "prevailing inclination" is to submit to

---

33. For a thorough examination of Reinhold's thought on the Holy Spirit, see King, *Omission of the Holy Spirit*.

God's will (2:200).[34] Whatever else justification and sanctification may do, they do not, for Reinhold, get rid of the fact that the sin of self-love is always the most basic thing about why we do what we do. Although Reinhold uses the language of justification, there is no clear sense in which the Spirit's work of regeneration actually affects the human heart, mind, and will.[35]

If Reinhold is critical of Calvin, he is even more so of the Roman Catholic position in general and Augustine specifically. The Catholic position, according to Reinhold, is that God's mercy in Christ turns the sinner from self-centered love to obeying God, enabling growth in grace and progress in sanctification (2:135).[36] Catholics rightly believe that love is no simple possibility in the heart of man, but they believe (falsely, for Reinhold) that it is God's possibility in the heart of the individual. Like Calvin, Catholics are mistaken because they do not see that self-love remains the most "basic attitude" in human action (2:136). Thus, the Catholic does not appreciate the "tragic quality of the spiritual life" that was discovered in the Reformation.

This tragic quality means that Augustine was mistaken to say that the church may be identified with the kingdom or city of God (2:138). The problem with Augustine's thought, for Reinhold, is not that he wrongly identifies or connects the church and kingdom, but that he connects them *at all*. Reinhold takes any identification to mean that the church does not stand under God's judgment, but is the place where the contradiction between "the historical and the divine" is overcome. Instead, Reinhold contends that the church is the place where God's mercy and judgment on the historical are mediated. As a result, the contradiction between the "historical and the holy" is overcome in principle but not in fact (2:139). Given that Reinhold does not offer a robust view of the Spirit's activity in regeneration and sanctification, it is no surprise that he offers little in the way of ecclesiology.

Reinhold also lacks an emphasis on the Spirit's future eschatological work. Christianity, according to Reinhold, sees history

---

34. He is referring to Calvin's *Institutes*, 3:14:9.

35. Cf. Yoder, *Reinhold Niebuhr and Christian Pacifism*, 21.

36. This generic description could be applied not only to Roman Catholic thought but Protestant orthodoxy as well (e.g., the view of sanctification put forth in the Belgic Confession).

after Christ as the interim between the revelation of history's meaning and the fulfillment of that meaning, thereby contradicting the social optimism of liberal Christianity. But this interim is not a historical, eschatological "already/not yet," in which the kingdom has been already inaugurated in Jesus but not yet come to its complete fulfillment. Instead, for Reinhold, it is an existential, dialectical "already/not yet" that describes an "inner contradiction" that is a "perennial characteristic" of human existence and history. Throughout the ages, Christians have expected a consummation of history because Jesus, Paul, and the early church all erroneously interpreted the eschaton as a future point in time (2:49–50). For Reinhold, the eschaton symbolizes our sense that eternal fulfillment impinges on the present moment. Every moment of our time brings us closer to the fulfillment of our life and the dissolution that is our death, but there is no *historical* consummation of all things. Likewise, there is no such thing as an actual resurrection of the body at a future time. The resurrection, according to Reinhold, is a symbol of the twofold nature of the human self. As spirit, the individual is in direct relation to the eternal. As embedded in nature and history, the individual stands in an indirect relation to the eternal (2:36). The tension between the "already" and the "not yet" is a productive paradox because it drives history and drives the individual self, but it is a motor that is itself stationary, never actually reaching an eschatological destination. We thus pray for God's kingdom to come, knowing all the while that "it is in fact always coming but never here."[37]

In sum, Reinhold's view of creation, fall, and redemption are linked to his view of humanity, which sees humans as creatures who are a paradox: finite and free. Creation then refers to the ideal possibility of original righteousness, which stands "outside of history" and judges every act in time (1:280). According to Reinhold, the fall is not a historically contingent event but an existential term that describes the anxious human who continually acts as though his acts are eternal, not just historical, and thereby exalts himself too high. Redemption is the paradoxical recognition that "the final exercise of freedom in the transcendent human spirit is its recognition of the false use of that freedom in action.

---

37. Niebuhr, *Interpretation of Christian Ethics*, 60.

Man is most free in the discovery that he is not free" (2:160). Creation, fall, and redemption are not movements through salvation history, but existential and dialectical descriptions of the life of each human and of all humanity.[38] This construal of creation, fall, and redemption is not left behind in Reinhold's social ethics but is in fact integral to them.

Two cities: Augustine and Reinhold Niebuhr

By comparing Reinhold to Augustine, we can better grasp the basis of Reinhold's social thought. For Augustine, there is no ontological inevitability to sin, as there seems to be in Reinhold's account. Reinhold's social thought is different from Augustine's on three points: for Reinhold, the self is a self-in-competition, justice is a power struggle, and war is inherently part of human social life. On each of these points, Augustine and Reinhold conceptualize creation and fall in different ways, and these greatly affect their views of human sociality.

For Augustine, the city of God is inhabited by those who recognize that the good can only be had insofar as it is shared. They do so because they know that the infinite God abundantly supplies the finite creation with an endless source of good.[39] Given the original goodness of creation (including humanity) and God's redemptive work, Augustine presumes that it was and is still possible for humans to live in such a way that communion—not deadly competition—characterizes their life in God's creation. The earthly city, for Augustine, is founded on the rejection of this common good and the invention of the notion of a purely private good, in which *my* good could be evil for *you*. Augustine's point is that what is truly good for one will be truly good for all and vice versa. Thus, the fratricidal Cain and Romulus (mythical founder of Rome) are prime examples of the human city that assumes that

---

38. As Gilkey indicates, this description is not without problems: in denying that Adam is the "historical cause of our ills," both Niebuhr and other theologians who follow him seem "unaware that this denial might push them into an ontological necessity, i.e., that the results of the fall are the consequences of creation" (*On Niebuhr*, 133, n. 7).

39. Augustine, *City of God*, 15.3–15.5.

there is a finite limit to the good. Both kill their brother because they assume there is a zero-sum competition between persons and groups, where the good of one *must* be the ill of the other. Notably, what Augustine characterizes as the earthly city over against the city of God, Reinhold sees as an inherent part of human life.

In discussing self-interest, Reinhold dismisses the notion of a self-in-relation that seeks communion and cooperation. For him, the self is always in competition and self-seeking at the expense of others. Echoing Immanuel Kant, he argues that obeying the moral law must be disinterested on the part of the self.[40] As self-transcendent spirit, humans are presented with (or, more accurately, present themselves with) the "law," namely, the transcendent possibilities of acting without interest (1:278). We see this, for example, in Jesus' call to the rich young ruler that demands "action in which regard for the self is completely eliminated" (1:287). But disinterested action is not only necessary, it is also the impossible possibility. It cannot be sustained in history because one must deal prudently with competing claims and interests (2:72). As Reinhold has defined it, to participate in history or society means the assertion of one ego interest against another. Stated differently, Reinhold contends that humans always operate with some measure of *eros*, a love that has some reference to the happiness of the self, whereas the *agape* love of the cross has no reference to the good of the self (2:82). Sadly, according to Reinhold, *agape* love cannot appear in history or society without being polluted by *eros* (2:108).[41] Consequently, in his use of the notion of disinterestedness, Reinhold does not outline a place for

---

40. In discussing the various formulations of the categorical imperative, Kant declares: "By the mere fact that they are categorical, [they] exclude from their sovereign authority every admixture of interest as a motive" and so "cannot possibly as such depend on any interest," (*Groundwork of the Metaphysics of Morals*, 99). Elsewhere, he states, "Reverence is the assessment of a worth which far outweighs all the worth of what is commended by inclination, and the necessity for me to act out of *pure* reverence for the practical law is what constitutes duty, to which every other motive must give way because it is the condition of a good will *in itself*, whose value is above all else" (*Groundwork*, 71).

41. Cf. *Moral Man and Immoral Society*, 18, 45.

the happiness and good of the self in ethical theory and action.[42] That is, because his view of the self is always a sinful self, all self-love or self-regard is bad; he does not have an account of proper self-love.

For Augustine, however, sin is not *any* self-regard; it is *self-centered* rather than God-centered self-regard.[43] The issue of valid self-interest is further clarified by John Milbank, who recognizes that in a fallen world, one will often have to sacrifice one's own happiness in order to do what is good.[44] The cross of Christ is a prime example of this. But Milbank differs from Reinhold in arguing that we should not posit an *absolute* disjunction between doing what is good and the happiness of the ethical agent. In other words, Milbank seeks to rehabilitate a proper happiness of the self as a valid goal of the moral life because of his Augustinian doctrine of creation and fall.[45]

Reinhold's absolute disjunction between doing the good and the happiness of the ethical agent is directly connected to his conflation of creation and fall.[46] Conversely, Milbank distinguishes between creation and fall in a way that sees self-sacrifice as a means to an end rather than an end in itself, noting that "in a corrupt, fallen world, the only way to the recovery of mutual interaction will pass through sacrifice unto death. But the point is that

---

42. For assessment of Reinhold and self-interest, see Hicks, "Self-Interest, Agency, and Deprivation," 147–67. Also, Valerie C. Saiving argues that Reinhold's identification of sin with self-interest and love with selflessness is a masculine way of framing the problem. Saiving, "The Human Situation: A Feminine View," 100–112. Although Niebuhr's stated goal is to criticize the powerful on behalf of the oppressed, Saiving's analysis suggests that his framework may unwittingly legitimize passivity in the face of oppression.

43. For a thorough examination of this aspect of Augustine's thought, see Schlabach, *For the Joy Set Before Us.*

44. Milbank, "The Midwinter Sacrifice," 31.

45. Milbank, "The Poverty of Niebuhrianism," in *The Word Made Strange*, 239.

46. If we were to follow the suggestion of Hicks, we could map liberalism's public/private dichotomy onto Reinhold's (and Kant's) duty/happiness split. Hicks, "Self-Interest, Deprivation, and Agency," 157.

this sacrifice is not in itself the good, but rather that which sustains a road to the good in adverse circumstances."[47] For example, Jesus' enduring the cross "for the joy set before him" (Heb 12:2) causes conundrums for Reinhold's thesis regarding disinterestedness. Milbank's line of thought, however, indicates that this text reveals that the *true* and *ultimate* good of the self is not in conflict with the good of the other. The cross then is not the inevitable path of divine love in *history*, but the inevitable path of divine love in the midst of *fallen* history. That is, the sinfulness of humanity, not the very nature of humanity, is the immediate cause of the cross. Due to his anthropology, Reinhold cannot imagine a created order in which persons with rightly-ordered loves desire God and pursue the common good in harmonious community (which includes rather than excludes the individual's own true good as well). Instead, he reads a consequence of sin and the fall—inordinate self-love rather than God-centered self-love—back into the very fabric of creation.

This explains in part why Reinhold sees justice as the precarious balance of conflicting self-interests.[48] The domains of politics and economics have to do with justice, not love.[49] Since mutual love is not a viable option in humanity's social-political life, justice is the next best thing by which the interests of each are guarded against unjust violations by others.[50] Society cannot be perfect, so justice entails the strategic use of coercion, conflict, and balancing competing interests.[51] Justice is therefore a perennial power struggle.

Both Augustine and Yoder agree that in a fallen world, this is how justice typically works. But if one has a biblical doctrine of creation and redemption, one can provide a broader account of justice. True justice, argues Augustine, involves rendering what is

---

47. Milbank, "The Ethics of Self-Sacrifice," 35.

48. Niebuhr, *Interpretation of Christian Ethics*, 128. Cf. "Justice through Revolution" and "Justice through Political Force" in *Moral Man and Immoral Society*, 169–230.

49. Niebuhr, *Interpretation of Christian Ethics*, 169.

50. Niebuhr, "Why the Christian Church Is not Pacifist," 116.

51. Niebuhr, *Interpretation of Christian Ethics*, 131.

due to each, including God.[52] Love, worship, and justice are therefore never truly separable. If we love and ascribe proper worth to our Creator God, God will enable us to have rightly ordered loves for all created things and thereby do justice in all our dealings. With a proper view of creation and redemption, love and justice are not two things we are paradoxically caught between, but two ways of saying the same thing: to do justice is to love any particular thing as it ought to be loved. Interestingly, Yoder explicitly emphasizes this same Augustinian point, noting that thinkers who see an absolute disjunction between love and justice do so precisely because they lack a proper doctrine of creation.[53] The fall brings about a relative disjunction between love and justice with the introduction of retributive justice. Yet, retributive justice cannot be a creational norm insofar as it would have been unnecessary in a world where all things are properly ordered under the reign of God. True human nature and the creational, natural law have no other norm than *agape*, which *is* true justice, loving something as it ought to be loved.[54]

For Reinhold, however, love cannot be the law of our being in the realm of politics, so war will be necessary. In other words, pacifism looks naive to Reinhold because of his anthropology. Once he has described humanity as the anxious combination of nature and spirit that inevitably produces sin and discord, war becomes a structural or ontological fact of human existence. Peace is not impossible because there are *sinful* humans; peace is impossible because there are *humans*. In response to liberal pacifism, which made too little of human sin, Reinhold makes it central. For him, the overt conflict of war is thus "a final and vivid revelation of the character of human existence."[55]

Notably, Augustine agrees that war between humans is an external revelation of the war that the fallen individual experiences internally as disordered loves. Similarly, the eternal destination of the unrighteous is war—the eternal experience of internal

---

52. Augustine, *City of God*, 19.21.

53. Yoder, *Christian Witness*, 83.

54. Ibid.

55. Niebuhr, "Why the Christian Church Is not Pacifist," 108.

and external discord. Hell is war and vice versa. Unlike Reinhold, though, Augustine sees this as the revelation of the character of *fallen* human existence, not simply of human existence. Peace with God and with others is how we were created by God, which is why Yoder's pacifism can be seen as deeply Augustinian.[56] Because of the way he construes the doctrine of creation and fall, Reinhold's theology and social ethics are ultimately unable to account for the *shalom* that is humanity's true nature and destiny.

H. Richard Niebuhr: The fall into culture

As with Reinhold, so H. Richard's views of creation, fall, and redemption are intertwined with his theology of culture. Given the influence of H. Richard's *Christ and Culture*, it is worthwhile to see how his theology of culture interconnects with other key doctrinal points. In particular, his view of creation and fall significantly affect his Christology and doctrine of the Trinity.

The five types

H. Richard's typology of how different Christians relate Christ and culture is well known. Before offering analysis of H. Richard's views, however, we should briefly summarize those types. The first type, "Christ against culture," sees the two terms standing antithetically to each other. H. Richard contends that Scriptures such as 1 John and thinkers such as Tertullian and Tolstoy exemplify this radical distinction between church and world. The second type, "Christ of culture," assimilates Christ and culture to each other. This type reads Christ as embodying the best and highest of civilization and reads culture as most human where it stands in accord with Christ. Positing no "cracks" in human existence, this view—exemplified by "cultural Protestantism"—largely ignores biblical themes such as fall, incarnation, judgment, and resurrection. The third type, "Christ above culture," synthesizes Christ and culture, affirming the dual responsibility of human beings both to obey Jesus and to recognize the cultural commands of the Creator God. For the synthesis, grace perfects nature but it does not annul nature. The fourth type, "Christ and culture in paradox," focuses on the

---

56. Schlabach, "The Christian Witness in the Earthly City," 235.

dialectic between God and humanity that results from human sin. This dialectic—rather than the duality of church and culture or nature and grace—means that the real focus is not on *what* we do but *why* we it.[57] The fifth type, "Christ transforming culture," sees creation, fall, and redemption as contemporary categories by which we understand culture. F. D. Maurice exemplifies the height of the conversionist type, and he does so by connecting universalism—the idea that all persons and cultural institutions partake of the kingdom of Christ—with eschatological immediacy—the idea that every moment confronts us with the divine.

The fall into culture

H. Richard views culture as both creational and fallen. H. Richard's definition of culture includes several things that virtually all theologians would consider creational, part of how God intended humans to be—things such as language, habits, ideas, beliefs, customs, social organization, education, speech, tradition, and sociality.[58] These are creational (or essential) to human life, not an accidental addition due to the fall. Of course, given human fallenness, sin affects every particular instantiation of culture. But as H. Richard continues his definition, he clarifies that culture is not only creational but also fallen. Culture is by definition anthropocentric, concerned with humanity as the measure of all things (35). This means that in the realm of culture, God cannot be worshiped for his own sake but for the sake of some other end desired by humanity. "Culture" in this sense is roughly equivalent to what the New Testament calls the "world," (32) what Augustine calls the earthly city,[59] and what Albert Wolters calls "misdirected" culture.[60] Culture wars are also inherent to culture: every particular culture (and person within each culture) seeks to erase its particularity by claiming that its good is *the* good of humanity (36). Because of such self-seeking, each culture is a site of conflict, where individuals pursue their own

---

57. Carter, *Rethinking Christ and Culture*, 48–49.

58. Niebuhr, *Christ and Culture*, 33 (further references to this text will be noted parenthetically in the rest of this chapter) .

59. Cf. Augustine, *City of God*, 15.7.

60. Wolters, *Creation Regained*, 49–52.

interest. Likewise, the world as a whole is a site of conflict, where each particular culture stands in conflict with others. Consequently, pluralism is important for H. Richard, whether between cultures or within a particular culture, because it attempts to respect each person's right to pursue his or her own "good." By defining culture in anthropocentric and antagonistic terms, H. Richard makes culture fallen by nature, rather than seeing anthropocentrism and conflict as results of cultural perversion.

Wolters articulates the conceptual tools needed to further elucidate this point.[61] For him, "structure" denotes those elements of human life and culture that are part of God's creational intention for his good creation. Structure refers to the essence or nature of a cultural practice. From the beginning, God intended that humans cultivate the earth and use their God-given potential to produce culture across the entire spectrum of human life. "Direction," by contrast, refers to whether human beings instantiate particular cultural practices in a way that is for God's glory and human flourishing or for sinful human ends. These terms are useful in analyzing H. Richard's criticism of the "Christ against culture" type.

For H. Richard, 1 John, Tertullian, and Leo Tolstoy stand against culture in a variety of ways.[62] 1 John draws a clear line between the church and world; Tertullian rejects political life, military service, and philosophical attempts to merge Christianity with Stoicism and Platonism; and Tolstoy rejects war, a society built on self-protection, and the taking of oaths. Yet, as H. Richard points out, these "radicals" inevitably use culture, despite any disavowals they might make. For instance, 1 John uses terms that Gnostic philosophers also use; Tertullian employs legal and philosophical language and concepts of Rome; and Tolstoy's pacifism reflects something of his Russian sense of mystical communion with all humanity and nature. Moreover, H. Richard argues that Christians always have to use language that is already in play in their culture (like "Messiah," "Lord," or "love"), and he argues that the fulfillment of the law of love requires cultural specificity

---

61. For a thorough discussion of this point, see Wolters's chapter "Discerning Structure and Direction" in *Creation Regained*.

62. These thinkers are addressed at length in Niebuhr, *Christ and Culture*, 45–65.

(70–71). That is, concrete acts of love require knowledge of what specific acts would count as "love" toward someone who occupies a specific place in a culture. Love cannot be embodied except in culture. Even if Christians were to attempt to withdraw from non-Christian society and culture, their life together would require organization, human achievement, and concern for temporal ends like food and shelter (72). So, for Reinhold, the radical position is naive because it thinks it can escape culture, and it is inconsistent because it sometimes rejects culture and sometimes accepts it.

We must notice, however, the equivocation in H. Richard's analysis. Rather than differentiate between conditions of creaturehood, or structure, and fallen cultural development, or misdirection, he sees only inconsistency. Among other things, 1 John rejects the lust of the flesh, the lust of the eyes, and the pride of life; Tertullian rejects participation in warfare; and Tolstoy criticizes unjust economic practices. These thinkers, however, are not rejecting culture *per se* as much as particular perverted cultural practices or—in Wolter's terms—misdirected culture. These practices are fallen perversions of true culture. The author of 1 John does not advocate contentless love that floats above culture; he says that the way Christians show love is by sharing goods with those who need them. This is not theoretical inconsistency but practical love. Tertullian does not argue that humans have no need of social organization; he states that upholding that organization by means of violence is not the calling of the Christian. Tolstoy does not argue that following Jesus means that humans do not need food and shelter; he contends that the process of obtaining food and shelter in the Russia of his day was characterized by profound injustice. This does not mean these thinkers are all correct in their conclusions. Whereas all spoke against what they took to be *fallen* aspects of their culture, H. Richard negatively assesses this position on the basis that one cannot escape *creational* aspects of culture.

The "against culture" position cannot be consistently held, according to H. Richard, because to do so one would have to cease being human, a further indication that he sometimes uses "culture" to refer to something creational, sometimes fallen. The reason that H. Richard can criticize the radicals' stance so powerfully is not because of their logic but because of his equivocation on the term *culture*. Whereas the radical position should be seen as debating *ethical* possibilities (and impossibilities), H. Richard has framed the debate so that being "against culture" is by definition an *ontological* impossibility. Moreover, by defining culture as inherently fallen, H. Richard has inscribed the fall back onto creation. By H. Richard's interpretation, the creation mandate to be cultivators (Gen 1:28) was the mandate to go forth and fall into culture.

Christ and concrete cultural norms

To understand H. Richard's goal in *Christ and Culture*, it is helpful to see where he ends that work: prescriptive pluralism. In other words, we can never give definitive answers about God's will for and within particular human cultures. He draws this conclusion for a variety of reasons, including our fragmentary knowledge, our relative amount of faith or unbelief, our position within history and society, and the relativity of our values (234). H. Richard therefore underscores humility with respect to his five types: no one can claim "This is *the* Christian answer" (231). Such a claim, argues H. Richard, usurps Christ's lordship, does violence to the Christian liberty of others, and presumes that our particular place in the church and in history allows us to have the eschatological fullness of God's word (232). H. Richard is right to be concerned, since Christians have many times confused their particular cultural manifestations with the fullness of God's kingdom. On closer examination, however, this prescriptive pluralism has profound effects on his views of Christ and culture. Christ is nothing more than a sign pointing to the Absolute, and culture is left devoid of any criteria regarding what transformation actually entails. Moreover, H. Richard favors the type, "Christ the Transformer of Culture," precisely because—as he describes it—it entails a prescriptive pluralism that refuses to make any substantive, binding claims about human life or morality.

H. Richard's Christ points away from culture to the Absolute God. H. Richard approvingly cites Joseph Klausner's assertion that Jesus abstracted religion and ethics from the rest of social life. Instead of addressing culture in any way, Jesus ignored it and "everything concerned with material civilization" (3). Jesus is the exemplar of radical monotheism, "that unique devotion to God and to that single-hearted trust in Him which can be symbolized by no other figure of speech so well as by the one which calls him Son of God" (27). H. Richard underscores that "in his single-minded direction toward God, Christ leads men away from the temporality and pluralism of culture" (40), pointing away from the values and conditioned nature of humanity's social life to the One who is "Unconditioned" (28). Elsewhere, H. Richard further describes this God as the "one beyond the many"[63] and the "principle of being itself."[64] Idolatry, then, treats the finite as absolute or the relative as the universal (211). This leads H. Richard to be quite pessimistic about the ability of the absolute to appear in the midst of the finite: "When the principle of being is God—i.e., the object of trust and loyalty—then he alone is holy and ultimate sacredness must be denied to any special being. No special places, times, persons, or communities are more representative of the One than any others are."[65]

This absolute disjunction between the absolute and the finite negatively affects H. Richard's Christology, leading some scholars to charge him with a Gnostic, Docetic, or Nestorian Christology (which essentially deny the humanity of Jesus) whereas others charge him with a liberal, only-human Jesus.[66] Those who charge him with denying or downplaying Jesus' humanity do so because of H. Richard's conclusion that Jesus is unrelated to culture. This

---

63. Niebuhr, *Radical Monotheism and Western Culture*, 24.

64. Ibid., 37. Glen Stassen notes that these terms are striking because H. Richard had previously criticized them as "abstract and pre-Christian." (Stassen, "Concrete Christological Norms," 175).

65. Ibid., 52.

66. The charges of Docetism, Gnosticism, and Nestorianism come, respectively, in Carter, *Rethinking Christ and Culture*, 64, and "The Legacy of an Inadequate Christology," 392; Friesen, *Artists, Citizens, Philosophers*, 300, n. 21; and Long, *The Goodness of God*, 82. Charges of a liberal Christology are made by Carter, "The Legacy of an Inadequate Christology," 395; Gardner, "Ethical Issues for the 1970's," 206; Irish, *The Religious Thought of H. Richard Niebuhr*, 42–46; Kliever, "The Christology of H. Richard Niebuhr," 45; Stassen, "Concrete Christological Norms," 176; and Wittmer, "Analysis and Critique of 'Christ the Transformer of Culture,'" 153.

conclusion can be reached only by ignoring Jesus' humanity. Those who charge him with having a merely human Jesus do so because H. Richard depicts Jesus as pointing away from himself to the Father. The New Testament, however, not only portrays the Son pointing to the Father, but the Father pointing back to the Son (e.g., Mark 9:7). Yoder weighs in on this issue, noting that H. Richard ignores several characteristics of Christ as depicted in the New Testament and classical theology, characteristics that "would have made impossible the interpretation of Jesus as 'pointing away' from the realm of culture, and thereby as needing the corrective of a 'more balanced' position."[67] Jesus did not come to point away from all culture to the Absolute but, at least in part, to point to certain cultural options and away from others. If H. Richard were to call attention to this, it would undermine his own position of prescriptive pluralism. Ultimately, H. Richard's prescriptive pluralism, the Absolute God of radical monotheism, and the Jesus who points away from any concrete culture are all of a piece.[68]

Christ, therefore, is important for H. Richard because he points to the transcendent God who destabilizes all historically particular configurations of culture. As Glen Stassen argues, H. Richard was acutely aware of the way that historical and cultural conditions affect all attempts to know and proclaim the truth. This recognition of our hermeneutic horizons need not mean an absolute relativism, however, and Stassen shows how H. Richard endeavored to outline norms that would validate the truth of Christianity from *within* history.[69] Nevertheless, Stassen also shows that because H. Richard reacted so strongly against Karl Barth's Christocentric

---

67. Yoder, "How H. Richard Niebuhr Reasoned," 60. Those characteristics are (1) Jesus is the incarnate Son of God whose teaching is authoritative and whose person is unique, (2) Jesus' death provides atonement for human sin and his resurrection provides the basis for new power in human experience, (3) Jesus is an exemplary human whose disciples are called to follow him not in "slavish mimicry but . . . free discipleship," and (4) by virtue of Jesus' resurrection and ascension, he is affirmed as Lord over nature and human history.

68. Stassen, "Concrete Christological Norms," 185.

69. Ibid., 156–72.

theology, he advocated not merely a hermeneutic of humility but a position of "equiprobabilist relativism."[70] That is, any and all positions become equally tenable. Thus, H. Richard became reticent to affirm the ability of any historically-located person or church to proclaim that any particular practice was definitively God's will for that place and time. Stassen's point is more fully seen in H. Richard's negative evaluation of the "Christ above culture" type and his positive depiction of the "Christ transforming culture" type.

For H. Richard, the "Christ above culture" type tends to claim too much. He acknowledges there is a divine law which humans access by reason, but holds that any particular formulation of this law in language and concepts will be culturally conditioned (145). The "Christ above culture" type continually forgets this and sees its own articulation of God's law as that law itself. Consequently, the "Christ above culture" type perpetually falls back into the "Christ of culture" type. Because what we call "God's law" is always our interpretation of God's law rather than the transcendent law itself, we must not only be humble but also suspend judgment about any particular cultural practice. If those in the "above culture" position were humble enough to acknowledge that their action is a purely symbolic human action, that would be fine. But when they claim their action may participate in the kingdom of God on earth, they are insufficiently circumspect. By contrast, proper pluralistic humility is a characteristic only of the transformationist type (147).

For H. Richard, the transformationist type speaks of Christ correctly because it is humble and pluralistic enough to disavow any certainty with respect to God's will for human culture. Humility and pluralism come from, in part, a disavowal of the doctrine of election. The Gospel of John, Augustine, and John Calvin all fall short of being true transformationists, according to H. Richard, because they continue to cling to this doctrine (204, 216–18). H. Richard notes that both Scripture and Christians often identify a particular people (Israel and the church) as set apart. Importantly, election is

---

70. Ibid., 176. In a 1960 address at Union Theological Seminary, H. Richard himself stated that he had spent the last decade intentionally leaning the opposite direction of Barth (174).

not only about eternal destiny, but about present cultural practices. For example, when God sets Israel apart, he gives them very specific guidelines as to how they are and are not to behave with respect to a whole variety of cultural practices. Election is problematic, according to H. Richard, because it focuses on one particular people or one particular cultural option.

For H. Richard, the true transformationist is a universalist—they believe all will be saved. Transformationists reject the notion that "the Christian life is cultural life converted by the regeneration of man's spirit" (which is the position of the Gospel of John). Instead, they reframe reality, seeing all humans and all cultural existence as already transformed (205). The transformation does not happen in the external world, but in the subjective viewer. There is irony here. H. Richard assumes that the kingdom of God cannot become a reality in his first four types.[71] The kingdom is possible, however, in the conversionist position precisely because conversionists do not claim anything binding about their way of life, for that would violate the principle of pluralism. H. Richard does not merely hold to a "diachronic pluralism." This idea affirms a proper contextual and creational diversity in which Christians give different answers to different cultural questions at different times and in different places. Instead, he holds to a "synchronic pluralism," in which Christians in the same culture confronting the same issue give different and often contradictory answers. With minor issues of Christian liberty, this is no problem, but with other issues, it raises the question of the church's faithfulness. H. Richard's position seems to imply that if one makes a claim about God's will regarding a specific ethical matter or cultural practice, one violates his prescriptive pluralism. Thus, to say "this is what you ought to do, too" is immediately to put oneself in the "against culture" or "above culture" position rather than the conversionist. Being a conversionist therefore means that one never actually tells someone they *ought* to do something (unless, ironically, that something is to stop telling others what to do).

H. Richard rightly wants Christians to recognize their fallibility, their historicity, and their ever-present hermeneutical matrix. These are all legitimate points. Nevertheless, he argues that by virtue of the fact that I am human and always interpreting, I can

---

71. Cf. Carter, *Rethinking Christ and Culture*, 68.

say something about what God requires of *me*, but I cannot go beyond that to pretend that I may be able to discern something that is morally binding for other people (239). Stated differently, H. Richard's "Christ the Transformer of Culture" does not indicate concrete Christological norms for culture. Instead, H. Richard uses "Christ" as a cipher to reject any concrete norms, precisely because those norms will always be formulated in human history, language, and concepts.

As a result, H. Richard's pluralism and universalism transform his understanding of the redemption of culture so that it becomes nothing more than an intellectual exercise of reframing what one is already doing in one's culture. "The sovereignty of God" and "the lordship of Christ" now mean that all our cultural institutions are *already* participating in God's kingdom (226, 256). H. Richard's claim that "there is no phase of human culture over which Christ does not rule, and no human work which is not subject to his transforming power over self-will" sounds right (227). But we must keep his other points in mind: Christ does not tell us anything concrete but points away from culture, and the notion of election must be rejected, whether it is with respect to persons or to cultural practices. For Reinhold, the fact that Jesus is Lord of all spheres of life means that I *cannot* give concrete criteria to distinguish between good and evil in this sphere. Christians will continue doing what they were already doing as a part of their culture, but with a new rationale to justify their actions. Under the guise of biblical language of sovereignty and lordship, Christians become passive toward the real evils of their particular culture and lose any criteria by which to judge faithfulness or unfaithfulness to their Lord.[72] In the end, what goes by the name of transformation is really accommodation.[73]

---

72. Stassen, "Concrete Christological Norms," 145; Wilson, "Christ and Cult(ure)," 183; and Wittmer, "Analysis and Critique of 'Christ Transforming Culture,'" 244.

73. Cf. Jacob Klapwijk's notion of "inverse transformation" in Klapwijk, "Antithesis, Synthesis, and the Idea of Transformational Philosophy," 147–148.

Orthodox trinitarianism or heterodox unitarianisms?

Just as the Christ of *Christ and Culture* is governed by the principle of pluralism, so H. Richard's doctrine of the Trinity is less about the persons that comprise the Godhead and more about the pluralism that ought to be accepted in the church. Throughout *Christ and Culture*, H. Richard repeatedly faults certain types for failing to be trinitarian. For example, he criticizes the "Christ against culture" type for overemphasizing Jesus and underemphasizing the Father as Creator and Governor of history, as well as the Spirit who is immanent in creation and the Christian community (81). He criticizes the "Christ of culture" type for forgetting that the Father transcends all particular cultures (114–15). He commends the "Christ above culture" type because at its best it faithfully represents the Trinity, although it generally slides back into the "Christ of culture" type (131). H. Richard prefers "Christ transforming culture" because it is properly trinitarian and therefore most accurately understands the biblical narrative of creation, fall, and redemption (192–93). This sounds promising, but closer examination reveals that H. Richard's doctrine of the Trinity is not so orthodox, which consequently raises questions about his theology of culture. Rather than making the coherence between Father, Son, and Spirit the basis of true ecumenical unity, H. Richard reads the contradiction between Arians, Marcionites, and spiritualists back into the very nature of the trinitarian God. We see this in how H. Richard articulates the relationship between the persons of the Father and Son, and between creation and redemption.

H. Richard proposes that we think of Christianity as an "association . . . of three Unitarian religions." By "Unitarian," H. Richard means simply that different Christians identify with and focus on one particular person of the Godhead and ignore the other two persons of the Trinity.[74] Thus, there are Unitarians

---

74. Niebuhr, "The Doctrine of the Trinity and the Unity of the Church," 372–73. The importance of this article should not be underestimated. In addition to its original publication in 1946, it was republished as "Theological Unitarianisms," *Theology Today* 40, no. 2 (1983): 150–57 and, even though already published twice, it was also included in H. Richard Niebuhr, *Theology, History, and Culture: Major Unpublished Writings*, (1996).

of the Father, of the Son, and of the Spirit. The Unitarianisms listed by H. Richard are not simply various stands of trinitarian-affirming Christians who emphasize one person or another in their practical piety. Instead, H. Richard includes positions that would deny the doctrine of the Trinity as traditionally understood. For example, he includes Arians, Deists, and Unitarians (in the more narrow sense) under the Unitarianism of the Father, and the chief example of Unitarianism of the Son is the early heretic Marcion, who divorced Jesus from the God of the Old Testament.[75] As in *Christ and Culture*, H. Richard emphasizes pluralism, arguing that the truth is the sum of all the positions presented. He asserts that we need the doctrine in order to emphasize that Christianity is "not the realized conviction of any of its parts but rather the common faith."[76] The doctrine of the Trinity shows that all the partial insights of the various Unitarianisms must be held together synthetically. "A doctrine of the Trinity, so formulated," H. Richard concludes, "will never please any one part of the church but it will be an ecumenical doctrine providing not for the exclusion of heretics but for their inclusion in the body on which they are actually dependent. Truth, after all, is not the possession of any individual of any party or school, but is represented, insofar as it can be humanly represented, only by the whole dynamic and complementary work of the company of knowers and believers."[77]

H. Richard's absolute pluralism creates problems when he articulates the relationship between the Father and Son. For H. Richard, the Father creates the world, governs history, grounds natural theology, and rules over nature and secular societies.[78] By means of human reason we can therefore look at the world and discern the Father's will for human life. The problem is that the conclusions of natural theology do not always match up with Scripture in general and the revelation given in Jesus in particular. For H. Richard, what

---

75. Niebuhr, "The Doctrine of the Trinity and the Unity of the Church," 373–74.

76. Ibid., 383.

77. Ibid., 384.

78. Niebuhr, *Christ and Culture*, 80–81, and "The Doctrine of the Trinity and the Unity of the Church," 373.

we know via creation—in the natural world and in human society by means of reason—differs from what we find in Christ. How is this contradiction between Father and Son, creation and Christ to be handled? H. Richard does not attempt to find coherence between the two, but emphasizes pluralism, which admits that the faith of the one church requires these opposing Unitarianisms. Yoder, however, rightly points out that "the intention of the post-Nicene doctrine of the Trinity was precisely *not* that through Father, Son, and Spirit differing revelations come to us. The entire point of the debate around the nature of the Trinity was the concern of the church to say just the opposite, namely that in the Incarnation and in the continuing life of the church under the Spirit there is but one God."[79]

H. Richard's pluralism profoundly affects his view of heresy and the doctrine of the Trinity. As the church of the fourth century attempted to be faithful to biblical language, they excluded certain stances as incompatible with Scripture. These positions were heresy. For H. Richard, however, heresy must be allowed so that, as Craig Carter puts it, the church would include "the Arians and liberals along with the Swedenborgians and pietists and . . . the mystics and metaphysical idealists. All are heretical in and of themselves, yet all are essential to the whole faith of the whole church."[80] H. Richard argues that any particular position, by definition, cannot possess the truth. Instead, truth is represented only by the whole dynamic and complementary spectrum of those who claim anything about who and what they think the Christian God is. Presumably, the position held by the particular group which confesses that God is one *ousia* (being/substance) and three *hypostases* (subsistences/persons) is insufficiently ecumenical because it is held by some particular people and not others. Since H. Richard sees the doctrine of the Trinity as a doctrine that allows for rather than excludes heretical views of God, it would seem to follow that the only anathema would be against those who would label themselves orthodox in any exclusive sense. Here we again see H. Richard's awareness of historical embeddedness and his hermeneutic humility become so strong that they lead him to

---

79. Yoder, "How H. Richard Niebuhr Reasoned," 62 (original emphasis).

80. Carter, *Politics of the Cross*, 124.

be an "equiprobabilist relativist" not only with respect to knowing God's will regarding particular cultures (as noted above) but regarding the capability of humans to make affirmations regarding the nature of God.

H. Richard ascribes contradictory content to Father and Son in part because his description of culture equivocates and conflates creation and fall. Since by culture he means something that is inherently both created and fallen and, because the Father is identified as Creator of human nature and culture, conflict between the Father and Son is inevitable. Whereas the "Christ against culture" type sees Christ as countering *fallen* culture, H. Richard reads that position as simply against culture, which resides under the rubric of the Father. So, just as the Unitarianism of the Father and Son are not to be brought into a coherent trinitarian unity, neither may Christ and creation be brought together in a coherent theology of culture. Indeed, just as the coherence produced by Nicene orthodoxy would exclude some ways of speaking about God, so coherence between Christ and creation would exclude some ways of being in culture, namely, those discerned as fallen. This is exactly what H. Richard's thought, with its pluralistic emphasis, seems to disallow.

In sum, H. Richard's thought has three shortcomings. First, his use of the term "culture" is equivocal. Sometimes he uses it to refer to creational aspects of culture and other times uses it to refer to the fallen direction that specific cultures take. Second, it leads to a Christ who is by definition unrelated to culture. A Christ who judges any and every particular form of culture equally is, in the end, a Christ who judges no particular form of culture. This explains why H. Richard's concept of "transformation" is abstract and lacks concrete criteria. Third, in his appeal to trinitarianism, H. Richard sets the Father as Creator and Son as Redeemer in competition and contradiction. Christ and creation thus become two alternate and competing authorities for the Christian's loyalty in culture, to say nothing of the Spirit as providing a third avenue of potentially contradictory revelation. For H. Richard's pluralism, some Christians follow the light of creation and others tread the way of Jesus. Trinitarianism, thinks H. Richard, accepts contradiction and competition between the persons of the Trinity, seeing the true church as a fold large enough to hold all heresies. H. Richard's conflation of creation and fall, his problematic Christology, his unorthodox trinitarianism, and his lack of substantive and discriminating criteria for cultural transformation are integrally linked. These theological problems cast aspersions upon H. Richard's theology of culture, making it an unsuitable option for a theology of culture that is both biblical and consistent with classical orthodoxy. Although it is trinitarian in language, it is not in substance.

Yoder observes that the relationship between the Jesus of *Politics* and Reinhold Niebuhr was one of "total theological encounter."[81] One could also say that Yoder's engagement with both Niebuhr brothers is one of total theological encounter, dealing with such basics as the doctrines of the Trinity and of Christ; of the meaning of creation, fall, redemption, and consummation; and of the role of the Spirit and the church in the life of the Christian. Yoder's difference was not simply a dispute about social ethics or pacifism, but about the deficiencies at the core of the Niebuhrs' theology. Yoder's own thought must now be spelled out more fully to see how his trinitarian theology of culture constitutes a more biblical and theologically orthodox alternative.

---

81. Yoder, *Christian Attitudes*, 317–18.

3

God's Word and Our Words: Yoder and the Creeds

The Niebuhrs use trinitarian language without substance; Yoder does not. To those operating with caricatures of Yoder's position, this claim may seem objectionable. They take his Anabaptism to be at odds with creedal Christianity and possibly trinitarianism, his focus on history to be at odds with the creeds' metaphysical and ontological language, and his anti-Constantinianism to be at odds with the man Constantine, who was firmly enmeshed in the proceedings of Nicea. Yoder's relationship to the creeds—and thus his Christology and trinitarianism—is a contentious topic. Some scholars question Yoder's Christological orthodoxy and criticize him for it, whereas others laud him for (in their view) his apparent heterodoxy.[1] At best, critics charge Yoder with indifference to the trinitarian and Christological orthodoxy of the Nicene and Chalcedonian Creeds and, at worst, hostility toward them.[2] Still

---

1. Finger, "Did Yoder Reduce Theology to Ethics?" in *A Mind Patient and Untamed*, 333; Reimer, "Mennonites, Christ, and Culture," 12; Reimer, "Theological Orthodoxy and Jewish Christianity," in *Wisdom of the Cross*, 435; Biesecker-Mast, "The Radical Christological Rhetoric of John Howard Yoder," in *A Mind Patient and Untamed*, 42; and Weaver, *The Nonviolent Atonement*, 92–96, and "The United States Shape of Mennonite Theologizing," 639–40.

2. When Yoder references the creeds, he generally means Nicea and Chalcedon, although he does reference the Apostles' Creed as well. He addresses Nicea and Chalcedon at length in *Preface to Theology*.

others argue that Yoder's thought is perfectly compatible with creedal orthodoxy.[3] If Yoder rejects the creeds and their doctrines of God, as both critics and friends sometimes claim, he cannot be characterized as "trinitarian." Although Yoder takes a complicated stance toward tradition in general and the creeds in particular, his thought fits with both Scripture and creedal orthodoxy, especially the trinitarian and Christological formulations of the Nicene and Chalcedonian Creeds.[4]

Why do some see Yoder as in line with creedal orthodoxy whereas others see him as downright anticreedal? Because they often jump straight to what Yoder says about the creeds without examining how his view of the creeds fits within the context of his broader theology, including his view of the nature of theological language and the authority of tradition. Yoder sees the creeds as legitimate translations of the New Testament because, like the New Testament, Nicea and Chalcedon enter into specific thought worlds and refashion those linguistic and conceptual worlds in such a way that Christians can affirm that Jesus is Messiah and Lord within that world. If we are no longer part of the thought worlds to which the creeds were addressed, can we dispense with them? Yoder would say no, not least because he himself sees that they must be addressed. The creeds, like the Bible, are both applicable and always in translation. The question is not whether they are dispensable but whether we have adequately translated and interpreted them so that we can understand precisely why they are indispensable.

In other words, the creeds go beyond the Bible precisely by *not* going beyond the Bible. They go beyond the Bible in that they communicate the gospel in new missionary situations that were not the context of the original writings of Scripture; but they do *not* go beyond the Bible in that they communicate that message faithfully. So, for those who take the Bible and the creeds seriously, Yoder's

---

3. Carter, *The Politics of the Cross*, 93; Nation, "Mending Fences and Finding Grace"; Weaver, "Missionary Christology," 423–39; and Slater, "Does Yoder throw the Christological baby out with the Constantinian bathwater?"

4. I am not the first to make the case that Yoder is compatible with creedal orthodoxy. This is done well in both Carter, *The Politics of the Cross*, and Nation, "Mending Fences and Finding Grace."

theology of culture does not represent a sectarian, antitrinitarian path but one that attempts to take seriously what Christianity has always claimed about the Father, Son, and Holy Spirit.

Yoder's appeal to creedal orthodoxy

A brief sampling of Yoder's works shows that he frequently appeals to Nicene and Chalcedonian orthodoxy both to support his own position and to assess the thought of others.[5] Unless we have good reason to do otherwise, a straightforward reading takes Yoder at his word when he affirms the teachings of the creeds and contends that his own thought is consistent with the creeds. Several examples reinforce this point. In *Politics*, Yoder claims that "the view of Jesus being proposed here is more radically Nicene and Chalcedonian than other views. I do not here advocate an unheard-of modern understanding of Jesus. I ask rather that the implications of what the church has always said about Jesus as Word of the Father, as true God and true Human, be taken more seriously, as relevant to our social problems, than ever before."[6] Elsewhere, Yoder also claims that his Christian pacifism stands or falls with the claim that Jesus is Christ, Lord, and true revelation of God.[7] Although Yoder acknowledges criticisms that the Jesus of *Politics* is a diversion from traditional Christology, he disavows them.[8] In fact, he argues that the Christology of *Politics* does "not mean a reduction; it rather sought to safeguard the wholeness of the classical Christology."[9] That is, Yoder does not deny but extrapolates the implications of Chalcedon: "We misunderstand the

---

5. He also appeals to the Apostles' Creed at several points. For example, see Yoder, "A Theological Critique of Violence," in *The War of the Lamb*, 39–40.

6. Yoder, *Politics of Jesus*, 102.

7. Yoder, *Nevertheless*, 125: Yoder's pacifism "would lose its substance if Jesus were not Christ and its foundation if Jesus Christ were not Lord." One epigram to this chapter is a quote from T. S. Eliot: "The hint half guessed, half understood, is Incarnation."

8. Yoder, "That Household We Are," 9.

9. Yoder, "The Power Equation, Jesus, and the Politics of King," in *For the Nations*, 138, n. 26. Cf. Yoder, *Politics*, 226. Carter also makes this point in *Politics of the Cross*, 130.

relationship between Christ's two natures if we wipe out the political side of his human existence."[10]

Yoder also claims to be more consistent with classical orthodoxy than those he sometimes criticizes. At the beginning of *Politics*, Yoder asks, "What becomes of the meaning of the incarnation if Jesus is not normatively human? If he is human but not normative, is this not the ancient ebionitic heresy? If he be somehow authoritative but not in his humanness, is this not a new gnosticism?"[11] There are two ways of functionally denying creedal Christology. Modern liberal theology is often overtly Ebionitic, notes Yoder, which means that it affirms Jesus' humanity but not his divinity. But many creedally orthodox Christians are covertly Gnostic. So, throughout Christian history, a central threat to Christology has not been an external Ebionism (e.g., modern non-Christians who think Jesus was merely a good moral teacher) but an internal Gnosticism or Docetism that emphasizes Jesus' divinity to the point that it eclipses or denies his humanity. Even today, theologically conservative Christians who argue vociferously that the divinity of Jesus must be confessed and named may either unwittingly ignore Jesus' humanity or implicitly (or perhaps even explicitly) deny the normativity of Jesus' humanity.[12] For the Chalcedonian Christian, argues Yoder, rejecting the normativity of Jesus' humanity is as theologically and ethically problematic as rejecting his divinity.

Yoder also combats H. Richard Niebuhr's "trinitarianism," as noted in the previous chapter.[13] The doctrine of the Trinity, Yoder

---

10. Yoder, *Discipleship as Political Responsibility*, 58.

11. Yoder, *Politics*, 10.

12. For example, see Carson, *Christ and Culture Revisited*, 52–59, 159–72. Carson clearly affirms the full humanity of Jesus. Carson, however, manages to address Jesus and the kingdom he announced without connecting this to a new way of being political and cultural. Although he finds Jesus advocating for a secular, demythologized state, Carson's main focus is on Jesus' humanity only as a vehicle to provide atonement for sin and therefore get the Christian to heaven rather than hell (58). This is not wrong in itself, but far too narrow. In a work by a New Testament scholar that addresses Christ and culture, it is a startlingly thin account of Jesus' humanity and all that entails for human life and culture.

13. Yoder's criticism is summed up in "How H. Richard Niebuhr Reasoned," 61–65.

argues, underscores the unity of will and purpose of Father, Son, and Holy Spirit. The three persons do not contradict one another. The three persons are distinguished, but they also act in unity. In contrast to H. Richard Niebuhr's contradiction-in-unity version of the Trinity, Yoder claims that his distinction-in-unity trinitarianism is consistent with creedal orthodoxy.

The creeds are relative

If Yoder's appeals to creedal orthodoxy were all that scholars had to go on, there would be no controversy regarding his relationship to the creeds. In a 1980 lecture, however, Yoder notes that in his "Preface to Theology" course lectures (now published), he takes "a narrative and relativizing approach" to the development of early Christian dogma, especially the Christological creeds.[14] He also highlights the political and procedural problems with the early councils, especially Constantine's involvement in Nicea.[15] These statements seem to support those who question Yoder's Christology, and those who use Yoder to criticize rather than affirm Nicea and Chalcedon.

Given this ambivalence, the debate about Yoder's stance vis-à-vis the creeds continues unabated. Yoder's view of the creeds, however, must be placed in the context of several necessary and clarifying questions that Yoder answers elsewhere: What is the nature and purpose of theological language? What is the authority of tradition within the church? What is the proper procedure for resolving theological questions and issues that arise within the church? What is the task of the theologian within the body of Christ? Yoder answers these questions and sets the stage for his view of the creeds in two key points. First, for Yoder, the gospel has been in translation from its inception. Second, Yoder describes the authority of tradition in a way that clarifies how important theological distinctions and formulations should be made and who should be involved in making them.

If the above issues are addressed, we can see in what sense Yoder both affirms and relativizes the creeds. Because they

14. Yoder, "That Household We Are," 9.

15. Yoder, Preface, 197.

faithfully translate and articulate the old message of Scripture in a new day, the creeds should be affirmed.[16] Because they are not Scripture, they are relativized. They are not masters but servants of the Word of God (understood first as Jesus Christ and second as Scripture). Importantly, for Yoder (though perhaps not for others) "relativizing" the creeds does *not* mean dismissing or ignoring or denying them but recognizing their proper place as servants of the good news, heralds of the gospel. Put differently, the *relativity* of the creeds means that they are *relatives* of Scripture, bearing a family resemblance. Just as children inherit family traits from their parents and reassemble them in new ways, so the creeds inherit biblical thought and speech patterns and reassemble them in new times and places to respond to new questions and to refute unfamiliar ways of proclaiming or translating the good news.

The missionary nature of the gospel. The need to translate words and concepts from one thought world to another did not begin with colonialism, modernity, or globalization. From the first disciples of Jesus until the present day, Christians have perpetually faced this challenge and opportunity. For example, the early Christians had to ask how one proclaims the gospel to those who are not Jews, who are not from the land of Palestine, and who have questions that were never posed to or about Jesus.[17] The proclamation of the gospel, Yoder notes, has two key characteristics.[18] First, Christians think that what they believe is true, not just for them, but for all people. Second, Christians have been compelled to tell others about this truth. From the disciples in the first century to the missionaries of today who depart from Georgia to Guatemala or from Chile to Chicago, Christians engage other people who have completely different languages, thought worlds, and frames of reference. The missionary task of proclaiming the good news of Jesus in new terms, times, and places does not arise as a new challenge in AD 325 with the Council of Nicea. This task commences already in the first century, in the missionary spread of the gospel and in the very pages

---

16. I am playing off the title of Yoder's "As You Go: The Old Mission in a New Day."

17. Yoder, "But We Do See Jesus," in *Priestly Kingdom*, 50.

18. Yoder, "That Household We Are," 2–3.

of Scripture. In the face of the perennial missionary task, Yoder's essay "But We Do See Jesus" notes that there are several responses one could take. If one thinks one has the truth but encounters a new and different thought world, what are the options? He lists and rejects six faulty options before looking to Scripture for how to properly go about the missionary task of proclamation.

The first option is a defensive fidelity to one's particular truth.[19] Before encountering a different thought world, the particular truth one holds just seems natural. But when confronted with new and different ideas, one's relation to one's truth claims is transformed. The truth one believes is no longer simply organic and natural (for example, the subconscious awareness that "I believe this, my parents believe this, and so does most everyone else I know"). Instead, the truth claim now calls for defensiveness and suspicion toward those who might challenge it.

A second option—on the other end of the spectrum—is to renounce one's previous position and to convert to the wider thought world. Since the wider world seems to be larger and stronger, it is often thought to be truer. Those converts to the wider world often take up the task of the "enlightened pedagogue," the third option. These converts are convinced that rational argumentation can lead people from their original "smaller" thought world to the "larger" one.

The fourth option is the *apologia*. One does not renounce one's truth claims or roots in a "smaller" world, but rephrases that truth in a way that makes it commendable to the mainstream value system. This position accepts the wider world's way of saying things and then tries to show how its minority position makes sense within that bigger logic. A fifth option constructs a new metalanguage, an attempt to take us beyond all particularities of previous conversations so that we become the creators of the newest, widest world yet. A sixth option is a pluralistic humility. One keeps one's truth claim but does not try to convince others of that truth. In other words, one alters what is typically meant by "truth" and instead opts for humility because the different truth claims generated by varying thought worlds are thought to be irreconcilable.

---

19. The following paragraphs are a summary of Yoder, "But We Do See Jesus," in *Priestly Kingdom*, 48–49.

Yoder argues that all of these answers are unsatisfactory because they presume the priority and truth of the supposed wider world. In reality, however, Yoder's points out that any so-called wider world is still another provincial way of speaking, thinking, and reasoning: "one adolescent's breath of fresh air is another's ghetto."[20] So, the question still remains, "How can particular truths be proclaimed publicly?"[21] Scripture provides a model.

In John 1, the author uses the term *logos*, implying that this term would have been part of his audience's understanding of reality. As a principle of order and rationality, the *logos* bridged the gap between the eternal and the temporal. John could have let the logic of this worldview dictate how he would conceptualize Jesus, but he did not. Instead, John breaks the rules of this cosmology by putting Jesus as *logos* both at the top of the cosmology—the *logos* is deity—and at the level of humanity—the *logos* became flesh, a scandalous claim to most hearers.

The writer of Hebrews 1 provides a second example of translating the gospel. In Hebrews 1, the author explores the cosmological chain familiar to the Jewish audience. God is at the top, with angels as messengers between heaven and earth. Humans are on the bottom, and priests are raised up to be mediators between earth and heaven. The author of Hebrews, however, does not place Jesus just below the angels, as the high priest or second Adam, but above them at the right hand of God. Importantly, this exaltation does not require the loss of his humanity since the exaltation is precisely because of his true humanity.

A final example comes from Colossians 1, which engages an audience who viewed the world as held together by a network of principalities and powers. One navigated this world with the aid of fasting, festivals, visions, and angel worship. The author of Colossians, rather than showing how Jesus can help his audience negotiate and manipulate the powers and principalities, argues instead that Jesus has broken their power. Jesus is not simply part of the cosmos but is its Lord.[22]

---

20. Yoder, "But We Do See Jesus," in *Priestly Kingdom*, 49.

21. Ibid.

22. Ibid., 52.

Based on these biblical texts, Yoder notes six moves that the biblical writers make to communicate their particular gospel message to their audience.[23]

1. The writers inhabit the new linguistic thought world, using its language and facing its questions.
2. Rather than fitting Jesus into the slots of that cosmology, the writer places Jesus above the cosmos as Lord.
3. The writers focus on the rejection and suffering of Jesus. He is Lord precisely because of his obedient suffering, not in spite of it.
4. The audience is called to participate in the self-emptying, death, and resurrection of the Son by the grace of God.
5. Behind and enabling the cosmic victory of the Son stands a variety of explanations: preexistence, coessentiality with the Father, possession of the image of God, and the participation of the Son in creation and providence.
6. The writer and readers share by faith in the victory of Jesus: "We are his house" (Heb 3:6).

Based on these observations, Yoder notes that the New Testament is missionary both in content and form:

A handful of messianic Jews, moving beyond the defenses of their somewhat separate society to attack the intellectual bastions of majority culture, refused to contextualize their message by clothing it in the categories the world held ready. Instead, they seized the categories, hammered them into other shapes, and turned the cosmology on its head, with Jesus both at the bottom, crucified as a common criminal, and at the top, preexistent Son and creator, and the church his instrument in today's battle. It is not the world, culture, civilization, which is the definitional category, which the church comes along to join up with, approve, and embellish with some correctives and complements. The Rule of God is the basic category. The rebellious but already (in principle) defeated cosmos is being brought to its knees by the Lamb.

---

23. Ibid., 53.

> The development of a high Christology is the natural cul-
> tural ricochet of a missionary ecclesiology when it collides
> as it must with whatever cosmology explains and governs
> the world it invades.[24]

Here is the crucial point: Yoder is saying that translation
of the good news of Jesus does not begin with the creeds in the
fourth century because the *Bible itself* is a missionary book and
Christianity has been a missionary faith *from the very beginning*.[25]
The text of the New Testament itself shows how to report the
story of Jesus as true for people who are not from the land of
Palestine, who are not Jews, and who have questions that were
never asked of Jesus.[26] Yoder does not hold to a "fall" from an
original pristine, untranslated (Jewish) message into some other,
contaminated (Greek) language. The good news of the gospel is
for all nations and has *always* been in translation, from the time
of Christ until the present day. To play on an Athanasian phrase,
there was no time when it was not this way.

The authority of tradition. If Yoder was a precritical biblicist
(assuming you can read the Bible apart from any tradition or interpretive lens) or a naïve restitutionist (assuming you can just ignore
history and go back to the first century church), we would expect
him to take a solely negative stance toward the creeds as "human
traditions." If, on the other hand, Yoder held to the inevitable
progress of church history, we would expect him to rubber-stamp
the creeds without thinking too much about them. Yoder does
neither and instead provides a nuanced view of the authority that
tradition does and does not have.[27]

For Yoder, the Bible and tradition can be distinguished.
However, Yoder also willingly acknowledges that tradition and
our interpretive lenses affect how we interpret Scripture. He points

---

24. Ibid., 54.

25. Yoder, "The Authority of the Canon," in *To Hear the Word*, 2nd
ed., 105. All future references are to this edition.

26. Yoder, "But We Do See Jesus," in *Priestly Kingdom*, 50.

27. The following paragraphs summarize Yoder, "The Authority of
Tradition," in *Priestly Kingdom*, 66–72, and integrate his argument there
with his remarks elsewhere on the subject.

out that the slogan "No creed but the Bible" is deceptive "if it is thought that in our own reading of the Bible we can avoid having any grid, any internal canon, of our own."[28] Indeed, Yoder contends that the best definition of fundamentalism is the refusal to acknowledge the "hermeneutic problem" that we all interpret the Bible through a particular grid.[29] Nevertheless, Scripture can never be completely conflated with our interpretation of it. We can never possess Scripture in the sense of not needing to continually check our own gloss on the text by returning to the text itself.[30] Yoder uses the analogy of a microscope and microbe.[31] The microbe can only be seen by using the microscope. The observer may even influence the microbe, dyeing it, putting it on a slide, even killing it, but that does not mean that the microscope becomes the microbe. Likewise, Yoder affirms that our reading of Scripture is always affected by prior interpretations in church history, contemporary concerns and priorities, and by our language and logic. Yet those realities do not make our interpretation of Scripture hopelessly subjective nor do they demand that the entire process of interpretation be controlled by a particular agent or office in the church.

Rather, because of these realities, God has gifted and equipped certain people within the church to be "agents of linguistic self-consciousness," or more simply, teachers. These individuals serve a key function: they enable and facilitate other members of the church to engage in the continual process of interpreting Scripture with discernment.[32] According to Yoder, these teachers have several duties. First, they must be aware of the fluid nature of language. This fluidity is why the book of James cautions against becoming a *didaskolos* (or teacher). Yoder explains: "Language is unruly in that playing around with words or trying to be consistent in our use of words or dealing with issues by defining terms is a

---

28. Yoder, "Thinking Theologically from a Free-Church Perspective," in *Doing Theology in Today's World*, 256–57.

29. Ibid., 257.

30. Yoder, "'There is a Whole New World'," in *To Hear the Word*, 4.

31. Yoder, "The Authority of Tradition," in *Priestly Kingdom*, 66.

32. Yoder, "The Hermeneutics of Peoplehood," in *Priestly Kingdom*, 32.

constant source of contestation and confusion."[33] The teacher must
be aware that words and concepts are not the same, that different people define and use words in different ways, and that words
and their denotations and connotations change over time. Second,
teachers must be aware of the language, concepts, and historical-
cultural context of the original text. Although they never leave their
own historical-cultural particularity behind, teachers should empa-
thetically enter the world of Scripture and inquire about the original
author, original audience, and how this text would have been interpreted and understood in its original setting. Third, the teachers of
the church must be aware of the language, concepts, and historical-
cultural setting of their own place and time. This does not mean that
they can jump out of their own interpretive skin, but it does mean
that they are self-aware. When we are aware of our own time and
place, we also recognize that there are particular agendas and questions we bring to the text that other times and places did not bring.

A key example is the relation of the Bible to social and political issues. Whereas previous generations may not have asked
these kinds of questions of the text, Yoder's generation did.[34] For
Yoder, asking questions of the text is not wrong, so long as we do
not presume ahead of time either to know that the Bible addresses
the issue or that it says what we want it to say. The *didaskolos*
brings together these duties, recognizing that the power of language is its vulnerability and fluidity and that its vulnerability
and fluidity is its power. Consequently, because language and history inevitably flow on,[35] the real issue is not tradition versus
Scripture, but faithful translation versus unfaithful translation.[36]

Faithful interpretations and appropriations of Scripture can take
a variety of shapes. Yoder calls this "fidelity without rigidity,"[37] a
kind of change that is like "fecundation" and the "organic quality of
growth from seed."[38] We ought to expect a rich and complementary

---

33. Yoder, "The Use of the Bible in Theology," in *To Hear the Word*, 82.

34. Yoder, "The Authority of Tradition," in *Priestly Kingdom*, 71.

35. Yoder, "The Use of the Bible in Theology," in *To Hear the Word*, 90.

36. Yoder, "The Authority of Tradition," in *Priestly Kingdom*, 67, 69.

37. Yoder, *Body Politics*, 10.

38. Yoder, "The Authority of Tradition," in *Priestly Kingdom*, 67.

diversity across time and space. The church in North America can learn from the church in other parts of the world as their particular concerns and contexts bring to light things that North American Christians might not otherwise see. Likewise, the contemporary church can learn much by listening to interpreters in other ages. If we are aware of the concerns, challenges, and appropriations of Scripture in ages past, we will avoid being completely subjected to the whims or agendas of our own time. A proper understanding of language and of context, however, suggests that if faithfulness is to mean anything, then unfaithfulness is a real possibility as well.

Infidelity to Scripture can happen in multiple ways, some worse than others. Sometimes unfaithfulness is unintentional, the result of linguistic or conceptual slippage over time.[39] For Yoder, this should not produce guilt but renewed attentiveness. At other times infidelity is more insidious: "We are not plagued merely by a hard-to-manage diversity, by a wealth of complementary variations on the same theme. We are faced with error, into which believers are seduced by evil powers seeking to corrupt the church and to disqualify her witness."[40] For Yoder, these are the types of "human traditions" criticized by Jesus in Matthew 15. The problem is not with tradition *per se*; it is that some Christians have invalidated the word of God for the sake of their tradition (v. 6). The agent of linguistic self-consciousness, like Jesus in Matthew 15, carries on the task of guarding Scripture against those who appeal to its authority wrongly.[41] For Yoder, if theologians take Scripture authoritatively, their primary task is not to defend Scripture's authority to those who do not see it as such. Rather, the theologian's primary task is to guard against those who *do* believe in Scripture's authority but use that authority to back up bad interpretations and translations of Scripture's meaning.

The good news about our potential (and actual) unfaithfulness is that we can repent and change. To make this point, Yoder

---

39. Ibid., 70.

40. Ibid., 69.

41. Yoder, "The Use of the Bible in Theology," in *To Hear the Word*, 83–84.

compares the "wholesome growth of a tradition" to a vine.[42] A vine needs consistent pruning to provide a new chance for the roots to strengthen the whole vine and enable it to flourish. Likewise, any living tradition needs to be pruned on occasion to allow the roots a new chance to enliven the whole vine. Yoder underscores that this is not "primitivism" or an effort to regain some "pristine purity," as though time should not move. Instead, he sees it as a "looping back, a glance over the shoulder to enable a midcourse correction, a rediscovery of something from the past whose pertinence was not seen before."[43] The church continually goes back to Scripture so that it can faithfully go forward as it should, bearing witness to its Lord.

Here is the crucial point: as with translation, so this process of looping back, returning to the origins of the church in Jesus' own life, death, resurrection, and ascension, is already going on *in Scripture itself*.[44] Particular authors wrote the Bible with particular (and polemical) agendas to particular audiences. In the years following the ascension, the early church was already dealing with the issue of sorting faithful teaching and tradition from unfaithful. Thus, Yoder contends that there was no time when the church was not already *ecclesia reformata semper reformanda*, looping back to its roots in Jesus in order to go forward faithfully.[45] This process did not begin at some later date in church history but was an immediate, essential task of the church from the very beginning.

One example of this looping back to go forward is found in Acts 15.[46] The early church struggled over the relationship between Jew and Gentile. But the church did not sidestep or ignore this issue; it confronted the issue directly. In doing so, those involved brought arguments from Scripture, shared their experiences, and listened to one another. As the people of God gathered together

---

42. Yoder, "The Authority of Tradition," in *Priestly Kingdom*, 69.

43. Ibid., 69. Cf. *Preface*, 179.

44. Yoder, "The Authority of Tradition," in *Priestly Kingdom*, 70.

45. Ibid. The Latin phrase is often translated, "The church reformed, and always reforming."

46. Yoder, "The Use of the Bible in Theology," in *To Hear the Word*, 91; cf. "The Hermeneutics of Peoplehood," in *Priestly Kingdom*, 33.

in open conversation, a consensus was reached. The church could say of that consensus that "it seemed good to the Holy Spirit and to us" (Acts 15:28). Importantly, in context of ecclesial conversation, the agents of linguistic self-consciousness do not stand alone or speak from an ivory tower, but bring one gift among many to bear on the process, with confidence that God continues to direct his church as its members discern the way to speak faithfully and embody the old message in a new day.

Yoder's assessment of the creeds

The preceding framework helps explain how Yoder can offer both positive and negative assessments of Nicea and Chalcedon. The creeds are relative because they are not Scripture; the creeds are our relatives because those involved in the formulation of the creeds did in their day what the New Testament writers did in the past and what we are trying to do in the present: faithfully testify in our language and culture to the truth of the gospel. Yoder's nuanced view explains both what the creeds are and what they are not.[47]

Yoder does have several criticisms of the creeds, though these do not outweigh the positives. First, Yoder contends that the councils that produced the creeds were not procedurally flawless.[48] The Acts 15 model of conversation and discernment is violated on two fronts. When the unbaptized Constantine called for the Council of Nicea, it may be that his motives had more to do with his own political agenda and less to do with concern for the church coming to terms with its Christology.[49] Moreover, given that he was not baptized, his participation in the deliberations raises procedural questions. So the consequences for being on the wrong side of the debates of the fourth century were not merely ecclesial, but

---

47. When I speak of the "creeds" in this section, I mean to refer only to the trinitarian and Christological formulas offered by Nicea and Chalcedon.

48. For a personal testimony regarding the difficulties and futility of councils, see Gregory of Nazianzus, *Ep.* 130, in *Creeds, Councils and Controversies*, 118–19.

49. Yoder, *Preface*, 197.

political.[50] The decision reached by the church in Acts 15 had the force of the Spirit behind it, not the sword of the Emperor. This significantly changes the tone of conversation as well as the stakes involved. Having independence from the emperor means, for an Acts 15 model, greater procedural freedom to seek the truth in conversation, which is why Yoder speaks approvingly of the critical leverage of some Arians and Nestorians against the empire (although he elsewhere notes that Arian theology is more accommodating to the Empire than is orthodox Christology).[51] If a group recognizes the need for independence of the church from the political authorities, they are more in line with Scripture's pre-scription for ecclesial deliberations than a group that does not. For these reasons, Yoder argues that before simply accepting the doctrinal content of the creeds, we ought to think about the pro-cedural authority of the councils.[52]

Second, the creeds do not carry the same weight of authority as Scripture. For Yoder, there is a difference between the words of Scripture and our words as we exposit and reflect on Scripture. If we accept the teaching of Scripture, the church has to find ways to sort out things that we hold based on the Bible: monotheism, the revelation of God in Jesus, and the continuing work of the Holy Spirit.[53] But there is a difference between the revelation given in Scripture and what happened at Nicea. For example, in the decades after AD 325, the Cappadocians helped to clarify (and establish the linguistic rules) that we ought to speak of three *hypostases* and one *ousia*. Obviously, we do not find those specific terms being used in this technical sense in Scripture. So however necessary the creeds might be, Yoder argues that they must not be equated with Scripture itself. In addition, Yoder notes that the form of Scripture

---

50. Yoder, *Preface*, 199.

51. Ibid., 223. Yoder makes clear that Arius had friends in high places, not least for the practical reason that "his theology fit the empire. If you lower your concept of Christ, then you can raise your vision of the emperor because the *Logos* was in both Jesus and the emperor . . . If Jesus is a little smaller, the king will be a little higher, and that is just what Constantine and his advisors wanted" (Yoder, *Preface*, 199).

52. Ibid.

53. Ibid., 204.

and the form of the creeds are different. The form of the gospel proclamation is generally narrative, about both who Jesus is and what he does. Nicea and Chalcedon are philosophical and onto-logical summary statements about who Jesus is. Although Nicea records his birth, death, resurrection, and ascension, Yoder worries that later generations have taken this to imply that the kind of life Jesus lived was immaterial, not intimately connected with his death, resurrection, and ascension.[54]

The creeds are not, thirdly, reasons to stop thinking and wrestling with the Bible's message in our own culture and historical context. In the fourth and fifth centuries, certain questions were generated and answered in the creeds. The questions and way of framing the problems arose out of that culture, language, and time. But we live in a different time and place, with different worldviews and language games. So, for example, as J. Denny Weaver reports, Yoder encouraged Weaver to think constructively about how to answer some of today's questions in today's language in a way that is consistent with and faithful to the Bible.[55] Yoder would not have taken this to be a strange idea, but simply what any theologian should do: be faithful to Scripture and think carefully about what it has to say to our world today. As noted above, the missionary ought not capitulate to the logic of one's time and culture but, following the pattern of Scripture itself, seek ways to transform and refashion the words and thought patterns of one's culture so that it is brought in line with Christ. We cannot guarantee our faithfulness before embarking on this process, which is why we must examine theology carefully, whether in the fourth or the twenty-first century.[56]

Fourth, the creeds are not self-evident in a kind of ahistorical, alinguistic way. This truth is apparent in any undergraduate or seminary class that discusses the Trinity. For the debate to be comprehensible to English speakers, students must have a linguistic scorecard comparing Greek, Latin, and English, such as the

---

54. Ibid., 220.

55. Weaver, "The John Howard Yoder Legacy," 457.

56. Ibid., 458.

one provided by Yoder in *Preface to Theology*.[57] The awareness of linguistic complexity enables us to bridge the distance from their time to ours and to understand why the Western church thought the East was in danger of tritheism and why the Eastern church thought the West was in danger of Sabellianism (which denies a proper distinction between the persons of the Trinity). Even in the fourth and fifth century, it was not a simple matter of reading the Bible and recognizing that the Greek or Latin language had one word that obviously fit God's oneness and another that obviously fit God's threeness. Moreover, Yoder points out that as the Cappadocians worked the matter out, they took two words that were often used synonymously in Greek—*ousia* and *hypostasis*—and began to use them in a more technical way, self-consciously appropriating the words and giving them a nuance that they often did not have in the general vernacular.[58] There is nothing wrong with doing so, Yoder contends, so long as we realize that the formula eventually arrived at was *not* something that was simply self-evident in the language and the culture of that day or in ours. It took a good deal of work on linguistic and logical precision to make clear exactly what trinitarian doctrine was saying and not saying. Fortunately, that is why the church has agents of linguistic self-consciousness.

Fifth and finally, the creeds are not necessary for ecumenical dialogue. Because Scripture, not the creeds, is the ultimate authority for Christians, Yoder argues that we do not need the creeds to talk to other Christians. For him, the Acts 15 model is sufficient. The basis for Christian unity is the work of Christ and the confidence that the Spirit continues to work as we gather around Scripture. The creeds signified that in the fourth and fifth centuries, but they do not bypass the need to continue that conversation today.

If one focuses only on these five things that the creeds are *not*, one might be tempted to think Yoder's overall stance toward them is negative. But it is not. Despite these limitations, Yoder highlights five positive aspects of Nicea and Chalcedon that, in the end, outweigh the negatives.

---

57. Yoder, *Preface*, 200.

58. Ibid., 200–1.

First, the creeds are procedurally valid and acceptable. Nicea had flaws, which Yoder is quick to note. But Yoder also notes that it is valid, not simply because the emperor convened it or the bishops attended it, but because at Nicea the church was doing what the church had done in Jerusalem as recorded in Acts 15. They were talking about how to affirm—in their language and culture—their commitment to God and to Jesus.[59] Although there may have been "dirty politics" going on, Yoder believes the church fathers were seeking the good of the church. In the care he shows toward explaining the different positions, Yoder honors the bishops and theologians who genuinely struggled with this question. They really were concerned with this issue as a theological issue, not simply using Nicea as a thinly-veiled mask for their will to power.[60] Moreover, Yoder is no perfectionist. If any church conversation had to be completely flawless with respect to procedure and motives, few or no decisions could be considered valid. Precisely because ulterior motives tend always to be in play, Yoder emphasizes dialogue and openness. The members of the church need to listen openly and talk openly with one another so that they can learn from and correct one another. The process of dialogical discernment is a spiritual discipline that helps lead us further along as individuals and as a community in the direction God desires. Although not flawless, the councils that produced the creeds are an example of this.

Second, the creeds are historically particular translations of the meaning of the Bible. What does Scripture demand we say? According to Yoder, several things: monotheism, distinctness of Father and Son, preexistence of the Son,[61] that Jesus is both human and Son of God,[62] that his work is the work of God and yet man,[63] that he is normative,[64] and that there is God the Father, Son, and

---

59. Ibid., 205.

60. Unfortunately, some theologians and historians who are less careful than Yoder do not avoid a simplistic *Da Vinci Code*-like interpretation of Nicea.

61. Yoder, *Preface*, 191.

62. Ibid., 219.

63. Ibid., 201.

64. Ibid., 204.

Spirit.[65] The language of the creeds does not repeat the exact wording of Scripture. Instead, Nicea and Chalcedon employed ontological, philosophical language that was rooted in Greek thought. Some thinkers do not approve of this. Yoder notes that some criticize Nicea and Chalcedon because those creeds accept "Greek garb."[66] Others criticize them because they are the product of verbal wrangling.[67] Still others criticize them because they employ language of ontology (such as "being" or "essence"), not language of *agape*.[68]

Here we must take some time to show why Yoder explicitly rejects all three of these positions.[69] What these criticisms get wrong is that rather than saying, "The creeds are a *bad* translation of Scripture's meaning," they say, "The creeds are a *translation* of Scripture's meaning." For Yoder, this difference is enormous. Charging Greeks with employing "Greek garb" in their language is no criticism; it would be just as silly to expect them to wear three-piece suits to the Council of Nicea as it would be to expect them to employ the reasoning and language of their contemporaries. So Yoder states, "It would have been the wrong question had the early Christians asked, 'Shall messianic Jews enter the Hellenistic world and adjust to its concepts?' Should Paul use Greek? The question was not whether to enter but how to *be* there: how in the transition to render anew the genuine pertinence of the proclamation of Christ's lordship, even in a context (*particularly* in a context) where even the notion of such sovereignty is questionable."[70]

Yoder would also concede that the creeds are the product of verbal wrangling, though he would not consider this a reproach because "words are the only tools you have to deal with truth. The problem was verbal in the first place."[71] Yoder does not mean that the problem was *merely* "verbal," in contrast to other problems

---

65. Ibid.

66. Ibid., 219. Cf. Yoder, "That Household We Are," 7.

67. Ibid., 202.

68. Ibid.

69. A. James Reimer's portrayal of Yoder misses this. For example, see Reimer, "The Yoder Legacy," 11.

70. Yoder, "But We Do See Jesus," in *Priestly Kingdom*, 56.

71. Yoder, *Preface*, 202.

regarding weighty and substantial matters. Rather, he is saying that the only way that humans can deal with questions about truth and reality is *through language*. In other words, people who accuse those involved with the creeds as wrangling over words (as though this is a bad thing) are misguided. Properly portraying the truth about reality, including the reality of God, will always involve wrangling over words. Moreover, the creeds' use of ontological language is not a problem in and of itself. The councils were addressing ontological questions, so they used ontological language. In addition, ontological language and language of *agape* are interconnected. So when Nicea states that the Son is *homoousios* with the Father "this is an affirmation of love; this is the way to say 'love' in the language of ontology."[72]

Yoder differs from J. Denny Weaver on this point. Weaver criticizes Nicea and Chalcedon for using ontology language rather than telling the narrative of the Gospels, saying that "virtually nothing" in the creeds helps shape the church to witness to God's kingdom. Weaver declares, "If all we know of Jesus is that he is 'one substance with the Father,' and that he is 'fully God and fully man,' there is nothing there that expresses the ethical dimension of being Christ-related."[73] There are two issues here. First, Weaver would have to do more work to spell out that his "if" is anything more than hypothetical. Who are those Christians who know only these two propositions about Jesus? Second, Weaver surprisingly overlooks the interconnections between theology, ontology, and ethics. For example, both Yoder and the fifth century church saw that Chalcedon has clear links to Christian discipleship. If Jesus really is fully human, then the ontological language of the creeds explodes into all arenas of theology and ethics that have implications for *our* humanity: soteriology, eschatology, politics, spiritual disciplines, and so on. Weaver backhandedly affirms the modern and Constantinian disjunction between theology and ethics by arguing that Chalcedon says virtually nothing about the reign of God or the shape of the church's witness. Such a reading seriously misunderstands what was at stake in the debate about Jesus'

---

72. Ibid.

73. Weaver, *Nonviolent Atonement*, 93.

true and full humanity. Yoder, however, clearly understands these stakes, which is why he repeatedly affirms that he takes Chalcedon with absolute seriousness.

In response to those in his own tradition who might dismiss the creeds, Yoder lists three mistakes that critics of Nicea and Chalcedon should *not* make:

1. Suggesting that the missionary invasion of the Hellenistic semantic world, which led to such a "translation," could have been or should have been avoided by remaining "biblical" in semantics or ontology;

2. Suggesting that developments toward a "high" Christology had not already begun within the apostolic canon itself;

3. Interpreting such developments as intrinsically contradictory to the Jewish messianic message of the first generations.[74]

Yoder adamantly makes these points because critics who argue any of the above (some of whom are his fellow Anabaptists) set themselves not only against the creeds but *against the New Testament itself.* For Yoder, all three of these moves were already happening in the New Testament, centuries before the creeds were composed. Yoder accepts the translations of the creeds—at least in part—because he accepts that the gospel has been, from the beginning, in translation. The real question is not whether to translate but whether one has translated faithfully or unfaithfully.

These comments make clear just what kind of "narrative and relativizing" approach Yoder takes to the creeds. There is a naive type of historicism that would relativize the creeds because of a modern notion of "progress." This naive historicism understands well the historical embeddedness of the creeds but implicitly presumes that humanity has just lately uncovered the timeless, eternal truth whereby we judge other periods of history. In other words,

---

74. Yoder, "That Household We Are," 7. It should be noted that the original context of this lecture is a conference on believers church Christology. With this in mind, it would appear that Yoder is working to help those in his own tradition see why many of their standard criticisms of creedal Christology would not apply.

naive historicism points out the speck in the eye of past generations while ignoring the log of historical embeddedness in its own. Yoder is no naïve historicist. The questions, the language, and the historical context of Nicea and Chalcedon may not be our questions, our language, or our historical context, but that does not mean they are wrong, misguided, or problematic. Scripture, not the prevailing mindset of any era, provides critical leverage in the context of *any* age. Though there are biblical grounds to criticize Nicea (e.g., the role of political coercion), Yoder sees many criticisms of the creeds as mistakes committed by those who are not self-aware enough to turn their criticism back on their own time and thought.

To return to the discussion of what the creeds are, Yoder would say that although the creeds are historically particular, they answer perennial questions that the church must face. The creeds are not the Bible, but they are generated and necessitated by the Bible: "The problem the doctrine of the Trinity seeks to resolve, the normativity of Jesus as he relates to the uniqueness of God, is a problem Christians will *always* face if they are Christian. The doctrine of the Trinity is a test of whether your commitments to Jesus and to God are biblical enough that you have the problem the doctrine of the Trinity solves."[75] One can dismiss the creeds by dismissing the world of the early church, including the philosophical and linguistic air they breathed, but that does not mean we can escape the issues that they were trying to clarify.[76] Why were the creeds needed? One could say that to have a church there must be creeds and so we need to go to Scripture to piece together a creed. But that is historically backward, Yoder notes.[77] As the early church read the Scriptures, questions inevitably arose. The church wanted to be faithful to the old message in a new day and to affirm in their time and place what needed to be said. That desire for faithfulness is what produced the creeds. Thus, the creeds are not a mechanism imposed externally on the church, but the organic result of what happens when the church reads the Bible, wants to

---

75. Yoder, *Preface*, 204.

76. Ibid., 219.

77. Ibid. Both advocates and critics of the creeds sometimes commit this error.

understand it, and seeks to witness faithfully in its own time and place to who God is and what God has done. In this sense, if any church desires to be faithful to the God revealed in Scripture, it will inevitably find itself undertaking the same task as the councils of Nicea and Chalcedon. Hence, Yoder argues that we need not fewer but more creeds and confessions: "The slogan ['no creed but the Bible'] is deceptive if it is thought to mean that we can get along without postapostolic formulations . . . The polemic point is not that such formulations should not exist. It is probably better that there should be more of them. Neither the ancient ones of Nicea, Athanasius, Chalcedon nor the modern ones of Augsburg, Thirty-Nine Articles, or the Westminster Confession should be a last word or a filter between us and the Scriptures."[78] In other words, the line between real faithfulness and unfaithfulness to the gospel is not one that can be drawn in the fourth or sixteenth century, nevermore to be redrawn. Since infidelity is a constant threat, the church's commitment to faithfulness must be ongoing.

Fourth, the trinitarian and Christological formulas offered at Nicea and Chalcedon are what the church *had* to say in its time in order to be faithful.[79] They are not only historically particular, they are *faithful* in the midst of their historically particular situation. Once one acknowledges that the Greeks had to speak Greek, then one must find ways within that thought world to say what must be said. Although noting the complexity of the fourth-century debates, Yoder rejects Monarchianism, Arianism, Sabellianism, Docetism, and Ebionism as unsatisfactory and concludes that the creeds were what the church had to say to articulate successfully the message of the New Testament in a different thought world.[80] By "relativizing" the creeds, Yoder does *not* mean that one could be Arian or Docetic

---

78. Yoder, "Thinking Theologically from a Free-Church Perspective," 256.

79. Yoder does not think that all creeds and confessions will necessarily be faithful. Moreover, he does not comment on the other canons or anathemas offered by Nicea and Chalcedon, other than simply listing the canons of the Council of Nicea (Yoder, *Preface*, 208–9). His focus is solely on the trinitarian and Christological teachings offered at the councils. To my knowledge, he does not analyze the other ecumenical councils, nor does he pass judgment regarding many later confessions.

80. Yoder, *Preface*, 201.

and still be faithful to the Bible's meaning. Moreover, Yoder does not make the case that there are a host of other philosophical or ontological ways to say what the creeds say. Though this does not preclude the possibility of doing so, it does indicate that, to this point in history, we have few if any examples. Hence, if you are going to speak the language of ontology, Yoder himself provides no better way to affirm what needs to be said than Nicea and Chalcedon.

Finally, although in one sense the creeds are not ecumenically necessary (as noted above) there is another sense in which the creeds are, for Yoder, necessary for dialogue with other Christians, especially those who do explicitly affirm the creeds. Because Yoder takes history seriously and because the path of faithful proclamation about who God is passes through the creeds, he refuses to simply discard Nicea and Chalcedon. This explains in part why Yoder repeatedly references Nicea and Chalcedon in his writings: not just as a bit of rhetorical trickery to confuse those who are creedally orthodox into buying into his ethics, but because Nicea and Chalcedon are faithful translations of biblical language and thought patterns and, as such, provide a touchstone between Yoder and other non-Mennonite Christians. There is a marked contrast between doing something that *complements* or *extrapolates* the creeds and doing something that is *at odds with* and *contradicts* the creeds. Yoder may do the former, but he would disavow the latter. Nicea and Chalcedon want to be faithful to Scripture; so does Yoder. Yoder takes the divinity of Jesus seriously; so does Nicea. Yoder takes the humanity of Jesus seriously; so does Chalcedon. This is why Yoder essentially says, "If you believe the Bible and take the creeds seriously, my arguments ought to make sense." Although Christians may criticize Nicea and Chalcedon, Yoder would caution that we must vigilantly examine our own translation of the gospel "with the same commitment to the man Jesus, and the same commitment to the unique God that they [the councils] had, or else we shall have left the Christian family."[81]

Having cleared one potential objection to seeing Yoder as presenting a trinitarian theology of culture, Yoder's Christology must now be examined. There we see the key to Yoder's trinitarian theology of culture—a key that clarifies the way that creation, culture and, indeed, all things hold together in Christ.

---

81. Ibid., 204.

4

Yoder's New Testament Christology

M any Christians ask, "How do Christ and culture relate?" or "How do creation and redemption relate?"[1] Many times these questions grow simply from the desire to be coherent. Other times, however, Yoder notes that these questions often reveal an insufficiently biblical view of Jesus, culture, creation, and redemption. That is, if we *begin* with the assumption that these are two basically unrelated topics, our very starting point will skew how we understand the relationship between creation and redemption. In his biblically grounded Christology, Yoder holds that in his humanity and his divinity Jesus not only relates directly to culture, but also serves as the linchpin for creation and redemption's coherence.

The humanity of Jesus: Messiah and culture

"At no point was [Christianity] directly concerned with the social upheavals of the ancient world . . . The central problem [of the

---

1. This is not to say that these are bad questions in and of themselves. Yoder's point is that questions become systemic problems for thinkers precisely because too little attention is paid to biblical texts that could possibly resolve these questions. For one reason or another, though, the relevant texts are ignored or downplayed. Yoder addresses questions like these in a variety of places, including "Creation and Gospel," 8–10; "How H. Richard Niebuhr Reasoned," in *Authentic Transformation*, 61–62; "Reformed versus Anabaptist Social Strategies," 5–6; "That Household We Are," 8.

New Testament] is always purely religious, dealing with such questions as the salvation of the soul, monotheism, life after death, purity of worship, the right kind of congregational organization, the application of Christian ideals to daily life, and the need for severe self-discipline in the interests of personal holiness."[2] This view of Jesus, articulated by Ernst Troeltsch in 1931, was widespread in North American Christianity in 1972 when Yoder wrote *Politics of Jesus* and continues to persist in many circles even today. This view sees Jesus as a religious savior, but not someone who addresses cultural questions concerning power, politics, wealth, decision making, and other related issues. Against this position, Yoder cogently argues in *Politics* that Jesus did not point away from these public or political issues but instead offered "one particular social-political-ethical option."[3] Moreover, because Jesus is fully human, the real question is not whether Christ and culture relate, but whether we respond in cultural obedience or rebellion to Christ.

In keeping with the spirit of Yoder's project and in order to highlight Jesus' humanity, we should speak of the Messiah and culture, rather than Christ and culture. Why should we make this change? *Messiah* is the Hebrew equivalent of the Greek word transliterated *Christ*. Both Messiah and Christ refer to the "Anointed One," so they mean the same thing. Many Christians today hear "Christ" as a reference to Jesus' divinity or to the exalted Christ. This is not wrong in itself, but it can detract from the way the term *Messiah* underscores both Jesus' Jewishness and his humanity.

Some critics perceive Yoder's emphasis on Jesus' humanity or on the political aspects of his ministry to be one-sided.[4] But it is not. Yoder is trying to show the broadness of the biblical view, whereas some traditions with a so-called high Christology actually have a more narrow view of Jesus than Yoder because they ignore

---

2. Troeltsch, *The Social Teaching of the Christian Churches*, 1:39.

3. Yoder, *The Politics of Jesus*, 11.

4. Reimer, "Mennonites, Christ, and Culture," 12. Cf. Craig A. Carter's treatment of charges of reductionism in *The Politics of the Cross*, 126–36.

the ethical and political aspects of his life.[5] So Yoder attempts to do justice to both the full humanity and the full divinity of Jesus.[6]

Jesus the Jew. According to Yoder, conversations about Messiah and culture should begin with the Old Testament's portrayal of Israel as the covenant people of God. Christian thinkers make a critical error when they forget that Jesus was a Jewish man, fully embedded in his time, history, and society. Indeed, for Yoder, the problem with many interpretations of Jesus is that they willfully ignore or simply set aside as irrelevant his Jewishness and all that it implies for his ministry and teaching. When Jesus' Jewishness is ignored, he can be construed in a variety of ways, such as a mendicant sage, a preacher of ahistorical individualism, a radical monotheist, or the founder of a new world religion.[7] These positions can be held only if we ignore the embeddedness of Jesus within the context of first century Judaism. As a result, Yoder declares, "The idea of Jesus as an individualist or a teacher of radical personalism could arise only in the (Protestant, post-Pietist, rationalist) context that it did; that is, in a context which, if not intentionally anti-Semitic, was at least sweepingly a-Semitic, stranger to the Jewish Jesus."[8] To avoid this mistake, Yoder emphasizes two foundational points regarding how Jesus, in his full humanity, relates to culture: continuity between Old and New Testaments and the purpose of Israel's calling. In addition, the practice of Jubilee and the wars of Yahweh provide test cases whereby we can see these two points played out in concrete ways.

Continuity and calling. Yoder, along with coauthor Richard J. Mouw, first emphasizes the promise-fulfillment relationship both between the Old and New Testaments and between Israel and the church.[9] The church should therefore be seen as a "theocratic

---

5. I have argued this in detail in "Spinning the Liturgical Turn: Why Yoder is Not an Ethicist," 173–92.

6. Yoder, *Politics*, 226.

7. See Ibid., 6–8, for a list of reasons Jesus is set aside as irrelevant to social ethics.

8. Ibid., 109. In the 1994 edition, Yoder notes interpretation of Paul has also fallen prey to an anti-Jewish bias (*Politics*, 227).

9. Mouw and Yoder, "Evangelical Ethics and the Anabaptist-Reformed Dialogue," 132. Mouw and Yoder see this as a point of similarity between the Mennonite and Calvinist traditions.

community" that is "the fulfillment of the promises given to Israel."[10] Despite perceived differences between Reformed and Anabaptist traditions, Mouw and Yoder point to a deep similarity between these traditions, in that they see God's work in both Old and New Testaments as directly relevant to the cultural and political life of humanity. Against a sharp division between the Old and New Testaments (as in dispensationalism), the political promises given to Israel are fulfilled in the New Testament; against a Lutheran two kingdoms view, there are not two different sets of norms for human community, but one.[11] Broadly conceived, then, the New Testament is the organic extension of the Old. If the Old Testament cares about disparate issues such as land use, humane treatment of animals, fairness in economic dealings, sexual conduct, and political power, then we should not expect that Jesus or the New Testament is exclusively concerned with the salvation of individual souls. The God who created all things is interested in the redemption of all things in both testaments.

Because of the continuity between Old and New Testaments, God's purpose for Israel impinges directly on the question of the Messiah and culture. God's purpose is missional: to be a blessing and light to all nations in their communal and cultural life (Gen 12:3; Isa 42:6; 49:6). Election entails mission. God does not call Abraham simply to bless him, but to commission him and his family to be a blessing to all peoples inasmuch as they love God and love their neighbors as they ought. Crucially, this mission is a corporate and communal one. Israel's life together (and later, the church's life together) should not be construed simply as an aggregate of individuals in personal relationships with God.[12] Rather, in Exodus 19:6, the people of Israel are set apart as a priestly kingdom.[13] The

---

10. Mouw and Yoder, "Evangelical Ethics," 132.

11. Ibid., 133.

12. Mouw and Yoder emphasize this point with respect to the church, again seeing it as a point of similarity between Anabaptist and Reformed communities. Cf. Mouw and Yoder, "Evangelical Ethics," 133. See also Yoder, "A Light to the Nations," 14–18.

13. Yoder references this text as one of Israel's charter texts in "Thou Shalt Not Kill," in *To Hear the Word*, 39. Exodus 19:6 also serves as the basis for Yoder's book title *The Priestly Kingdom: Social Ethics as Gospel*.

priesthood of Israel was not merely the priesthood of one tribe, the Levites, nor was it simply a cultic priesthood. As the entire people of Israel lived out their life together—from Sabbath observance to sacrifices to social justice—they were priestly representatives of God's ways to the rest of the world. Yoder sees the Torah, which addresses all these matters, as "grace and liberation" because it reveals God's will for a vast spectrum of human life.[14] Consequently, God's covenant purposes in calling Abraham are inherently social, political, and cultural.

For Yoder, the transition from the Old to New Testament is not a move from law to grace, but from grace to grace.[15] That is, the gracious gift of Torah is exceeded by the gracious gift of Christ, who is the fulfillment of Torah, and the Spirit, who is the seal of the New Covenant which frees us to obey the central meaning of Torah: love of God and neighbor (Jer 31:33; Ezek 11:18-19). Yoder points out that Jesus does not rescind the central commands of the Old Testament, but he actually sharpens and deepens them.[16] This should not be taken as a new legalism but as true freedom; what could be more freeing than living out God's intentions for human life?[17] When Jesus comes as the Messiah of Israel and as the goal to which the Law and Prophets point, he comes with a social agenda that is "as broad as the entire Torah,"[18] representing a "paradigm

---

14. Yoder, "Thou Shalt Not Kill," in *To Hear the Word*, 46.

15. In a cryptic yet pregnant comment, Yoder states, "The sixteenth century made *law* an issue in a way that predisposes us to be unfair to much that went before." Yoder, "Gospel Renewal and the Roots of Nonviolence," in *The War of the Lamb*, 49. Cf. Yoder, "The Hilltop City," in *He Came Preaching Peace*, 102.

16. Yoder, "Jesus the Jewish Pacifist," in *The Jewish-Christian Schism Revisited*, 70; and "Gospel Renewal and the Roots of Nonviolence," in *War of the Lamb*, 49.

17. Cf. Yoder, *Discipleship as Political Responsibility*, 61. Yoder elsewhere makes the point that God does not simply free his people *from* something, but *for* something. So, Sinai follows Exodus. Yoder is therefore suspicious of any theology, liberation or otherwise, that makes an undefined "freedom" or "liberation" the ultimate goal. Yoder, "Exodus and Exile," 304.

18. Yoder, "Jesus: A Model of Radical Political Action," in *War of the Lamb*, 78.

of renewal taking up into itself all of the concreteness of the deu-teronomic vision of faithful community under God."[19] For Yoder, whatever is happening in the New Testament ought to be under-stood in connection with God's intentions in the Old Testament, and this includes the whole spectrum of social, political, and cul-tural issues dealt with in the Torah and the Prophets. When the Messiah comes, he comes to a people who see their social, politi-cal, and cultural life not as extraneous but as essential to their covenant relationship with God.

Jubilee and the wars of YHWH. It hardly needs to be said that a straightforward reading of the Old Testament leaves no doubts that Israel's God is concerned with social, economic, and political prac-tices. What does need to be said, according to Yoder, is that when the Messiah comes he will address these concerns. Yoder wrote extensively regarding the Old Testament.[20] In particular, two prac-tices he addresses—Jubilee and holy war—helpfully illustrate that the God of Israel is directly concerned with matters of culture and society. Moreover, Israel's prophets directly connect the messianic era to these two concerns. With respect to Jubilee, Isaiah 49:8-9 states, "This is what the LORD says: 'In the time of my favor I will answer you, and in the day of salvation I will help you; I will keep you and will make you to be a covenant for the people, to restore the land and to reassign its desolate inheritances, to say to the cap-tives, "Come out," and to those in darkness, "Be free!"'" (NIV). With respect to concerns of war and conquest, Zechariah 9:9-10 states, "Rejoice greatly, Daughter Zion! Shout, Daughter Jerusalem! See, your king comes to you, righteous and victorious, lowly and riding on a donkey, on a colt, the foal of a donkey. I will take away the chariots from Ephraim and the warhorses from Jerusalem, and the battle bow will be broken. He will proclaim peace to the nations. His rule will extend from sea to sea and from the River to the ends of the earth" (NIV). Jesus spoke and ministered in a context where these concerns and issues would have been prevalent. When the Messiah comes, he will have to address these expectations.

19. Yoder, "The Power Equation, Jesus, and the Politics of King," in *For the Nations*, 141–42.

20. For a thorough engagement of Yoder's reading of the Old Testament, see Nugent, *The Politics of Yahweh*.

The practice of Jubilee, as outlined in Leviticus 25, included at least four key practices.[21] First, the year of Jubilee entailed a Sabbath year for the land. The people could eat the produce of the field, but they were commanded to neither sow nor reap. If the people kept God's statutes, God would bless them in the sixth year so that they would be sustained through the Sabbath year (Lev 25:20-22). Second, the year of Jubilee included remission of debts. When someone sells their land or themselves into indentured servitude to pay off a debt, that debt should be forgiven in the year of Jubilee (Lev 25:28, 40). This forgiveness of debts leads to the next two practices. A third facet of Jubilee was the liberation of servants. For those who have sold themselves as servants to their fellow Israelites and cannot afford to redeem themselves or have a family member redeem them, the year of Jubilee is a year of release (Lev 25:39-43). Importantly, in the midst of this practice, God wants the people to recognize that *all* people of Israel are *God's* servants. Even if they are in debt, they are to be recognized as ultimately God's people. This is what Pharaoh failed to see. Servitude and indebtedness are not to be absolute characteristics of Israel's society, but relative practices that get readjusted at least every fifty years. A fourth and final practice of Jubilee is the redistribution of land (Lev 25:23-34). The land is ultimately God's land, not the people's. Therefore, when the land is sold to pay off debt, this is never a final sale, but a temporary one. In the year of Jubilee, the land goes back to the original family and tribe. This ensures that the people of Israel are not dispossessed of their inheritance by their own people.

The prescriptions for the year of Jubilee make it clear that God is concerned with the social and economic organization of the people of Israel. Their care of the land is his concern. The Sabbath year not only allows the land to rest, it also gives the people the opportunity to show that their economic life is sustained by neither greed nor the drive to survive, but by a fundamental trust that their God will provide for their needs. In the remission of debts, liberation of servants, and redistribution of property, God has provided a way for Israelite society to make relative economic

---

21. Yoder looks for allusions to the year of Jubilee in the Gospels in "The Implications of the Jubilee," chapter 5 of *Politics*.

adjustments every fifty years. This prevents a scenario where some families or tribes become perpetual servants and others become perpetual masters. The people own neither their land nor their servants absolutely, since both the people and the land are God's. The God of the year of Jubilee is a God who is concerned with the mundane matters of land, work, debt, and remission of debts.

A second practice of Israel was that of the wars of YHWH.[22] Rather than being embarrassed about the reality of Israel's wars, Yoder pays close attention to the text of Scripture in order to give a thick description of that practice and place it in the overarching narrative of Scripture.[23] When looking at the wars of YHWH, Yoder wants to avoid both a narrowly legalistic focus on war as well as a sharp dualism between Old and New Testament ethics.[24] Although other pacifists may make this move, Yoder does not.[25] Instead, he focuses on continuities and developments within the trajectory of the biblical narrative as it moves from Old to New Testament.[26] The appropriate way to address the question of the wars of YHWH is to understand them on their own terms, without

---

22. Yoder refers to this phenomena both by its designation from the social sciences—holy war—and its designation from the guild of biblical studies—wars of YHWH. He indicates that he prefers the latter in "Jesus the Jewish Pacifist," in *Jewish-Christian Schism Revisited*, 88, n. 10. Yoder addresses holy war in "If Abraham Is Our Father," in *Original Revolution*, 91–110; "'To Your Tents, O Israel': The Legacy of Israel's Experience with Holy War," 345–62; "Texts that Serve or Texts that Summon? A Response to Michael Walzer," 229–34; "Is Not His Word Like a Fire? The Bible and Civil Turmoil," in *For the Nations*, 85–86; and "From the Wars of Joshua to Jewish Pacifism," in *The War of the Lamb*, 67–76.

23. Yoder, "Texts that Serve," 233. Yoder calls this the "cultic density of ancient semitic experience" which, he notes, "is something deeper than the components which we can make contemporaneously comprehensible in terms of the politics of nation building or the ethics of bloodshed."

24. Yoder, "From the Wars of Joshua to Jewish Pacifism," in *War of the Lamb*, 68. He lists Tolstoy and Petr Chelčický as representatives of this dualism.

25. Yoder, "From the Wars of Joshua to Jewish Pacifism," in *War of the Lamb*, 68.

26. Yoder, "If Abraham Is Our Father," in *Original Revolution*, 105.

imposing twenty-first century questions and concerns on the text. The first task is not to let our categories judge Scripture, but to let Scripture inform and shape our categories of thinking. When we do this we see God's attention to how, if, and when Israel takes up arms. This care shows that God is concerned with Israel's political and military situation.

Yoder lists six marks of the wars of YHWH, listed here verbatim:[27]

1. The people were mustered by the sound of the trumpet. There was no standing army, no professional military class. There were in Israel no soldiering skills; only a volunteer militia. In some cases (Gideon, for example) the combatants might be very few.

2. "The city and all that is in it shall be devoted to JHWH for destruction" (Josh 6:17). To "devote to destruction" (the root use of *herem*) is first a cultic event, invoking or ascribing the status of tabu, whereby the lives and goods in question become the property of the deity. It is this ceremonial consecration, occurring before the battle, which we cannot understand if we modernize the cultic dimension out of the story.

3. The assembled warriors are called on to trust JHWH as the real actor in the event, who will only act on their behalf if they trust him. Then they go into battle in the confidence that God will "give the enemy into your hand."

4. Then God does give the victory. The enemy panics and usually flees. Sometimes the Israelites participate in the bloodshed of mopping up, sometimes not.

5. Then the sacrifice, which had been promised before the battle, is consummated by the destruction of (some or all of) the lives and goods of the enemy. Obviously what there was there to be destroyed would vary enormously, as "the enemy" was sometimes a fortified city, sometimes an armed camp, sometimes a bedouin village.

---

27. The following list is quoted directly from Yoder, "Texts that Serve," 232–33.

6. Then the event ended with a divine demobilization: "To thy tents, O Israel."

The central point behind the wars of YHWH (which are very different from the later wars of Israel's monarchy) is found in Exodus 14:13: stand firm and see the salvation of YHWH, because YHWH will fight for you. This motif is central to the exodus of Israel from Egypt, the wars of Joshua, and the miraculous deliverances in the time of the Judges. It can also be seen in the time of the monarchy with Asa (2 Chron 14), Jehoshaphat (2 Chron 20), and Hezekiah (2 Chron 32). Ezra exhibits the same posture of trust in God when he refuses to accept Artaxerxes's horses and soldiers as a protective consort for those returning to Jerusalem (Ezra 8).[28] Other facets of Israel's narrative also serve to reinforce the need to trust God for survival, including Abraham's willingness to sacrifice Isaac (Gen 22),[29] Abraham's relinquishing of better land to Lot (Gen 13), Isaac's relinquishing his wells to Abimelech (Gen 26), and the stories of Joseph and Daniel.[30]

The wars of YHWH clarify what it means for God to call his people to have faith in God's covenant promises. Israel's faith is not simply a religious virtue, but a political one:

> Faith or *emunah*—a near synonym of trust, *batach*—is a politically, even militarily, operative quality or activity. "To believe" is not primarily to assent to propositions about the divine being, or about some state of affairs, or about anything. Nor is it merely inward attitude. "To believe" is to be ready to risk one's survival, to wager one's dignity or one's identity on the confidence that YHWH will intervene in one's favour. "To believe" is to risk one's well-being on the hypothesis that right behaviour will be "with the grain" of the cosmos, despite appearances.[31]

---

28. All these examples are noted by Yoder in *Politics*, 77–84.

29. Yoder, "If Abraham Is Our Father," in *Original Revolution*, 101–02.

30. Yoder, *Politics*, 84.

31. Yoder, "To Your Tents, O Israel," 350. Cf. Yoder, *Politics*, 125, n. 31: "When the author [of Hebrews 11] defines 'faith' as assurance of the hoped-for and conviction of the unseen, the 'hoped-for' and 'unseen' realities are not some otherwise unknown truth, proposition, or

Yoder's point is that faith and unbelief necessarily manifest themselves in differing stances toward military might and action. Faith in God's faithfulness to his covenant promises is seen in Joshua's victory at Jericho, Gideon's defeat of the Midianites, and Hezekiah's deliverance from the Assyrians. Disbelief toward God's covenant promises is seen not only in pagan cultic practices, but in Israel's reliance on pagan military practices and alliances to ensure their survival. "The just shall live by faith" is, after all, not first a statement about the salvation of individual souls, but about the posture God's people ought to have in the face of military defeat, destruction, and the apparent impossibility of God's purposes for his people to continue (Hab 2:4).

From the biblical text, Yoder argues that practices such as Jubilee and holy war make it very clear that the God of Israel is concerned with every aspect of Israel's life. This includes their willingness to trust him for their food and let the land lie fallow. It includes their concept of property. It includes their willingness to freely forgive debts at the appropriate time. It includes whether or not they forge military alliances with other nations and import foreign military technology such as horses and chariots. It includes whether and how the people will take up arms to ensure their survival. When the Messiah comes, will he address these social, political, and cultural concerns? Yoder's answer is a resounding yes.

Jesus the Messiah. Yoder's argument in *Politics of Jesus* and elsewhere is quite simple: the Bible teaches that Jesus the Messiah is directly relevant to questions of culture, including politics, economics, and social ethics.[32] Building on research in the biblical studies guild, Yoder surveys nine episodes in Luke's Gospel and provides ample evidence that, as Israel's Messiah, Jesus is relevant to questions of politics, culture, and social ethics.[33]

---

prediction but the concrete vindication of obedience. 'Faith' is obeying when it is not 'visible' that it 'pays' or 'works.'" Yoder also notes in this context that Hebrews sees Jesus as the culmination of the series of people who had exemplary faith.

32. Yoder, *Politics*, 11.

33. The following is a summary of chapter 2, "The Kingdom Coming," of Yoder, *Politics*, 21–53.

In the first notable episode, Mary, Zechariah, and John the Baptist all point to a hope that is not simply "spiritual," if by spiritual we mean something disconnected from issues of culture and politics. In other words, when God acts, it will inevitably affect how human society is ordered. So Mary states,

> He has shown strength with his arm,
> He has scattered the proud in the imagination of their hearts,
> He has put down the mighty from their thrones,
> And exalted those of low degree;
> He has filled the hungry with good things,
> And the rich he has sent away empty. (Luke 1:51-53)[34]

Although Jesus' fulfillment of the hopes of Mary, Zechariah, and John the Baptist may have been different from their expectations, the difference was *not* that they were expecting a sociopolitical Messiah and that Jesus was a spiritual Messiah. Rather, Luke includes this material to show that "the pious hopes which awaited Jesus were those in which the suffering of Israel was discerned in all its social and political reality, and the work of the Awaited One was to be of the same stuff."[35]

This expectation continues in Jesus' baptism, commissioning, and temptation, which all have royal overtones. In Luke 3, the Father calls Jesus his Son, a term that, in the Old Testament, often refers to Israel's king (e.g., Ps 2:7). Yoder suggests that Luke 3:22 merges the theme of kingship from Psalm 2:7 with the suffering servanthood of Isaiah 42:1. According to Yoder, "Thou art my Son" is "the summons to a task. Jesus is commissioned to be, in history, in Palestine, the messianic son and servant, the bearer of the goodwill and promise of God."[36] In Luke 4, this term is again used, this time by the tempter, who challenges Jesus with the phrase, "if you are the Son of God." According to Yoder, the temptation of Christ is not primarily a test of his divinity, but a test of what kind of king he would be. Yoder points out that the tempter was not an Enlightenment evidentialist looking for proof of a Nicene or Chalcedonian definition of sonship. Rather, the

---

34. I quote the text as given in Yoder, *Politics*, 21. Yoder does not specify which translation he is using.

35. Yoder, *Politics*, 23.

36. Ibid., 24.

temptations put to Jesus are all wrong ways of being God's anointed king. The economic temptation involves turning the stones to bread, feeding the crowds, and becoming king. The social-political temptation involves bowing the knee to the tempter and ruling over all the kingdoms of the earth. The religious reformer temptation involves Jesus casting himself from the pinnacle of the temple, thereby appearing as a heavenly herald. Jesus' response, Yoder notes, was not to deny that he was the true Son of God, the Messiah, or the rightful King: "He does not say, 'You are expecting a king and I am not a king.' No, he says, 'You do right to expect a king, but expect a different kind of king.' He claims that this is the fulfillment of the messianic expectation rather than its rejection."[37] In claiming this, Jesus makes himself directly relevant to questions of power and politics.

Jesus reinforces this in his Nazareth sermon. In reading Isaiah 61:1-2, Jesus reveals the platform of the kingdom he proclaimed: "The Spirit of the Lord is on me, because he has anointed me to proclaim good news to the poor. He has sent me to proclaim freedom for the prisoners and recovery of sight for the blind, to set the oppressed free, to proclaim the year of the Lord's favor" (Luke 4:18-19, NIV). When people expected the Messiah, they expressed it in social terms, connected with the year of Jubilee.[38] This hope is not "that Jesus is going to take Palestine off the end of the scale of temporal sequence but rather that there is to come into Palestine the equalizing impact of the Sabbath year."[39] Jesus' message was not simply inward and individualist. Nor did he simply point to God and away from any concrete concerns of the culture and society. Instead, Yoder contends, the kingdom expected by Jesus is "a visible socio-political, economic restructuring of relations among

---

37. Yoder, *Preface to Theology*, 244. The ascension further shows that the disciples' view of Jesus was not too political but too provincial. Jesus' ultimate goal was not simply to sit on a throne in Jerusalem as King of Israel but to sit at the right hand of the Father as Lord of the universe.

38. Cf. Yoder's chapter "The Implications of the Jubilee," in *Politics*, 59–75, for a further exposition of Jubilee themes in the Gospels. Yoder's exposition of these themes is primarily a summary of Trocmé, *Jesus and the Nonviolent Revolution*. For further confirmation of this thesis, see Ringe, *Jesus, Liberation, and the Biblical Jubilee*.

39. Yoder, *Politics*, 30.

the people of God, achieved by divine intervention in the person of Jesus as the one Anointed and endued with the Spirit."[40]

Jesus extends and reaffirms the Nazareth platform when he calls the twelve as the firstfruits of restored Israel and when he delivers the Sermon on the Plain. Jesus gives blessings and woes, according to the format of Israel's covenant blessings and curses, including blessings on the poor and the hungry. Jesus' instructions to his followers call them to love their enemies and forgive debts in imitation of their heavenly Father (Luke 6:35-36).

When Jesus feeds the five thousand in the desert, the crowds resuscitate the economic temptation as the path to kingship (John 6:15 makes this especially clear). Immediately after the feeding, Jesus tells his disciples that he will suffer and die, and he "sets his face" to go to Jerusalem for that purpose (Luke 9:51, KJV). Jesus confronts and rejects the Zealot temptation, but he also rejects withdrawal into the desert or into mysticism. The path that leads to the cross is "the political alternative to both insurrection and quietism."[41]

When Jesus teaches about the cross and the cost of discipleship, he reinforces that following him involves a new social, political, and ethical option. Jesus knows that Herod seeks to kill him (Luke 13:31-32) and that Jerusalem had turned against him (Luke 12:49–13:9; 13:33-35). Jesus therefore wants his disciples to realize that they are called to the kind of life that leads to the cross.

Yoder adamantly insists that "bearing one's cross," in the historical context of Jesus and his first hearers, means something different than it has in Protestant pastoral care:

> [Our cross is not] any and every kind of suffering, sickness, or tension, the bearing of which is demanded. The believers' cross is, like that of Jesus, the price of social nonconformity. It is not, like sickness or catastrophe, an inexplicable, unpredictable suffering; it is the end of a path freely chosen after counting the cost. It is not . . . an inward wrestling of the sensitive soul with self and sin; it is the social reality of representing in an unwilling world the Order to come.[42]

---

40. Ibid., 32.

41. Ibid., 36.

42. Ibid., 96.

Although other meanings may be, to some degree, legitimate extrapolations of the meaning of the cross, Yoder does not want us to forget that crucifixion is the preferred form of torture and capital punishment for those who would dare to challenge the sovereignty of the powers that be.

When Jesus calls his disciples to take up their cross, they are called not to lord it over others but to be, like Jesus, one who serves.[43] That is, he is calling them to operate on the same plane as Caesar but to inhabit it differently. "Lording it over" and "serving" are two different answers to the same question of how to be God's Messiah and followers of the Messiah. As such, this question shows the inherently social nature of the gospel:

> In none of the accounts where this word [of serving rather than lording over] is reported does Jesus reprimand his disciples for expecting him to establish some new social order, as he would have had to do if the thesis of the only-spiritual kingdom were to prevail. He rather reprimands them for having misunderstood the character of that new social order which he does intend to set up. The novelty of its character is not that it is not social, or not visible, but that it is marked by an alternative to accepted patterns of leadership. The alternative to how the kings of the earth rule is not "spirituality" but servanthood.[44]

To be a disciple of the servant Messiah means a willingness to be a servant to others.

Jesus' determined path leads him to what Yoder terms the "epiphany in the Temple." Jesus' entrance into the temple is preceded by the triumphal entry, in which the crowds use explicitly messianic language: "Blessed is the king who comes in the name of the Lord" (Luke 19:38). Yoder notes that Jesus not only enters the temple and drives out those who sold there, but that he also begins teaching daily in the temple (Luke 19:47). This, Yoder contends, is a symbolic takeover of the temple by the One who rightfully has jurisdiction over it. Notably, Jesus' adversaries could not bring a legitimate

---

43. Cf. Yoder, "The Christian Case for Democracy," in *The Priestly Kingdom*, 155–59.

44. Yoder, *Politics*, 38–39.

charge against him. Whatever he did, he did in a legal fashion. As the Gospel of Luke comes to its climax, Luke reinforces the clash of kingdoms occurring in the life and ministry of Jesus.

This clash comes to a head at Gethsemane, where Jesus must fully and finally renounce the temptation to messianic violence. Yoder asks, What would it have meant for Jesus' "cup to pass" from him? What would it have meant to gain the crown by means other than the cross? A righteous holy war is the most viable option. Accompanied by the heavenly hosts and his own band of followers, Jesus would be installed as the messianic king in Jerusalem and, with the backing of Israel's God, would cast the pagans from Israel's land. As Jesus had resisted this temptation earlier in the feeding of the five thousand and the triumphal entry, so again he resists the tempter and accepts the will of his Father, who loves his enemies and sends rain upon both the just and the unjust.

Jesus' execution and exaltation are the result of his victory over temptation. Jesus is executed as "King of the Jews," a tribute, Yoder holds, to Jesus' willingness to unsettle the established order of the reigning Jewish and Roman authorities. Although Jesus threatened their sovereignty, his threat was atypical in that it did not involve armed revolt. In any case, Jesus' crucifixion demonstrates that his public ministry made it plausible that he posed a serious enough threat to the Roman Empire to merit execution.

Moreover, in Jesus' own interpretation, his execution is simultaneously his exaltation. When the resurrected Jesus explains himself to the disciples on the road to Emmaus, they did not fully reckon with the necessity of the Messiah's suffering: "like Peter at Caesarea Philippi, they were failing to see that the suffering of the Messiah *is* the inauguration of the kingdom."[45] So Jesus asks them, "Was it not necessary that the Messiah should suffer these things and enter into his glory?" (Luke 24:26).[46] As Yoder points out, the ascension has not yet happened, so the Messiah's glory must be something other than and previous to that (although this does not exclude the ascension by extension). We truly understand the full glory of resurrection and ascension

---

45. Ibid., 51.

46. Scripture text quoted from Yoder, *Politics*, 51.

only when we see those things as the result of the glory revealed in Jesus' suffering on the cross.[47] As Yoder forcefully puts it:

> Here at the cross is the man who loves his enemies, the man whose righteousness is greater than that of the Pharisees, who being rich became poor, who gives his robe to those who took his cloak, who prays for those who despitefully use him. The cross is not a detour or a hurdle on the way to the kingdom, nor is it even the way to the kingdom; it is the kingdom come.[48]

For Yoder, Luke makes it abundantly clear that Jesus' life, teachings, ministry, and crucifixion, as well as his resurrection and ascension, have direct bearing upon social, political, and economic matters. Yoder concludes that Jesus, as prophet, priest, and king, was "the bearer of a new possibility of human, social, and therefore political relationships."[49] Although one might be inclined to (or want to) write off as unreal, irrelevant, or impossible the kingdom Jesus proclaimed, this is neither good exegesis nor good systematic theology. As Israel's fully human Messiah, Jesus is directly related to culture. The real challenge that Scripture presents to us, for Yoder, is not to relate two unrelated entities, the Messiah and culture; the real challenge is whether we will answer the Messiah's call to follow *him*, with all that that entails for our relationship to culture.

The Messiah who issues this call, however, is not only the Jewish Messiah. The Jewish authors of the New Testament use language to describe the Messiah that is generally reserved for God alone. Following Scripture, Yoder's Christology focuses not only on the humanity of Jesus but also on his divinity.

The deity of Jesus: Logos and creation

Yoder's Christology repeatedly draws on New Testament texts that outline the work of the preincarnate Son: John 1, Colossians 1,

---

47. Yoder, *Preface*, 122, refers to John 3:13; 12:32; 13:31ff.; 17:1-5; and Acts 3:13 as texts that identify the cross with Jesus' exaltation and glorification.

48. Yoder, *Politics*, 51.

49. Ibid., 52.

Hebrews 1, and Philemon 2. By examining Yoder's interpretation of these texts, we see several points that are crucial to Yoder's theology. For starters, the exegetical evidence supports a close link between Christ and creation because Christ is active in the work of creating and sustaining all things. And since the Word is the one by whom all things were created, we must pay attention to the shape of the life lived by the incarnate Word. Furthermore, Yoder affirms Christ's divinity. As God in the flesh, Jesus is the preeminent revelation of who God is. Although some accuse Yoder of having a low Christology that denies the divinity of Jesus, that position is untenable.[50] Third, because the divine Son is intimately involved in creation, pitting creation and redemption against each other is the height of folly. Unfortunately, Yoder declares, the connection between Christ and creation is a claim "which, in a systematic way, most theologies to our day do not really believe."[51] Yoder notes that several thinkers (including Martin Luther, Reinhold Niebuhr, and Emil Brunner) draw a sharp distinction between creation and redemption, which are seen to have two different, if not opposing, ethical implications.[52] Although the theological or ethical systems of these thinkers pit Christ and creation against each other, Yoder contends that Scripture does not.

Jesus the Creator. Before we turn to relevant New Testament texts, we must see how Yoder links them to Proverbs 8:

> Does not wisdom call
> Does not understanding raise her voice?
> On the heights beside the way,
> In the paths she takes her stand
> Beside the gates in front of the town,
> At the entrance of the portals she cries aloud:
> To you, O men, I call,
> And my cry is to the sons of men . . .
> I, wisdom, dwell in prudence,
> And I find knowledge and discretion.
> The fear of the Lord is hatred of evil . . .

---

50. See Reimer, "Mennonites, Christ, and Culture," 12; and Finger, "Did Yoder Reduce Theology to Ethics," in *A Mind Patient and Untamed*, 333.

51. Yoder, "Glory in a Tent," in *He Came Preaching Peace*, 82.

52. Ibid.

> I have counsel and sound wisdom,
>   I have insight, I have strength.
> By me kings reign,
>   And rulers decree what is just;
> By me princes rule, and nobles govern the earth . . .
> The LORD created me at the beginning of his work,
>   The first of his acts of old.
> Ages ago I was set up,
>   At the first, before the beginning of the earth.
> When there were no depths I was brought forth.
>   (Prov 8:1-4, 12-16, 22-24).[53]

Yoder makes several observations here. Wisdom personified is the "coherence of creation" and the "agent of God in the rest of creation."[54] Further, wisdom is not merely creaturely, but divine: "it partakes of the nature and authority of God" (184). Third, although divine, wisdom plays out in the human and material realms, in the sense that Proverbs is about the practical skills of living well (186). So Proverbs speaks of a wisdom that is (1) divine, (2) involved in creation, and (3) a guide for how humans ought to live. Although the relevant New Testament texts do not directly cite Proverbs 8, Yoder contends that this notion of wisdom stands behind the New Testament texts that speak of the Son as *logos*, as divine, and as agent of creation.

For Yoder, the hymn of Philippians 2:5-11 is also vital to understanding the person and work of Christ:

> In your relationships with one another, have the same mind-set as Christ Jesus: Who, being in very nature God, did not consider equality with God something to be used to his own advantage; rather, he made himself nothing by taking the very nature of a servant, being made in human likeness. And being found in appearance as a man, he humbled himself by becoming obedient to death—even death on a cross!

---

53. This is the text of Proverbs 8 as found in Yoder, *Preface*, 184. The editors of that volume note that the quotations of Scripture in *Preface* have been standardized and that Yoder does not consistently use one translation (Hauerwas and Sider, "Introduction," 27). Unless otherwise noted, I will use the biblical text as given in *Preface*.

54. Yoder, *Preface*, 184. Further references to *Preface to Theology* in this chapter will be placed parenthetically in the text.

> Therefore God exalted him to the highest place and gave
> him the name that is above every name, that at the name of
> Jesus every knee should bow, in heaven and on earth and
> under the earth, and every tongue acknowledge that Jesus
> Christ is Lord, to the glory of God the Father. (NIV)

Yoder points out that Jesus' refusal to grasp this equality
can be taken in two different ways. First, *kenosis* (or emptying)
is often seen as a metaphysical emptying. As Son of God, Jesus
gives up certain divine qualities, powers, and attributes to become
human (83). Jesus, the divine Son, not only becomes human but
suffers death on a cross. Second, Paul's language of "equality with
God" also draws a parallel between the humanity of Adam and
the humanity of Jesus. Adam succumbed to the serpent's temptation to "become as God" (Gen 3:5). In contrast, Jesus accepted his
place as creature and refused to grasp at equality with God.

Although Yoder sees Philippians 2 as comparing the humanity of Adam and Jesus, he also contends that this text affirms the
preexistence and divinity of Christ (124).[55] Yoder points out that
if one focuses only on the humanity of Jesus, Philippians 2 could
be given an adoptionist interpretation: Jesus was elevated to the
position of Son *because of* his obedience. This, Yoder contends,
does not do justice to Jesus:

> The phenomenon of Jesus Christ reported in the early
> story is too unexplainable, too unique . . . to have been
> only another human, like others from the beginning. The
> idea of Jesus beginning life like other people is not enough
> to explain what he did. Or, to say it from the side of the
> monotheism of Jewish Christianity within which the church
> arose, the idea of a man becoming or being made God is
> unacceptable. The only alternative is for God to take the
> initiative and become a man among humans. (124)

For Yoder, when we think of the person and work of Christ,
we must acknowledge that he is divine, at work well before the
incarnation.[56]

---

55. Cf. "The Form of a Servant," in *He Came Preaching Peace*, 91–92.

56. Cf. Yoder, "'But We Do See Jesus': The Particularity of Incarnation
and the Universality of Truth," in *Priestly Kingdom*, 52.

In Colossians 1, the author of that epistle (Paul or otherwise) specifically focuses on the Christ's work in creation. In speaking of Christ, he states,

> The Son is the image of the invisible God, the firstborn over all creation. For in him all things were created: things in heaven and on earth, visible and invisible, whether thrones or powers or rulers or authorities; all things have been created through him and for him. He is before all things, and in him all things hold together. And he is the head of the body, the church; he is the beginning and the firstborn from among the dead, so that in everything he might have the supremacy. For God was pleased to have all his fullness dwell in him, and through him to reconcile to himself all things, whether things on earth or things in heaven, by making peace through his blood, shed on the cross. (Col 1:15-20)

Yoder makes three pertinent observations about this text. First, Christ is the agent of creation. Second, whatever order is in creation results from Christ's sustaining work: "In him everything 'systematizes,' everything holds together. This 'everything' that Christ maintains united is the world powers. It is the reign of order among creatures, order which in its original intention is a divine gift."[57] According to Colossians 1, it is not simply the Father or the Spirit (or both) who upholds the created universe, but the Son. Third, because Christ upholds the regularity and order of creation, this allows for the possibility of nature, history, and society. These areas are not simply the domain of the Father or Spirit, but of the Son. Importantly, this does not preclude the work of the Father or Spirit in creation and providence. Yoder is not trying to say that *only* the Son creates and sustains, but rather that creation cannot be separated from Christ on valid trinitarian grounds. Indeed, any biblically sound trinitarianism emphasizes the Son's role in creation.

In Hebrews 1, the author also presents Christ as directly related to creation. When commenting on this text, Yoder first highlights that the book of Hebrews is about continuity and fulfillment. What God is doing through the Son stands in continuity with how God spoke in the past. Jesus' sonship, however, goes

---

57. Yoder, *Politics*, 141. Cf. Yoder, *Preface*, 123.

beyond how God communicated in the past. According to Yoder, the Old Testament used the term "son of God" to refer to both angels and kings and, in the New Testament, to the Messiah (116). Given these varied meanings, Hebrews 1 makes several striking statements about Jesus as the Son of God:

> In these last days he has spoken to us by a Son whom he appointed the heir of all things, through whom also he created the world. He reflects the glory of God and bears the very stamp of his nature, upholding the universe by his word of power . . . To what angel did God ever say, "Thou art my son . . . ?" Or again, "I will be to him a father, and he shall be to me a son?" . . . Of the Son he says, "Thy throne, O God, is forever and ever." (Heb 1:2-3, 5, 8)[58]

According to Yoder, this is a distinctive use of the term "son of God" (117). Jesus is not "son of God" like the angels; he is equal to the Father. Whereas angel and kings can be called son of God in the sense of "dependence upon or subjection to God," the author of Hebrews singles out Jesus as the unique Son of God who "bears the very stamp of his nature," an identity with the Father that differentiates him from all others (116–17). In this sense, Jesus' sonship is qualitatively different from the sonship of angels or past kings. So Yoder underscores that the author of Hebrews makes abundantly clear that the Father addresses the Son as "God." Jesus is the agent of creation and truly divine.

In John 1, Yoder finds final proof that any dichotomy between creation and Christ cannot be sustained:

> In the beginning was the Word, and the Word was with God, and the Word was God. He was with God in the beginning. Through him all things were made; without him nothing was made that has been made. He was in the world, and though the world was made through him, the world did not recognize him. (John 1:1-3, 10)

Yoder points out that John uses a word often used in Greek philosophy, *logos*, to point to something unique. Yoder notes that *logos* generally has a variety of meanings, including reason, the

---

58. As quoted in Yoder, *Preface*, 117.

rationality of God that underlies the universe, and the communicative aspect of God. Although the emphasis on God as Creator and the notion of God's creative wisdom is not innovative, John uses this term in a new way to proclaim that the truth and power we see in Jesus is the very truth and power of God that created and sustains all things.[59] John thus goes beyond what would have been normal and acceptable for both Greeks and Jews in the proclamation that the *logos* became flesh. Yoder observes that this claim about the incarnation goes on to become, in 1 John, the "key to faithfulness" and the "center" of the apostolic witness (1 John 1:1-2; 4:1-3) (121). In this way, John affirms that Jesus is both truly human and yet more than merely human. In Yoder's words, John clearly shows that the Word is "preexistent" and that he shares in "the divine work of creation."[60] Based on John 1, Colossians 1, Hebrews 1, and Philippians 2, we must not presume that the person and work of Christ began only in the first century, for that would do injustice to Scripture. Yoder thus follows the New Testament in affirming the Son's preexistence, divinity, and work in creation (208).

Jesus the preexistent One. Yoder also underscores Jesus' divinity in his discussion of the Son's preexistence. Yoder repeatedly affirms the Bible's claims about Jesus' divinity, but some readers, including Thomas Finger, still argue that he reduces Jesus so that any "transcendent dimension" in Yoder's Christology is absent.[61] Contrary to Finger's claims, however, Yoder not only affirms the deity of Jesus in his exegesis of Scripture, but he repeatedly emphasizes the biblical support for the divinity and preexistence of the Son in his survey of the trinitarian developments and heresies of early church history. To argue that Yoder denies a transcendent dimension to Jesus makes nonsense of the language of Yoder and of the theologians he discusses.

In his survey of Tertullian, Yoder points out that Tertullian tries to develop ways of thinking and speaking that accurately reflect "what the biblical text demands must be said: the elements

---

59. Yoder, "Glory in a Tent," in *He Came Preaching Peace*, 82.

60. Ibid., 81.

61. Finger, "Did Yoder Reduce Theology to Ethics?" 333.

of preexistence, distinctness, and monotheism" (191). Yoder is not merely listing what Tertullian perceived the biblical text to be demanding, but what Yoder himself takes the biblical texts to be demanding, namely preexistence, distinctness between Father, Son, and Spirit, and monotheism (193). Tertullian marks the real beginning of the doctrine of the Trinity, Yoder argues, because he pushes toward something new: "a way of affirming distinction and unity at the same time without being silly or contradictory" (191). For Yoder, this must be done to make sense of the biblical text.

Later, when outlining Sabellianism, Yoder states that it must be tested against the texts outlined above, especially concerning the concept of preexistence. A basic point of Sabellianism is that "God takes the form of a mold that the world provides" (192). This view mistakenly believes that "there is no preexisting Son, but only the Son when the shape of Jesus is there" (193). Yoder points out that the Sabellian view also struggles to account for how the cross was salvific because it fails to "take seriously the preexistence of Christ" (194). Moreover, this position could also lead to the problematic view that the Son has no enduring existence once the Spirit is manifest. Sabellianism fails the test of faithfulness to Scripture, in Yoder's view, precisely because it does not adequately account for the preexistence of the Son.

Finally, Yoder surveys the work of Arius, noting that Arius was concerned with preserving God's transcendence (196–97). Arius held two propositions: (1) God does not need to have the Son to be God for that would destroy divine independence and (2) the Son cannot be made out of God. Arius's conclusion, therefore, is that the Son was created *ex nihilo* like all other things. Yoder criticizes Arius for holding that Jesus earned sonship based on his obedience. According to Yoder, Arianism problematically undermines Scripture's teaching about the Son's divinity and preexistence. This "dismantled not only the systematic, dogmatic, and philosophical statements of the second and third centuries, but began to go back and challenge some of the things that the New Testament itself had said" (197). Arius is a specimen of "naive" biblical reading that does not adequately account for the way that Scripture's Christological claims demand a rethinking of ontology (208).

Although Yoder recognizes that the actual word "preexistence" does not appear in the New Testament, he is equally clear that "the concept of preexistence [is] affirmed in the biblical documents" (208). Indeed, Yoder notes that a high Christology characterizes the oldest texts of the New Testament (139). Hence, later Christological and trinitarian developments of the church must be tested according to whether they do justice to the text of Scripture. Yoder recognized the difficulty confronted by the early church theologians, who were faced with the daunting challenge of encapsulating the New Testament's claims about Jesus, about the one true God, and about the distinction between the Father and Son. Though a difficult task, Yoder affirms that a key test of fidelity to Scripture is whether these theologians rightly affirmed Jesus' divinity and preexistence.

Based on the textual evidence outlined in this section, Thomas Finger's claim that Yoder has no "transcendent dimension" of Christology is baffling.[62] Contrary to Finger's argument, Yoder claimed that the biblical authors dismantled the transcendent referent *as commonly understood,* but not that they jettisoned transcendence (or divinity) completely. For example, John 1 does not simply tell people what they already know about the *logos,* but says that the *logos* has taken on flesh. If Yoder is really saying that there is no transcendent referent to John 1's *logos,* then it is hard to see how either the original audience or contemporary readers can make sense of John 1. Did Yoder really think that the apostle's claim that "the *logos* was *theos*" has no transcendent referent, but referred only to human "characteristics, activities, relationships, and potentialities"? If so, Yoder was a weak linguist, theologian, and philosopher indeed. Yoder, however, does not think that. He thinks that John "dismantled" the transcendent reference *as understood by the non-Christian interpretation* of this ontology. The writer did not throw away this ontological conceptuality, but hammered it into a Christological shape. John 1 does not say, "Let me fit Christ into this pre-Christian logic," but rather "how does Christ change the shape of this logic?" Thus, although Finger interprets Yoder as denying that the biblical writers "refashioned" Hellenistic conceptualities to express new

---

62. Ibid.

transcendent content, Yoder himself explicitly describes the biblical writers as doing this refashioning work, in which the writers "seized the categories, hammered them into other shapes, proclaiming Jesus at the top of the cosmology as divine and the bottom of the cosmology as human."[63]

Implications of Yoder's Christology

Yoder convincingly makes the case that the Bible presents Jesus as directly relevant to both culture and creation. As Israel's Messiah, Christ's work of redemption was not purely "religious," understood as pointing away from politics, economics, and culture. Moreover, because Jesus is the enfleshed *logos* who creates, orders, and sustains creation, creation and redemption are necessarily connected in him. Based on the exegetical evidence, Yoder draws several conclusions.

The Son and creation. A properly trinitarian doctrine of creation must include the Son as an active participant.[64] As Jan Rohls puts it, the Son's mediation of creation "excludes the possibility of regarding creation as the work of the Father alone."[65] When Christians lack a trinitarian doctrine of creation, they sometimes do so by misreading the Apostles' or Nicene Creeds, both of which speak of the Father's work in creation but not the Son's. Yoder does not fault these creeds for speaking of the Father as Creator, but he notes that the New Testament emphasis on the Son as agent of creation is missing (162). Although the Christian tradition as a whole is careful to affirm a trinitarian doctrine of creation, with the Son playing an essential role, some theologians are not, which leads to a second, more insidious problem.

In the last several centuries, some theologians (including the Niebuhrs) struggle to affirm the deity of Christ and therefore to pay due attention to John 1, Colossians 1, and Hebrews 1. For *a priori* systematic reasons, theologians do not include these texts when they discuss the relationship of Christ and creation, and the Father

---

63. Yoder, "But We Do See Jesus," in *Priestly Kingdom*, 54.

64. I do not attempt to address here the role of the Spirit in creation in Yoder's theology.

65. Rohls, *Reformed Confessions*, 55.

and Son. This skews the doctrines of the Trinity and of creation. This failure to affirm Christ's deity then *generates* the "problem" of how to relate the Father and Son, Christ and creation, or creation and gospel.[66] If we willingly allow the New Testament to speak on its own terms, the problem dissolves. Because Yoder affirms the full deity of Christ as proclaimed in the New Testament, his doctrines of the Trinity and of creation stand in line with Scripture. The Word who became flesh and tabernacled among us is none other than the Word who was in the beginning.

The Father and redemption. If certain thinkers put the Son on the sidelines in creation, they also neglect the Father's role in redemption. These moves are equally problematic. Yoder thus underscores that the Father and Son are unified not only in creation but in redemption.[67] This affects how we think about the wisdom and power of the Creator God. When we look at Jesus, we see who the Father is. Yoder explains that

> Christian belief is not content to see Jesus as truly the servant of men; we confess Him as Son of God. He is not only a demonstration of perfect manhood but at the same time the manifestation of the Godhead. It follows that God himself must be understood after the fashion not of a sultan or a judge, but of a servant. He who said "I am among you as one who serves" also said "He who has seen me has seen the Father." We must overcome the sub-Christian conception of God as a sort of distant, uninterested, or vengeful monarch who would just as soon see us all perish if it were not for the more humane or more friendly intervention of His Son. God the Father is Love; God the Father was in Christ reconciling the world to himself and not reckoning our sins against us; God the Father so loved the world that He gave His only-begotten Son.[68]

---

66. For example, in Niebuhr, "The Doctrine of the Trinity and the Unity of the Church," 371–384, Niebuhr speaks only of the Father as Creator.

67. Yoder also thinks the Spirit is equally involved, but that is not my focus in this section.

68. Yoder, "The Lordship of Christ and the Power Struggle," in *The Lordship of Christ*, 508.

To look at Jesus is never just to see Jesus, but also to see the Father, because the life, ministry, and death that Jesus undertook for our sakes was a mission given to him *by the Father*, as Jesus states in John 18:11, "Shall I not drink the cup the Father has given me?"[69]

Moreover, in the concrete life and teaching of Jesus the Messiah, the Father is revealed. Indeed, one might claim that Yoder is one of the most Johannine of modern theologians, constantly working out the implications of Jesus' words in John 14:9: "Anyone who has seen me has seen the Father." Specifically, Jesus makes the claim that by loving their enemies, his followers are directly imitating their heavenly Father (Matt 5:43-48). As Yoder points out, "the thought that we might be like God the Father is not a frequent one in the New Testament."[70] When Jesus loves his enemies, we see the Father's love for us. Christ's rejection of justified violence or holy war is thus not merely his choice, but that of the Father:

> The decision of Jesus not to be a violent zealot Messiah now comes to be seen as the surfacing, the manifestation, the incarnation of the deep reality of God's own nature . . . As you see the grain of a piece of wood at its edges, Jesus' choice not to rule the world violently is now seen to be the surfacing of an eternal divine decision . . . an eternally binding and freeing decision of the Son, very God of very God, to enter into our history. Then self-emptying is not only what Jesus did. It is not only what the eternal divine Son did. If it is that, then it is the very nature of God. The Creator of the universe is a servant. The Almighty loves his enemies.[71]

Given the unity of Father and Son in creation and redemption, the New Testament sees the cross and resurrection as not only a local, historical event, but also as a revelation of something universal about God's interaction with his creation: "What happened

---

69. Yoder references this point in *Politics*, 46.

70. Yoder, "The Moral Axioms of the Kingdom Coming," in *To Hear the Word*, 30. Cf. Yoder, "Jesus: A Model of Radical Political Action," in *War of the Lamb*, 79.

71. Yoder, "The Form of a Servant?" in *He Came Preaching Peace*, 93.

in the cross is a revelation of the shape of what God is, and of what God does, in the total drama of history. They affirm as a permanent pattern what in Jesus was a particular event . . . God has the same shape as Jesus, and he always has had. The cross is what creation is all about. What Jesus did was local, of course, because that is how serious and real our history is to God. But what the cross was locally is universally and always the divine nature."[72] In other words, the very nature of God is self-giving love. Out of God's abundant self-giving love, God creates, orders, and sustains the world; out of this love, God makes covenants and binds himself to frail and fallen human beings. The cross and resurrection are the apex of God's interaction with humanity. The cross and resurrection make clear the full extent of God's self-giving love, and they are fully consistent with the character and nature of God as revealed in creation and covenant history. The connection between creation and redemption is clear in the prologue of John's Gospel, which testifies that "what God always was continues. And what the Word of God was always trying to do in creation and in the garden of Eden and in Abraham and in Moses and in the prophets—shining on faithfully even though the darkness did not receive it—continues."[73]

The normativity of the Messiah. Because Jesus is divine, he is also the normative human being. The New Testament, according to Yoder, demonstrates that God did not simply speak by the words of the Son, but by the "being and presence" of the Son (333). Hence, revelation is not simply a part of what Jesus was doing; rather, the sum total of Jesus' life *is* revelation. Furthermore, Jesus, as God in the flesh, is not only the revelation of God but also the revelation of true humanity: "The humanity of Jesus is a revelation of the purpose of God for the person who wills to do God's will,"[74] including God's will with respect to our life as cultural and social beings. A biblical view of Jesus as fully human and fully divine, Yoder argues, results in seeing the humanity of Jesus

---

72. Yoder, "Glory in a Tent," in *He Came Preaching Peace*, 85.

73. Ibid., 88.

74. Yoder, "Christ, the Light of the World," in *The Royal Priesthood*, 185.

as normative for our humanity. A mistake in either an Ebionitic or Gnostic-Docetic direction leads one astray. These views lose the full revelation given in Jesus by focusing exclusively on either the divine or the human nature of Christ.

According to Yoder, the Ebionitic view reduces Jesus to a good rabbi, "dissolving Jesus' uniqueness into a sub-case of history in general" (173). An Ebionitic social ethic emphasizes Jesus as a good teacher and moral example but undercuts his ultimate authority by denying that he was truly divine. Sometimes when Christians refuse to allow Jesus to affect the church's social-political practices, a covert Ebionism is at work. Jesus is a fine example, but not really binding for us because in the end he is not really different in any way from us. In other words, the Ebionite sees the *commonality* of Jesus with all other humans as a reason for discounting his normativity for the Christian's cultural life.

On the other hand, a Gnostic or Docetic approach focuses on his divinity, but "dissolve[s] Jesus into one more example of revelation" (173). This Gnostic social ethic sets aside the normativity of Jesus by emphasizing his divinity, and thus the *difference* between Jesus and all other humans. This often happens when conservative creedal Christians claim that Christians should not attempt to imitate Jesus' ethical life because he was *unique*. Although Yoder affirms the uniqueness of Jesus' person and work, Yoder also emphasizes that, as a full and complete human being, Jesus must be seen as normative. Thus, the social ethics of the Christian community should correspond to those of Jesus.[75] As Nigel Wright helpfully explains, "Discipleship involves conformity to Christ in his death. Unique though it may be, it is also uniquely normative. In the Anabaptist tradition, and arguably in Scripture, the cross is not only an event but a divine principle with prototypical meaning, determining the life and fate of disciples."[76] Yoder fears that many thinkers have missed this prototypical aspect of Christ's

---

75. Yoder, *Nevertheless: The Varieties and Shortcomings of Religious Pacifism*, 134. Chapter 7 of *Politics*, "The Disciple of Christ and the Way of Jesus," is devoted to examining the numerous New Testament passages in which the Christian is called to imitate, participate in, and follow Jesus Christ.

76. Wright, *Disavowing Constantine*, 93.

cross, presuming that "because Jesus is seen as the Word made flesh, he cannot be seen as normative person."[77]

In contrast, Yoder argues that *precisely because* Jesus Christ is the Word made flesh, he should be seen as normative human being. As Yoder forcefully phrases the question, "What becomes of the meaning of incarnation if Jesus is not normatively human? If he is human but not normative, is this not the ancient ebionitic heresy? If he be somehow authoritative but not in his humanness, is this not a new gnosticism?"[78] When Yoder affirms the full deity and humanity of Jesus, it logically leads to affirming Jesus' authoritative and normative humanity.

Christ and creation. Yoder's analysis of the New Testament's Christology shows that we must not draw a sharp dualism between creation and redemption, whether in theology or ethics. Although the next chapter unfolds this point in greater detail, this chapter clarifies one of Yoder's central theological rules: New Testament Christology will not allow us to pit creation and redemption against each other, either as sources producing contradictory knowledge of God or as sources producing contradicting norms for human social and cultural life:

> If truly, as John says, the Word without which nothing was made that was made became flesh and tented among us in the man Jesus, then no a priori dichotomy between creation and gospel can be accepted. If truly, as Paul said in citing an ancient hymn in his plea to the Philippians, the norm for how we are to be minded is yielding authority rather than seizing it, in favor of taking on the form of a slave, there is no ground for a mandate to do the opposite.[79]

Indeed precisely because the Word became flesh, with all the cultural concerns of humanity, Christians are enabled to go about "the redemption of *creation*."[80] Yoder unpacks this further:

> It is one of the standard reproaches addressed to minority Christianity that it does not take seriously the possible

---

77. Yoder, *Politics*, 226.

78. Ibid., 10.

79. Yoder, "Creation and Gospel," 8.

80. Yoder, "That Household We Are," 8 (emphasis mine).

goodness of creation and the duties of building a culture. That argument would only hold if it were fair to separate creation from redemption and confuse it instead with fallenness. When the early witnesses make Messiah Lord of the cosmos, they reclaim what can be reclaimed of the original creation vision, precisely by denying that there exists an autonomous creaturely world needing to be served in its own terms. They confess instead that the claim of the cosmos to autonomy is its rebelliousness, and that its subordination to the Lord Yahweh has begun with the kenosis of the incarnation, with the cross, and moved forward with the resurrection and ascension . . . Both historically in the experienced cultural creativity of minority communities, and in the theological integrity of the linkage of redemption and creation, the gospel formulation of the cultural mandate is that which flows from this high Christology.[81]

In other words, if Christians are redeemed by Christ and ambassadors of reconciliation, then they must discerningly participate in the cultural life for which humanity was created. The way of Christ runs with the grain of the universe precisely because Christ is both Word and Lord of the universe.[82]

Nevertheless, worries persist that Yoder's focus on Christ eclipses creation and that Yoder himself has a deficient doctrine of creation. Does he ignore other lights, such as orders of creation or natural law? Does he diminish a truly biblical theology of creation? Yoder does indeed possess a robust doctrine of creation and his focus on Christ enriches rather than impoverishes the connection between creation and redemption and his resulting theology of culture.

---

81. Ibid., 8.
82. Yoder, *Politics*, 246.

5

The Power of Jesus and the Politics of Creation

Yoder's focus on Jesus is well known. What is less known is that Yoder provides both suggestive clues and explicit statements that help chart his doctrine of creation and theology of culture. Many commentators accuse Yoder of lacking a sound doctrine of creation and thereby having a deficient theology of culture.[1] These thinkers rightly raise the question of the relationship between Jesus and creation with all that that entails for theology and social ethics. The central question, as Richard Mouw succinctly puts it, is this: "When we live out these patterns of discipleship [the politics of Jesus] are we also reestablishing the politics of the original creation?"[2] Yoder answers in the affirmative, charting the connection between creation and redemption. Humans were created to exercise the peaceful power of Christ, and the Powers were created to be dynamic servants of peace and flourishing.

---

1. Budziszewski, "Four Shapers of Evangelical Political Thought," in *Evangelicals in the Public Square*; Charles, "Protestants and Natural Law," 33–38; Charles, *Retrieving the Natural Law*, 137–41; Haas, "The Effects of the Fall on Creational Social Structures," 108–29; Reimer, "'I came not to abolish the law but to fulfill it,'" in *A Mind Patient and Untamed*, 245–73; Schlabach, "The Christian Witness in the Earthly City," in *A Mind Patient and Untamed*, 221–44; and Wright, *Disavowing Constantine*, 163–66.

2. Mouw, "Creational Politics," 191.

Power and the Powers

What are the "Powers?"[3] They are the nexus of earthly and heavenly powers, both the visible and invisible spiritual forces that, for good or for ill, enable ordered human life.[4] To explain this in further detail, Yoder points to the New Testament's language and concepts. Biblical authors (primarily Paul) use language of "Powers" in a variety of contexts and with a variety of other terms.[5] Some terms have political overtones, such as *principalities*, *powers*, *thrones*, and *dominions*. Other terms are more "cosmological" (Yoder's term): *angels*, *archangels*, *elements*, *heights*, and *depths*. Still others are more religious, such as *law* and *knowledge*. As they address a variety of issues in different contexts, Biblical authors often juxtapose

3. Yoder draws heavily on Berkhof, *Christ and the Powers*. Yoder translated this work from Dutch. On this topic, Yoder references Hendrik Berkhof, G.B. Caird, G.H.C. MacGregor, and Markus Barth (*The Politics of Jesus*, 136). He also points to Karl Ludwig Schmidt, Willem A. Visser 't Hooft, Oscar Cullman, and Wolfgang Schweitzer (Yoder, "Behold My Servant Shall Prosper," in *Karl Barth and the Problem of War and Other Essays on Barth*, 161). Elsewhere, he cites James Stewart, Anders Nygren, Karl Barth, Clinton Morrison, and D.E.H. Whiteley ("Letter to John Stott," [Dec. 7, 1978], from the personal collection of Mark Thiessen Nation, 2). Since Yoder wrote *Politics*, Walter Wink has done a thorough study of the Powers in *Naming the Powers: The Language of Power in the New Testament* (Philadelphia: Fortress Press, 1984); Wink, *Unmasking the Powers: The Invisible Forces That Determine Human Existence* (Philadelphia: Fortress Press, 1986); and Wink, *Engaging the Powers: Discernment and Resistance in a World of Domination* (Minneapolis: Fortress Press, 1992).

4. The Old Testament lays a foundation for seeing the Powers as the nexus of earthly and heavenly powers in texts such as Ps 82; Dan 10:10-14, 18-21; Isa 24:21-23, and the Septuagint version of Deut 32:8. Thanks to John Nugent for noting these references.

5. The following paragraph is a summary of Yoder, *Politics*, 137. For "Powers" language in the New Testament, see Matt 24:29; Luke 12:11; Rom 8:38, 39; 13:1-4; 1 Cor 2:8; 15:24-26; Eph 1:20-23; 2:1, 2; 3:10; 6:12; Col 1:15-17; 2:15, 16; Titus 3:1; and 1 Pet 3:21–4:1. Terms associated with this semantic domain and conceptual field include *archē*, *archōn*, *exousia*, *dynamis*, *kosmokratores*, *kyriotēs*, *onoma*, *pneumatika*, *stoicheia*, and *thronos*. Yoder often uses the generic term *Powers* to refer to this linguistic and conceptual cluster.

these terms with one another, sometimes suggesting parallelism, other times not. This language, Yoder acknowledges, is complex.

The linguistic and conceptual complexity of "Powers," Yoder suggests, may be helpfully compared to the contemporary concept of "structure."[6] This complex term has a wide range of meaning, depending on the context in which it is used. In social and political fields, it can point to institutions, agencies, and offices. In some such situations, it is less concrete but still very real, in the way "Wall Street" can refer to a phenomenon far more complex than a street in New York City. In the field of psychology, one might speak of the structure of someone's personality to describe the patterns and responses that individuals have developed over time. In the field of architecture, "structure" refers to a physical artifact. In the field of linguistics, it denotes the grammar, syntax, and logic of a specific language. So, Yoder draws an analogy with the New Testament language of power and the Powers: "The concept 'structure' functions to point to the patterns or regularities that transcend or precede or condition the individual phenomena we can immediately perceive . . . It is this patternedness that the word 'structure' tries to enable us to perceive within all the varieties of its appearance. Similarly, 'power' points in all its modulations to some kind of capacity to make something happen."[7] Yoder willingly acknowledges that the New Testament language of Powers is not always as precise and unambiguous as a systematic thinker might like. Regardless, we can still examine Paul's meaning when he uses such terms and begin to understand what he meant.[8]

For Yoder, the Powers are crucial as a viable alternative to other theological and biblical constructions: "It would not be too much to claim that the Pauline cosmology of the powers represents an alternative to the dominant ('Thomist') vision of 'natural law' as a more biblical way systematically to relate Christ and creation."[9] Although

---

6. Yoder, *Politics*, 137.

7. Ibid., 138.

8. Ibid., 137, n. 2.

9. Ibid., 159. Cf. also Yoder, "Regarding Nature," in *The Teachings of Modern Protestantism on Law, Politics, and Human Nature*, 427–30. Also available online at http://theology.nd.edu/people/research/yoder-john/documents/REGARDINGNATURE.pdf (accessed January 4, 2010).

Yoder primarily reports on other scholars in *Politics of Jesus*, his other writings develop more fully his own distinctive view of the Powers, in which he argues for a doctrine of creation and theology of culture that draws upon the biblical language of power and the Powers. Yoder's doctrine of the Powers reveals that he has a positive account of creation. Far from pitting creation and redemption against each other, he shows their coherence in his view of the Powers.

Importantly, in explaining what the Powers are, Yoder argues for a holistic rather than a reductionistic view. He makes this case most thoroughly in personal correspondence with John Stott.[10] Stott worries that many commentators on the Powers commit to demythologizing Scripture based on modern prejudices. Those scholars therefore latch onto Powers language with reference *solely* to visible societal and political structures, disregarding the spiritual and invisible nature of the Powers.[11]

Yoder explicitly denies any "demythologizing" work on his own part: "For me there is a vast difference between saying, in conversation with my contemporaries, that Paul should make sense to them on their secular/causal level, and denying with them that there is anything not on their level. That latter denial would for me be logically illegitimate for general philosophical and theological reasons."[12] Yoder thinks that the Bible speaks to us today, and that an attentive eye to Scripture and a missionary ear to one's culture will see how it does so. This assumption, however, is very different from the methodological assumption of some of Yoder's contemporaries that the reigning worldview of modernity (or any other period) gets to stand as judge over against Scripture.

Furthermore, moderns often draw a sharp divide between a host of concepts: visible and invisible, natural and supernatural, immanent

---

10. Yoder, "Letter to John Stott," (Oct. 27, 1976); "Letter to John Stott," (June 28, 1978); John Stott, "Letter to John H. Yoder," (Oct. 27, 1978); and "Letter to John Stott," (Dec. 7, 1978). From the personal collection of Mark Thiessen Nation.

11. Stott, "Letter to John H. Yoder" (Oct. 27, 1978). Stott's worry is published formally in Stott, *God's New Society*, 267–75.

12. Yoder, "Letter to John Stott," (Dec. 7, 1978), 3. Yoder also notes that language of the Powers is more nuanced than that of modern social science (Yoder, *The War of the Lamb*, 64).

and transcendent, secular and religious, politics and spirituality, among others. In terms of the Powers, some commentators (Stott included) frame the debate so that the Powers must be understood as *either* personal, invisible, angelic beings or as impersonal but visible structures. Yoder argues that this dichotomous way of thinking has to be overcome if we are to read rightly the text of the New Testament. Whereas some modern commentators deny any reference to the invisible and transcendent dimensions in the text, others see them as referring solely to the invisible and transcendent dimensions. Or, better yet, they cannot see how the two are inextricably linked. Yoder's point is that this false dilemma is itself a characteristic of modern thinking, but not of the biblical text.[13] Writing to Stott, Yoder states that the solution is to see the biblical language of the Powers as

> a natural wholesome unity. To pry apart the empirical and more-than-empirical dimensions, which enables you to call the unity [between the two] an uneasy compromise, is itself the fruit of a post-platonic cultural development which has to be debated. I said before that I did not see any of us as denying the "heavenly" dimension, just because we feel that we can move from the first century into ours in identifying the earthly dimension. It is you, not [Hendrik] Berkhof and [Markus] Barth, who think that we must choose between the two, and as far as I can see from here you are thinking that on the basis of a post-reformation western cosmology rather than a biblical wholeness.[14]

Yoder is not reductionistic because, for Yoder, institutions are not merely empirical or merely visible or public. Every institution and every political and cultural practice concentrates and suffuses power—a power that enables humans to serve God and empower one another or a power that attempts to supplant God with idols and overpower other humans and creation. Because both humans and Powers are dynamic not static, Yoder provides a complex account of how the power of creation gets warped in the fall and set free in redemption.

---

13. Ibid., (Dec. 7, 1978), 7–8. For example, Psalm 82 connects God's judgment of the rebellious heavenly court with earthly kings. Moreover, the judgment of both is connected with the failure to do justice. Thanks to John Nugent for this reference.

14. Ibid., (Dec. 7, 1978), 4.

Power given: creation

The first characteristic of the Powers is that they are rooted in God's good creation and not essentially fallen. Colossians 1:15-17 is a central text: "He [Jesus] is the image of the invisible God, the firstborn of all creation, for in him all things were created: things in heaven and on earth, visible and invisible, whether thrones or powers or rulers or authorities; all things have been created through him and for him. He is before all things and in him all things hold together." Drawing on this text, Yoder asserts that the Powers are part of creation, which is characterized by "the reign of order among creatures, order which in its original intention is a divine gift."[15] Yoder further explains, again connecting the biblical language of Powers with structures: "There could not be society or history, there could not be humanity without the existence above us of religious, intellectual, moral, and social structures. *We cannot live without them.*"[16] God's works of creation and providence are not manifested through a series of arbitrary, immediate, or erratic divine interventions, but through the regularity and order of the Powers.[17] In this respect, Yoder compares them to orders of creation: "With the Reformed doctrine of the orders of creation, [Hendrik] Berkhof's Paul affirms that all human being is structured, that that structured quality is, itself, not an accident nor the fall, but a part of the divinely given creatureliness so that the whole is always more than its parts."[18] God meant the Powers to be servants of human flourishing, enabling humans to use their God-given power in the right way and through the right channels.[19] So for Yoder, "the Powers as such, power in itself, is the good creation of God."[20]

---

15. Yoder, *Politics*, 141.

16. Ibid., 143 (emphasis original). Cf. also Yoder, *The Christian Witness to the State*, 83; and "Reformed versus Anabaptist Social Strategies," 6.

17. Ibid., 141.

18. Yoder, "Behold My Servant Shall Prosper," in *Karl Barth*, 162.

19. Yoder, "On Not Being in Charge," in *Jewish-Christian Schism Revisited*, 175.

20. Yoder, *Politics*, 154.

Importantly, Yoder uses the term *power* not only to describe what *is* but to talk about what *should be*. It is not only a fact *of* creation, but part of God's intent *for* creation. In this way, power is a key part of both the origin and essence of what it means to be human.[21] Yoder acknowledges that "power" can be used in a variety of ways, most basically to refer to the ability to do just about anything.[22] As a result, we must always define concretely what we mean when we talk about "power" or "powerlessness."[23] Yoder drives this point home: Jesus "was not interested in either approving of power in general or disapproving of power in general. He was interested in exercising the power of love and eschewing the powers of destruction and selfishness."[24] Why did Jesus opt for the one route and not the other? He did so because "some kinds and forms of power are intrinsically good as a celebration of God's creative purpose, and others are intrinsically fallen as an instrument of pride and self-serving."[25] For Yoder, creational power goes with the grain of the universe, including the power of servanthood,[26] the power of forgiveness, the power of peoplehood,[27] the power of truth-telling, the power of creativity that sees beyond false and fallen dilemmas,[28] the power of a vision of the universe that sees it open to God,[29] and, of course,

---

21. Yoder's account of human power is strikingly similar to the exegetical conclusions reached by Middleton, *The Liberating Image*.

22. Yoder, *Politics*, 138.

23. Yoder, "Behold My Servant Shall Prosper," in *Karl Barth*, 156.

24. Ibid., in *Karl Barth*, 156.

25. Ibid., in *Karl Barth*, 164.

26. Yoder, "The Lordship of Christ and the Power Struggle," in *The Lordship of Christ*, 511; "Behold My Servant Shall Prosper," in *Karl Barth*, 155; and "The Evangelical Mandate for Social Action," in *For the Nations*, 191. Cf. also "Turn, Turn," in *He Came Preaching Peace*, 137.

27. Yoder, "Jesus and Power," 453.

28. Yoder, "The Spirit of God and the Politics of Men," in *For the Nations*, 229.

29. Yoder, "The Political Meaning of Hope," in *War of the Lamb*, 62.

the power and wisdom of the cross.[30] In the light of creation and cross, fallen "power" is no power at all but simply the lust for domination.[31] This type of power cannot be maintained over the long haul; under it, things fall apart.[32] In contrast, Yoder contends, true creational power is the power of love and service, for that is the power of the Creator God and the Crucified King: "Our concern should be doxological. It should be commitment to celebrating as inseparable the power and the love of YHWH who is at once the almighty liberator of the slaves, defender of the widow, the orphan, the foreign, and the loving *abba* of Jesus the Anointed. *That* power and *that* love are not opposites . . . they are two faces of the same reality."[33]

The power of the Word. The goodness of the Powers and the goodness of creation are no surprise, because God is the Creator. As the previous chapter highlights, creation is not only the provenance of the Father but the Son as well. For Yoder, this ontological point has epistemological implications: "What is known in Jesus is what was behind creation."[34]

By connecting Christ with creation, the biblical authors did not mean, according to Yoder, that their audience should use Christ simply to rubber-stamp their preconceived notions about "creation" and "culture." For Yoder, we see in the incarnation that God calls us to leave some loyalties and practices behind. God calls Abraham out of Chaldea and into a pilgrim posture, and he calls Israel out of Egypt and into the Promised Land.[35] Incarnation follows the same pattern as election and exodus in that God validates some ways of living and rejects others. The incarnation, therefore, does not validate the best and highest in human culture apart from Jesus. Instead, the incarnation provides the baseline by which we judge all cultural practices to see if they

---

30. Yoder, "The Wisdom and the Power," in *He Came Preaching Peace*, 37–46.

31. See Yoder, "The Political Meaning of Hope," in *War of the Lamb*, 54.

32. Cf. Yoder, "The Political Meaning of Hope," in *War of the Lamb*, 62.

33. Yoder, "'To Your Tents, O Israel,'" 362 (emphasis added).

34. Yoder, "Glory in a Tent," in *He Came Preaching Peace*, 82.

35. Yoder, "Let the Church Be the Church," in *Royal Priesthood*, 172.

conform to God's creational intentions for humanity as revealed supremely in Jesus.[36]

Yoder's focus on Jesus does not exclude other routes of true knowledge, including the revelatory status of nature, common sense, the lessons of history, and generalizations arising out of the observation of social process. Yoder refuses the false notion (and stereotype of Anabaptists) that "those other kinds of wisdom are to be smashed or cursed."[37] He argues, instead, that they must be tested against the wisdom of God in Christ. If those other kinds of wisdom are truly from God, then they will line up with Christ. Yoder reminds us that Scripture affirms that God's revelation in creation does not and *cannot* conflict with Jesus.[38] Consequently, Yoder charts a close biblically-grounded connection between creation and redemption.

The gift of power given. In the beginning, both the Powers and humanity were without sin. We have few clues to what this would have been like, but Yoder reflects on what this original goodness of human power and the Powers would have looked like with reference to questions of justice, family, and farming.[39] Yoder's thoughts on these three topics provide helpful insight into his own doctrine of creation.

Yoder first addresses the hypothetical question of what prefall society could have been and whether retributive justice would be part of it.[40] He makes abundantly clear that order and organization are part of God's creational intentions for human life and society.[41] He notes that, without sin, no one would commit offenses and no one would make selfish demands for vengeance. As a result,

---

36. See also Yoder, *Politics*, 99.

37. Yoder, "Radical Reformation Ethics," in *The Priestly Kingdom*, 120.

38. Yoder, "Glory in a Tent," in *He Came Preaching Peace*, 85–88.

39. Yoder acknowledges that thought experiments about the good creation without sin are largely speculative but useful for heuristic purposes. This will be the case no matter the theologian. Yoder stands out, however, for trying to bring his speculation into conformity with New Testament teachings about Christ's role in creation.

40. What follows is a summary of Yoder, *Christian Witness*, 83.

41. Yoder, "Reformed versus Anabaptist Social Strategies," 6.

there would be no need for the sword or for retributive justice. Moreover, distributive justice would ensure that all received their fair share, which each would willingly accept as sufficient. Yoder notes that when Reinhold Niebuhr, Paul Tillich, and others see justice and love as competitors, they do so because they do not begin with creation but with the fall.[42] These thinkers conceive justice as something that emerges on the site of conflict created by sin. In contrast, Yoder points to the possibility of a creationally-rooted justice that is *not* merely about conflict and competition, but cooperation. In his conception, true justice is loving someone or something as it ought to be loved, and true love is giving someone or something its proper due.[43]

Yoder then addresses the power of male-female relationships. For Yoder, the first chapters of Genesis present a "vision of social wholeness which is structured matriarchally."[44] Several textual points serve to reinforce this: the woman was created in a special act, her creation is described in more detail, she fills a gap that completes the original creation, and the man cannot live without her. The serpent comes to the woman and the man eats the fruit she offers because she is the decision maker in this area and, as most anthropological models suggest, the culture of gardening and gathering depends on the work of women.[45] In addition, the task of mothering calls for a loving, ordering, caring nature.

As a result, the fall is, for Yoder, a fall to male domination. Just as sin introduces strife into human-serpent and human-earth

---

42. Cf. Yoder, "Against the Death Penalty," in H. Wayne House and John Howard Yoder, *The Death Penalty Debate: Two Opposing Views of Capital Punishment*, Issues of Christian Conscience Series, ed. Vernon Grounds (Dallas: Word, 1991), 143.

43. In this way, Yoder's account converges with Augustine in Book 19 of *The City of God*.

44. Yoder, "Feminist Theology Miscellany #1: Salvation through Mothering?" Cf. Yoder, "You Have it Coming" in *The End of Sacrifice*. By "matriarchy," Yoder does not mean a mirror image of postfall patriarchy, but the type of servanthood and care for others seen in Jesus or in the Father, who, Yoder notes, is no patriarch (Yoder, "Salvation through Mothering?" 6).

45. Yoder does not say whose anthropological research he is using.

relations, so it produces strife in the male-female relationship. Yoder does not romanticize mothering or argue that certain characteristics are essential to one gender. He notes, however, that if one compares typical gender stereotypes—authority versus compassion, rationality versus relatedness, manipulation versus interaction, distancing versus identification—with the kind of mutual love exemplified in Jesus and commended by the apostles, the kind of love called for can be mapped onto the "feminine" column of this list.[46] Whatever dominion and power looked like in male-female relationships before the fall, it looked less like the kings of the Gentiles, who lord it over their subjects, and more like the Lord who wept over Jerusalem and longed to be a protective mother hen toward her lost chicks.

Finally, Yoder addresses the power involved in humanity's relation to the earth, plants, and animals.[47] As God's representatives on earth, the male and female are given responsibilities. The vegetation requires work but also provides food. The animals must be named and ordered. Yoder sees God's empowering of humanity in the naming of the animals. Power and responsibility are given to humanity to extend the divine creative initiative by exercising their rationality and language in the ordering process. God both gives order to creation and simultaneously calls humanity to participate in the ordering processes of creation.[48]

This kind of dominion or rule, Yoder notes, should not be confused with the exploitative, abusive domination that appears later in the biblical narrative. In the hospitable environs of the garden, "the fruits are fitting food, the animals are friendly neighbors (not to be eaten, in the vision of Eden); we are capable of ordering this cosmos, and its good is the same as our own."[49] Within this order, humans also recognized their limits, which is how Yoder interprets the forbidden tree. The tree is a potent sign that humans are not ultimately in control, but they exercise their God-given

---

46. Yoder, "Salvation through Mothering?" 6–7.

47. Yoder, "On Generating Alternative Paradigms," in *Human Values and the Environment*, 57–58.

48. Ibid., 58.

49. Ibid.

power as the image of God. The posture God desires of humanity in Genesis 1–2 looks remarkably Christlike in that they (at least for a time) did not see godlikeness as something to be seized but accepted their proper place as having relative but not absolute power.[50] This right posture with respect to God allowed them to live in harmony with each other and with creation.

The power of faith and hope. Yoder's belief in the foundational goodness of creation and the Creator God manifests itself in a further way. In ethical theory, Yoder sees the unity of means and ends growing out of an abiding faith in God as Creator and in the cosmos as God's creation. In two separate works, "The Political Meaning of Hope"[51] and "The Lessons of Nonviolent Experience,"[52] Yoder addresses nonviolence in the context of Reinhold Niebuhr's dilemma between faithfulness and effectiveness. For Niebuhr, the Christian will either be faithful and ineffective or compromising but effective. Yoder explains how overturning this false dilemma depends on faith in God and confidence in the foundational goodness of God's creation. Such faith produces a stance of hope—hope that faithfulness to God's ways will not disappoint.

Drawing on Gandhi, Martin Luther King Jr., and James Douglass, Yoder argues that we need not submit to the logic of the social sciences, whose use of "effectiveness" determines Niebuhr's analysis. The alternative, Yoder contends, is to begin with a view of the cosmos that is bigger than any human tools of analysis. Rather than trying to pick things apart so that we can better manage history, Gandhi, King, and Douglass all *begin* with a "deep commitment to the unity of ends and means."[53] Yoder calls this stance "cosmological faith."[54] For Yoder, faith trusts that God has

---

50. Ibid.

51. Yoder, "The Political Meaning of Hope," in *War of the Lamb*, 53–65. Cf. also "The Power Equation, Jesus, and the Politics of King," in *For the Nations*, 134–36.

52. Yoder, *Christian Attitudes to War, Peace, and Revolution*, 353–68.

53. Ibid., 364–65. On the practical effect of the problematic divorce between means and ends, see Goudzwaard, Vander Vennen, and Van Heemst, *Hope in Troubled Times*, 121–23.

54. Yoder, "The Political Meaning of Hope," in *War of the Lamb*, 60.

created the cosmos with a wholeness to it, and therefore any attempt to make sharp divisions between means and ends only makes things fall further apart. Yoder's point is simple but powerful: if the creational nature and destiny of humanity and all creation is shalom, then the means to that end has to be integrally connected to it.

Paradoxically, because this cosmological faith has a proper vision of the whole and of the *telos* of creation, it informs truly effective action. Despite the danger of being seen as a pragmatist (just doing what seems to "work" in the short run), Yoder refuses to abandon the language of effectiveness. He does so partly because effectiveness always needs to be defined in terms of the ends it seeks and partly because many forms of violence that claim to be effective are just as much based on faith as his own vision.[55] That is, violence does not really work either; people just have faith that it does (often despite the very clear evidence it does not). At the same time, Yoder's faith and hope are supremely unpragmatic insofar as they are not *grounded* in pragmatism or effectiveness, but in God. For Yoder, that divine ground explains why embodying Christlike, peaceful power works:

> To say with King, "love is the most durable power in the world," or "there is something in the universe that unfolds for justice," is not to claim a sure insight into the way martyrdom works as a social power, although martyrdom often does that. It is a confessional or kerygmatic statement made by those whose loyalty to Christ (or to universal love, or to *satyagraha*) they understand to be validated by its cosmic ground. Suffering love is not right because it "works" in any calculable short-run way (although it often does). It is right because it goes with the grain of the universe, and that is why *in the long run* nothing else will work.[56]

Recognition of the goodness of creation allows us to maintain a deeper faith and a stronger hope that, ultimately, "things hold together."[57]

---

55. Yoder, *Christian Attitudes*, 361.

56. Yoder, "The Political Meaning of Hope," in *War of the Lamb*, 62 (emphasis original).

57. Yoder, *Christian Attitudes*, 365.

Power perverted: the fall

For Yoder, the fall into sin entails the fall of power. Insofar as humans are granted power as God's representatives to cultivate his creation in a variety of ways, the fall is also the fall of culture. Things fall apart when the first Adam grasps after power that he should not have. In that act, Adam oversteps his limits. He seeks power that belongs to God alone.[58] Before this grasping, the creation was ordered with God as king and humans as his stewards, caring for the garden, the animals, and one another.[59] The act of rebellion disrupts the power flow and thereby also these relationships: the man and woman are now at odds, the humans and the wisest animal (the serpent) are now at odds, and the humans are at odds with the earth that brings forth their food. Most significantly, Adam and Eve reject their calling to be the *imago Dei*, to be God's representatives. In other words, the loving, self-giving power that flows from God to humanity is distorted and diverted by the humans. Rather than passing it on, humanity attempts to grasp it, hold it (as if one could hold the raging flood of God's loving power), and divert it. Fallen humans thus distort true power so that it flows to wrong ends, a flow that both produces and is generated by the Powers.

Power(s) idolized: the fall of the Powers. Although Yoder argues for the primordial goodness of the Powers, they are fallen.[60] Instead of helping hold things together, they divide and conquer humanity (e.g., Rom 8:38; Eph 2:2; Col 2:20; and Gal 4:3). Because of sin, "the structures which were supposed to be our *servants* have become our *masters* and our *guardians*."[61] The Powers, originally meant to be servants of human flourishing, have been invested with ultimate value and meaning that only God should have. Having turned aspects of the good creation into idols, we cannot live *with* them, as they harm and enslave humanity.[62] This fallenness goes deep according to Yoder: "[It] is structural: they

---

58. Yoder, *Preface*, 83–84.

59. Yoder, "Generating Alternative Paradigms," 58.

60. Yoder, *Politics*, 141.

61. Ibid. (emphasis mine).

62. Ibid., 143.

are warped. It is functional: they do not do their duty. It is noetic: we are not able to perceive by looking at things as they are what they really should be."[63] Just as the creational reality of the Powers is more than the sum of their parts, so the fallenness of the Powers is not merely the result of fallen individuals exercising power.

Yoder is clear about the devastation wrought by the fall on power and the Powers. He is equally clear, however, about the enduring reality of their createdness and God's providence. Even in their fallenness, the Powers continue to "exercise an ordering function."[64] Why is this? Simply put, their creational nature is *more* essential, more primordial, than their fallen perversion. Creation is more basic (ontologically) and prior (temporally) to the fall of the Powers.[65]

Acknowledging the accidental (rather than essential) nature of the Powers' fallenness clarifies how the Powers relate to chaos.[66] Yoder asserts that, though fallen, the Powers can have a preserving influence because, like humanity, they cannot escape the reality of their creatureliness—a reality that God uses to preserve creation from absolute chaos.[67] So "our lostness and our survival are inseparable, both dependent upon the Powers."[68] Consequently, humanity's relationship to the Powers cannot be reduced to wholesale affirmation or rejection.[69] Rather, Christians embark on the complicated process of discerning, engaging, and living out the gospel in relationship to the Powers.[70]

---

63. Yoder, "Behold My Servant Shall Prosper," in *Karl Barth*, 163.

64. Yoder, *Politics*, 141.

65. Guenther Haas mistakenly claims that Yoder sees creation and fall dialectically (Haas, "The Effects of the Fall on Creational Social Structures," 115–116). It is true that, after the fall, the Powers are simultaneously good and evil, but most Reformed thinkers claim that as well. At several points, Yoder states that the most basic characteristic of the Powers (ontologically, temporally, or otherwise) is their createdness.

66. See Mouw, *Politics and the Biblical Drama*, 94.

67. Yoder, *Politics*, 143.

68. Ibid.

69. Yoder, "How H. Richard Niebuhr Reasoned," in *Authentic Transformation*, 45, 52.

70. Yoder, *Politics*, 155.

This complexity explains why a New Testament view of the Powers is preferable to a traditional notion of orders of creation.[71] For Yoder, the Powers are dynamic, not static. So, the New Testament doctrine of the Powers describes the present state of the Powers as created, fallen, and still under God's providential control. Often, thinkers have conceived of creation orders in a static way, with certain institutions having a kind of essence that remains untouched by human sin and history and simply needs to be embodied in reality.[72] Yoder suggests that the Powers are more malleable and dynamic, in that they interface with human choice and responsibility, influencing and being influenced by humanity.[73] Adam was both placed in a world not of his own making and commanded to play a role in ordering that world. Even after disobeying God, he did not cease to be human or to exercise an ordering function. Instead, that ordering is now aimed toward the wrong ends. And this same dynamic of order and disorder produces the current state of affairs.

The complex interaction between humanity and the Powers has two implications. First, the solution to the fallenness of power and the Powers is not simply to get a Christian in the right position of power. That is not enough and far too individualistic a view of how cultures and societal structures change.[74] As Cornelius Plantinga puts it (offering a gloss on Hendrik Berkhof), "Mere personal goodness cannot lick them."[75] Something more has to happen: the Powers themselves have to be defeated, placed as penultimate rather than ultimate in God's creation. Second, and conversely, because the Powers are dynamic, human actors do have real power. If we are aware that something could be otherwise, we will not deify (or demonize) any particular institution. We will also be aware of our own responsibility to potentially act otherwise than a Power dictates. So whereas Reinhold Niebuhr talks about a "tragic necessity," or a necessary but unfortunate sin,

---

71. The following summarizes Yoder, *Politics*, 144.

72. See Yoder's comments on the state in *Politics*, 193.

73. Yoder, "Behold My Servant Shall Prosper," in *Karl Barth*, 164.

74. Ibid., 165.

75. Plantinga, *Engaging God's World*, 64.

Yoder would say that humans never *must* do something contrary to humanity's creational nature and the way of Jesus.[76] For Yoder, the real tragedy is seeing sinful behavior as necessary for life in God's world.

The tragedy of the fall manifests itself in a legion of social, cultural, and political ways. Whereas in creation we are called to worship God and serve others, in a fallen state, we esteem some created good above God. Consequently, we offer up other persons as sacrifices to various causes, ideas, and forces—including the Powers. The result, according to Yoder, is that "general labels like 'freedom' or 'justice,' 'socialism' or 'capitalism,' 'order' or 'humanism' become positive or negative values *in their own right*, causes to combat for or to destroy. The modern word for this is 'ideology.' The biblical word that fits best is probably 'idol.'"[77] Yoder contends that causes, concepts, institutions, and practices must be rightly ordered under God. The Powers are meant to be powerful as humans are meant to be powerful: by serving and not lording over humanity. When we exalt any Power as ultimate and independent from God, we commit idolatry. This idolatry will eventually consume both the idolaters and those whom they sacrifice upon the altar of these Powers-turned-gods.

Power diverted: the fall of culture. The fall of human power and the Powers drastically affects culture. Yoder's comments on the origins of culture are often cryptic, but some things can be gleaned from his narration of the early chapters of Genesis. The power and ordering role of humanity in the garden does not go away. It does, however, result in humans developing creation and ordering their lives in a self-serving way, such that we are out of tune not only with God but with our fellow humans and the rest of the biophysical creation. The fall of culture can be seen in Yoder's commentary on the narrative of Adam, Abel, Cain, and Cain's descendants.[78]

---

76. For the phrase "tragic necessity," see Brown, "Introduction," in *The Essential Reinhold Niebuhr*, xviii.

77. Yoder, "The Spirit of God and the Politics of Men," in *For the Nations*, 232 (emphasis added).

78. Yoder addresses this narrative most fully in "Generating Alternative Paradigms," 58–59, and "The Voice of Your Brother's Blood," in *He*

Adam worked in the garden in harmony with the earth and its produce, a model that Yoder sees at work in many Anabaptist and Amish farming communities. Adam's caretaking and order-keeping, however, was without the postfall toil spoken of in Genesis 3:17-19.[79] In this sense, prefall agriculture (and thereby the root of culture) was in tune with the biophysical creation and God's creative intent for human life. Insofar as Cain tills the soil and harvests the crops, his work continues that of Adam. After the fall, however, the relationship of harmony and fruitful abundance has been replaced with a struggle, a scratching open of the earth in order to survive. Thus, both Adam and Cain's postfall cultivating is ambivalent, close to nature but not naturally in tune with it. Nevertheless, Yoder contends that tilling and harvesting are no sin. In fact, the cultivation done by the farmer requires one to be keenly in tune with the earth, the rhythms of the seasons, and the need for crop adjustments.

Yoder contends that Abel, however, was even more in line with God's creation and creative intent for human life. As a shepherd, he is a throwback to the prefall attunement of humanity to the rest of creation. He wisely moves his flock to find vegetation and watering places that the earth provides. This pilgrim culture, Yoder suggests, is closer to God's original intent for human life and harmony with the earth than is Cain's. For Yoder, Abel's nomadic shepherding suggests a wisdom and harmony with what the earth gives forth, whereas Cain's farming wounds the earth in order to wrest sustenance from it. Importantly, Yoder suggests (rather than spells out) that Cain's sin is not his farming but his refusal to recognize Abel's practice was closer to God's original intentions for human life.[80] Rather than respond by seeking greater conformity

---

Came Preaching Peace, 57–68. The following summary is taken from these two texts.

79. Yoder states that "Adam makes the transition from nature to culture." Cf. "On Generating Alternative Paradigms," 59. From the context, it is impossible to tell whether Yoder is speaking of a prelapsarian or postlapsarian transition.

80. On the face of it, the vegetarianism of Cain seems preferable to the flock-herding of Abel. Clearly, the killing of animals (for sacrifices or for food) is a postfall phenomenon. But since God does not grant permission

with God's creational intent, Cain murders his brother, thereby furthering the divide between himself and his brother, the earth, and God.

The virtue of caretaking is all of a piece, so when Cain shows himself to be an unfaithful keeper of his brother, he shows himself to be an unfaithful cultivator of the earth.[81] In being hostile to his brother, he makes the fields hostile to him. The accusation of the soil forces him to flee to the city. From there, Cain's story and lineage go on to provide the basic components of history, including the protective threat of vengeance (the state), the city (civilization), the arts (Jubal's music), technology (Tubal-Cain's metallurgy), and war (Lamech's escalating vengeance). Yoder notes that this is all done in the line of Cain and suggestively states that "urbanization—the creation of cities—with the representative skills of metalworking and music—is seen as the culmination not of human solidarity or of reconciliation but of estrangement. The city is not the product of a town's growing large; it is founded by a fugitive. From this we could develop a whole book about the theology of culture."[82] This civilizing process took place, according to Genesis 4:16, "away from the presence of the LORD." This line of Cain, the unfaithful cultivator, developed culture.

The power God gave to humanity in creation is thus warped when it gets woven into the cultural life of humanity. For Yoder, there is no culture "as such" or institutions "as such" beyond the touch of history. The only culture and cultural institutions humans have ever known, therefore, are fraught with deep ambivalence. Despite such ambivalence, two additional points are worth noting.

First, the story of Cain is not only about sin but about grace as well. In response to Cain's sin, God offers a mark of preserving grace. The ambivalence of Cain and Cain's line is therefore

---

to eat animals until Genesis 9:3, does Yoder think that Abel's shepherding was not for the sake of eating the flocks, but simply caring for the animals and helping them find food wherever they could? That would seem to be the only plausible explanation that would make sense of Yoder's statements in this text.

81. Yoder, "The Voice of Your Brother's Blood," in *He Came Preaching Peace*, 62.

82. Ibid., 59.

just that: ambivalence, not pure, unadulterated evil. Second, the prophetic vision of redeemed life has a clear place for civilization and technology, a culture that hearkens back to prefall attunement with God and nonhuman creation. "To civilize," Yoder notes, is to transfer knowledge and to educate someone. So when Micah 4:2 speaks of the nations learning the ways of the Lord, this is true civilization. True civilization and culture entail not just a technological how-to but a moral knowledge that enables humanity to live as it ought in relation to God, other humans, and all creation. In a fascinating observation, Yoder notes, "The skills of smelting and smithing will be devoted no more to arming but to farming. The sharp edges will still be needed. In fact the edge of an agricultural implement needs to last longer and to cut more often than a weapon. So to make coulters instead of swords, and pruning knives instead of spears, will mean a technological advance, not a slowing down . . . Thus the prophets' vision is not primitivism or 'back to nature.' It calls for the more expert and more productive use of the skills of smelter and smith."[83] The hope for the prophets is neither a disembodied heaven nor a romantic utopia, but the "transformation of human existence within and not beyond its economic, cultural, and political nature."[84] This hope for transformation does not go unfulfilled.

Power unleashed: redemption

In creating humanity, God intended us to use power in accord with God's will to perpetuate shalom among humanity and all creation. After the fall, humanity diverted the flow of power, such that we erect idols and pursue the wrong ends or pursue apparently good ends by using wrong means. For Yoder, redemption neither annihilates the Powers nor eradicates human power. Instead, redemption rehabilitates both true human power and the Powers. Redemption involves walking by faith, believing that there is an ultimate unity of ends and means, of creation and redemption, and of Father, Son, and Spirit. Redemption means that we see Jesus and, in seeing him, we see that all things hold together in him.

---

83. Yoder, "The Hilltop City," in *He Came Preaching Peace*, 99.
84. Ibid., 101.

The power of Jesus. How does the redemptive work of Christ relate to the Powers? Jesus does not let the fallen Powers dictate his life; he lives independently of their idolatrous pull. Although he was *subordinate* to their rule, he did not *submit* to their rule, a fact that led to his victory and established his rule over the Powers.[85] Furthermore, he also resisted the greatest temptation the Powers could offer: the illusion that he could attain a good end by less-than-righteous means. For Jesus, loving God and his neighbor was more important than serving any Power. Because the Powers were originally meant to be servants of humanity's call to love God, other humans, and all creation, Jesus refused to let them gain mastery over him and would not sacrifice his neighbor to any Power, a refusal seen most clearly in his rejection of holy war against Rome.[86] Jesus' scandalous claim is that even the Roman enemy is not to be sacrificed to any Power, because in sacrificing another human being to a Power, one abandons the call to love, in which humanity and all creation are held together.[87] Jesus thus renounces the task of social engineering: "There is no such disincarnate or ideal value worthy to demand the sacrifice of the concrete personal and communal values of our real neighbor. Those abstractions will remain valuable in the measure in which they help us better serve our neighbors. They become sinful when we are asked to sacrifice our neighbors to them."[88] In other words, humanity was not made for the Powers, but the Powers were made for humanity.

Jesus' rejection of the *fallen* "Powers that be" is neither a rejection of the Powers as such nor of creation. Indeed, since the Powers are part of creation, God cannot and will not destroy, set aside, or ignore the Powers.[89] Redemption must be, as Yoder explicitly says, the "redemption of *creation*."[90] This can be seen in

---

85. Yoder, *Politics*, 144–45.

86. Ibid., 141.

87. Ibid., 45–53.

88. Yoder, "The Spirit of God and the Politics of Men," in *For the Nations*, 232.

89. Yoder, *Politics*, 144.

90. Yoder, "But We Do See Jesus," in *Priestly Kingdom*, 61 (emphasis added).

Yoder's discussion of the power exercised by Jesus. As true God and true human, Jesus unfurls the true power given to humanity. So the church marches under the banner of the champion and pioneer of the true humanity, who exercises the power of creation as the true *imago Dei*.

Some might be skeptical about characterizing Yoder this way because sometimes he sounds like he rejects the notion of power and historical agency. That is, he seems to accept Reinhold Niebuhr's faithfulness-effectiveness dichotomy and opt for the faithfulness side. For example, Yoder declares that "Jesus was so faithful to the enemy-love of God that it cost him all his effectiveness,"[91] that Jesus abandoned "any obligation to be effective in making history move down the right track,"[92] and that Jesus, and his disciples following him "accept powerlessness."[93] If taken on their own, such statements could be construed as advocating withdrawal from society, culture, and politics and preferring "pure" obedience to God over active involvement in society and culture. So Yoder could be interpreted as arguing that both Jesus and his disciples renounce all agency and power in history and culture. But this is a misreading of Yoder.

Yoder makes abundantly clear that Jesus, as Messiah, as the true *imago Dei*, and as the true human, does not reject power but reveals how to exercise the right kind of power.[94] Jesus is both unique incarnation and normative human being. As a man, the chief question Jesus faced, according to Yoder, was what kind of king or ruler he would be.[95] The temptation narratives discussed in the previous chapter illustrate this point well. For Yoder, Jesus did not renounce power, but redefined what true power is, in contrast to the temptation to grasp the wrong kind of power. Indeed, Jesus' temptation highlights that Yoder sees Jesus' entire life, death, resurrection, and ascension in terms of the right exercise of power: what kind of ruler will God's chosen one be?

---

91. Yoder, *Politics*, 233.

92. Ibid., 235.

93. Ibid., 237.

94. Cf. Yoder, "Jesus and Power," 453.

95. Yoder, *Politics*, 25.

This question is not just about what it means to be Israel's rightful king; it is about what it means *to be human*. Jesus' kingship was unique, but it was also prototypical of what it means to be human.[96] Adam was given dominion and called to exercise power in the proper way: loving care for the rest of creation and loving reciprocity with the woman, with whom he shares the divine image. Importantly, exercising power is not just the task of a select few.[97] To be human is to exercise power. Adam and Eve were God's representatives to the rest of creation as the *imago Dei*. Adam misused his power, however, by grasping after godlikeness. So when Jesus faces down the tempter, this time in the desert rather than the garden, he is not merely opting for a different way of being Israel's Messiah or king; he is opting for a different way of being human. Jesus, who had every reason to consider himself equal with God, gave up that right in order to exercise true power—the power of loving, self-giving servanthood. The power of God is thus seen most clearly in the cross and resurrection. This speaks volumes about what it means to be the *imago Dei* and what it means to follow Jesus.

This power is not confined to Jesus alone because, as Yoder notes, Jesus is the "firstfruits of authentic restored humanity."[98] Because Jesus is truly and fully human, his humanity affects ours. Thus, "Jesus is Son of God in a sense not completely distinct from our being sons and daughters of God."[99] Yoder is not trying to downplay the uniqueness of Jesus but to honor the language of John 1:12, which states, "Yet to all who did receive him, to those who believed in his name, he gave the right to become children of God;" and Romans 8:29, which states, "For those God foreknew he also predestined to be conformed to the image of his Son, that he might be the firstborn among many brothers and sisters." Because of Jesus' kingship, Christians can participate in his reign as a royal priesthood and priestly kingdom. This kingdom

---

96. The following paragraph draws upon Yoder, *Preface*, 81–84.

97. Cf. Richard Middleton's examination of this point in the historical and cultural context of the *imago Dei* of Genesis 1 (*The Liberating Image*, 93–184).

98. Yoder, *Politics*, 145.

99. Yoder, *Preface*, 71.

does not abdicate power but taps into the source of true power: "Jesus did not free His disciples from violence to make them pure and weak, but because He called them to use other, stronger resources."[100] Consequently, the church does not ask "[whether] to enter or to escape the realm of power, but what kinds of power are in conformity with the victory of the Lamb."[101] Although some may call this type of power "weakness," the point is not linguistic but Christological: "When [Jesus] prefers servanthood to domination, as His path and therefore ours, it is immaterial whether we call that 'powerlessness' or 'omnipotence'; it is God's way."[102]

The power of creation. If Jesus reconnects and restores the original power that humanity was called to exercise in creation, then the politics of Jesus is nothing less than the power of creation unleashed to fulfill God's original intent. It cannot be emphasized enough that this crucial point is repeated by Yoder in a multitude of ways and variety of contexts. Living in line with the Lamb's victory is not alien or in contradiction to creation, but coheres with creation at the most basic level. Because God created the world and continues to be involved in history, creation is from the beginning oriented toward an "open future." This means that our ethical reasoning must factor in God and the possibility of what *could be*, as opposed to simply focusing on what *is*.[103] Our hope in and obedience to God is thus not "groundless optimism,"[104] but trust in God's promise that "an ethic of *torah* or *halakah*, or an ethic of discipleship" is more rooted in the true "nature of things" than is social engineering.[105] Jesus' acceptance of the cross and resurrection was, according to Yoder, *both* an eschatological decision based on where God is taking the world *and* an ontological, creational decision based on "a truer picture of what the world *really* is."[106] Thus, Jesus' call to

---

100. Yoder, "Jesus and Power," 453.

101. Yoder, "Behold My Servant Shall Prosper," in *Karl Barth*, 167.

102. Yoder, "Jesus and Power," 454.

103. Yoder, "Ethics and Eschatology," 125–26.

104. Yoder, "The Spirit of God and the Politics of Men," in *For the Nations*, 230.

105. Yoder, "Ethics and Eschatology," 126.

106. Yoder, "Are You the One Who Is to Come?" in *For the Nations*, 211.

follow his path of cross and resurrection is "ontologically founded, connected to the arc from creation to apocalypse."[107]

This coherence between the politics of Jesus and the power of creation means that nature and grace are not oppositional, but complementary: "The way of discipleship is the way for which we are made; there is no other 'nature' to which grace is a *superadditum*."[108] In other words, "the behavior God calls for is not alien to us; it expresses what we really are made to be."[109] Yoder wants to make sure that we are defining "nature" as *creational* rather than as *fallen*:

> When society has been defined as the nation and social order as patriarchy, then it is no longer true that grace completes nature; in the face of that definition of "nature," the word of YHWH has to be like a fire, like a hammer that breaks rocks into pieces. Yet when the "nature of things" is properly defined, the organic relationship to grace is restored. The cross is not a scandal to those who know the world as God sees it, but only to the pagans, who look for what they call wisdom, or the Judaeans, who look for what they call power. This is what I meant before, when I stated that the choice of Jesus was ontological: it risks an option in favor of the restored vision of how things really are . . . The cross is neither foolish nor weak, but natural.[110]

This view of creation explains why cross-bearers are the ones working with the grain of the universe.[111] This does not mean,

---

107. Yoder, "That Household We Are," 7.

108. Yoder, "The Hermeneutics of Peoplehood," in *Priestly Kingdom*, 36. It should be clear that, contrary to J. Daryl Charles, Yoder does not pit nature and grace against each other ("Protestants and Natural Law," 36).

109. Yoder, "Are You the One Who Is to Come?" in *For the Nations*, 212.

110. Ibid., 212. Cf. Ernst Troeltsch's distinction between two meanings of "natural law." There is an *absolute* natural law, applying to the primitive state as the law of humanity's unfallen nature, and a *relative* or secondary natural law, which applies to humanity's fallen state. This relative natural law is both the result of sin and (limited) remedy to sin (*The Social Teaching of the Christian Churches*, 1:158–64).

111. Yoder, "Armaments and Eschatology," 58.

for Yoder, that suffering is somehow good as an end in itself.[112] Rather, it means that the shalom of creation is regained only by self-giving love, which in a sinful world most generally means suffering, as attested supremely by Jesus but also by mothers and martyrs, farmers and prophets.[113] Thus, to truly be the *imago Dei*, we must follow the path of *imitatio Christi*.[114] Yoder states, "In our access to it [shalom], it looks more like Jesus than like Eden, more like Jesus than like the feudal order that Luther called "creation," or the bourgeois order that Kuyper called "creation," or the racist order that Botha calls "creation"; but that does not mean we need to choose between creation and redemption. It means rather that the disjunction is wrong, as those definitions of creation are wrong, as any definitions of creation based on the way things are [i.e., in the fallen world] must be wrong."[115]

What is revealed, renewed, and restored in the politics of Jesus is therefore nothing less than the politics of creation. We cannot see the pristine creation, and we cannot see the fullness of the eschaton, but we do see Jesus. His resurrection and ascension, which validate his kingship, are the proof that the lust for dominance over others is no power at all, but one of the basest forms of enslavement.[116] The kingdom of the One who comes and tabernacles among us is a kingdom that endures, while kings and empires are ground to dust through their vain attempts to construct kingdoms that go against the grain of the universe.

Power reenlisted: transforming culture. Because God is sovereign and because Jesus is Lord, the Powers can be put to use. "[They] are not merely defeated in their claim to sovereignty, and humbled," according to Yoder, "they are also reenlisted in the original creative purpose of the service of humanity and the praise of

---

112. Yoder notes this in several places, including Yoder, *Politics*, 96, 129, 236, 238.

113. Yoder, "Are You the One Who Is to Come?" in *For the Nations*, 212.

114. I owe this way of phrasing the matter to J. Richard Middleton, "The Liberating Image?" 24.

115. Yoder, "Creation and Gospel," 10.

116. Cf. Yoder, "Behold My Servant Shall Prosper," in *Karl Barth*, 155–56; and Augustine, *City of God*, 19.15.

God."[117] Some Christians point to the work of the Father in creation and are naively optimistic about the Powers; others point to the work of the Son in redemption and are naively pessimistic about the Powers. Yoder's alternative is creational and Christological realism. That is, Christians can engage the Powers, not based solely on a doctrine of creation *apart from* Christ, but from the good news that, because of Jesus, the relationship between humanity, God, and the Powers has changed. This change is as broad in scope as creation: "Because Christ the risen Lord rules not only over the church which is his body, but also over the world which is the terrain of his combat, this approach does yield the wherewithal for talking beyond the confines of the church. Its relevance is not limited to those who believe in Jesus or even to those who hear about Him."[118] The transformed relationship between Christ and the Powers, and thus a transformed relationship between *humanity* and the Powers, results in the possibility of the authentic transformation of culture. God's intentions for his creation can once again be fully pursued. For Yoder, the Powers are reenlisted as the following takes place.

First, the church proclaims Christ's victory over the Powers in word and deed. The gospel is good news, which requires heralds. Christians must report "the meaning of an event rippling out from Golgotha" to those who have not yet heard.[119] This good news assumes that God's will for human life can be known because God has revealed it in Scripture, which provides the standard by which we are able to judge ourselves.[120] This interpretive task is always done with fear and trembling, but also with faith that the Spirit continues to lead the church. If the church denies that God's will can be known, what does it have to offer the world? That denial would compromise both its message about the person and work of Christ and its message about Christian discipleship. Without

---

117. Yoder, "But We Do See Jesus," in *Priestly Kingdom*, 61. It is a misreading of Yoder to say that "Christ does not redeem the Powers," as Guenther Haas does ("The Effects of the Fall on Creational Social Structures," 116).

118. Yoder, "Behold My Servant Shall Prosper," in *Karl Barth*, 164.

119. Ibid.

120. Yoder, "How H. Richard Niebuhr Reasoned," in *Authentic Transformation*, 71, 77.

Scripture as a "bar and a fulcrum not of [our] own making," transformation becomes a muddled term that justifies cultural capitulation rather than being a concrete message with real criteria for the church's life and practice in particular cultures.[121]

The church not only reports a message; its life together *is* a message.[122] The very presence of the church constitutes a witness to the Powers that their sovereignty has been broken. For example, the unity of the Jew and Greek together in one body is a visible proclamation to the Powers that Christ is Lord.[123] The incarnation and the ongoing work of the Spirit provide the basis for the continuing sanctification of the church: "the possibility of obedience is therefore a statement not about our own human capabilities, but about the fullness of the humanity of Jesus and the believers' identity with Him through the Spirit in the church."[124] Empowered by the Spirit, the church learns new ways of being cultural and political, including how power ought to be used, how to deal with conflict, how to use material goods in a proper way, and so on. As it does this, the church's life together constitutes both a new cultural option within the wider society and a body that seeks the peace of the city in which it is found.[125]

As the church proclaims Christ's victory in word and deed, the Powers must be dealt with on a case-by-case basis. Given the creational realities of historical development and cultural diversity, Christians should not expect that their dealing with different facets of culture will be uniform. There is no reason, biblically or theologically, to assume that if we affirm one particular aspect of culture then we must affirm them all:

> There have been those who confound creation and fall, society and the state, the plowshares and the sword, and

---

121. Yoder, "How H. Richard Niebuhr Reasoned," in *Authentic Transformation*, 77.

122. Ibid., 72–73.

123. See Yoder, "Behold My Servant Shall Prosper," in *Karl Barth*, 165; *Body Politics*, 29–30; and *Politics*, 218–23.

124. Yoder, "How H. Richard Niebuhr Reasoned," in *Authentic Transformation*, 73.

125. Ibid., 75; and *Politics*, 154.

conclude that he who refuses to be a soldier should cease to farm as well, since responsibility for culture is all of a piece; that to reject usury is to condemn property, or that to censure nationalism is to emigrate. From such alternatives we are freed; we serve our brethren culturally, rejoicing in the grace of creation, without deifying culture; we serve our adversaries nonresistantly, rejoicing in the grace of the cross.[126]

Yoder contends that God's judgment "redeems ('transforms') the Principalities and Powers by rescinding their claimed autonomy. It transforms them by denying their monolithic unity in favor of discerning discrimination."[127] Following Christ requires constant discernment that can never be jettisoned in favor of a typological answer to all potential scenarios (as in H. Richard Niebuhr's *Christ and Culture*). As a result, "sometimes the power of servanthood will be exercised in the face of the wider society's pressure as an intractable nonconformity, sometimes as an attractive alternative paradigm. Sometimes Caesar will encounter conditional subordination, sometimes conscientious support, sometimes disobedience, sometimes (though seldom) a provisional takeover, sometimes an exodus."[128] The church must discern in the power of the Spirit how it can live in conformity to the Word in each particular time, place, and culture.

Yoder's "asymmetrical," rather than monolithic, approach to the Powers and culture is necessary, *not* because of a disjunction between creation and Christ, but because of the fall. For Yoder, sin damages some areas of culture more than others: "what we take to be typical of some realms of creatureliness may be farther from the original divine purpose than what we take to be definitional for others. It may be that when we define the state as quintessentially the sword, and define the family as a covenant of permanent monogamy, the latter definition is closer to God's original purpose for human

126. Yoder, "The Lordship of Christ and the Power Struggle," 511–12. Cf. "Behold My Servant Shall Prosper," in *Karl Barth*, 167.

127. Yoder, "How H. Richard Niebuhr Reasoned," in *Authentic Transformation*, 76.

128. Yoder, "Behold My Servant Shall Prosper," in *Karl Barth*, 167.

sociality than is the former."[129] Yoder's mention of "God's original purpose" for human sociality is important. The proclamation of God's kingdom is not only a *new* creation, Yoder declares, but a reinstatement of "God's original intent."[130] The reenlisting of the Powers is thus a *new* creation, a *new* age dawning in the midst of the old insofar as this establishes social and cultural relationships "as they were meant to be" in the creative intent of God.[131] This reopens the possibility for humans to use their God-given power in right relation to God, other humans, and all creation. Like the church's looping back to the Bible in order to move forward to the future, this affirmation of God's intent in creation does not seek "to take history 'back to Go' but rather enables authentic progress."[132] Because "Jesus is both the Word (the inner logic of things) and the Lord ('sitting at the right hand')," humanity's calling in redemption to pioneer, renew, and re-form culture stands in continuity with humanity's original creational calling. The politics of creation are most fully revealed in the power of Jesus.

Power regifted: the *Haustafeln*. What does this power look like when fleshed out in concrete social situations? Although Yoder's notion of "revolutionary subordination" is controversial and often seen as reinforcing social conservatism, a careful reading of Yoder helps us see how human power gets refashioned in light of Christ.[133] Thus, the question is not *if* but *how* and *to what end* power is used.

The *Haustafeln,* or "household codes," of the New Testament are generally perceived to be socially and culturally conservative

---

129. Yoder, "Behold My Servant Shall Prosper," in *Karl Barth*, 165. Interestingly, Yoder's distinction between the family and the sword-bearing state bears similarities to both Augustine and Abraham Kuyper. See Augustine, *City of God*, 19.15 and Kuyper, *Lectures on Calvinism*, 91. Budziszewski is thus mistaken when he states that Yoder lumps the institutions of marriage, family, slavery, and the state all together, as though there are no distinctions between them ("Four Shapers of Evangelical Political Thought," 114–15).

130. Yoder, *Preface*, 246.

131. Ibid.

132. Yoder, "The Power Equation, Jesus, and the Politics of King," in *For the Nations*, 140, n.29.

133. Yoder, "Revolutionary Subordination," in *Politics*, 162–92.

with regard to the family and social roles.[134] Admittedly, from very early on in church history, these texts have been interpreted this way. Hence, the New Testament authors are sometimes charged with conservatism, patriarchy, and oppression. Yoder, however, offers an alternative interpretation. In contrast to a revolution that simply offers a mirror image of oppression or a position that justifies oppressive hierarchies, Yoder's revolutionary subordination arguably reconnects with the reciprocal power of creation and opens the way for creative, loving transformation. The *Haustafeln* give direction on how Christlike, creational power should be manifested in concrete relationships.

The first question Yoder addresses is: who exercises power? Significantly, these texts assume that all humans are called to exercise power and historical agency, not just those who are in places of privilege. So the admonitions of the *Haustafeln* are addressed first to those considered "subject" according to the culture of that day: the slave before the master, the children before the parents, the wives before the husbands.[135] In other words, the *Haustafeln* empower the underdog: "Here we have a faith that assigns *personal moral responsibility to those who had no legal or moral status* in their culture, and makes them decision makers."[136] According to Scripture, the status of these persons is *not* in fact defined by an idolatrous Power such as slavery or patriarchy. Those Powers cannot define the Christian. In appealing first to slaves, women, and children, the *Haustafeln* assume and affirm Christ's victory over the Powers. Power does not simply work its way down from Caesar above, but grows up from below.[137] This dynamic, Christlike agency shows that all human beings are viable movers of history and emphasizes that, to those members of society least likely to view themselves as bearers of power or history, God says, "You *are* powerful, you *are* important, you *are* the bearers of the true meaning of history."

---

134. The relevant texts are Eph 5:21–6:9; Col 3:18–4:1; and 1 Pet 2:13–3:7.

135. Yoder, *Politics*, 171.

136. Ibid., 172 (emphasis original).

137. Yoder, "Armaments and Eschatology," 53.

The subordinate persons addressed by the *Haustafeln* become truly free when Jesus enables them to love freely. This reveals to what ends the power of Jesus works. By loving freely those who least deserve it, this power opens the possibility that the oppressive relationship will be broken and transformed, thereby setting creation and history "on the move" again toward its proper *telos*.[138] Far from constituting a message of bondage and oppression, this call to moral agency is a freeing and empowering vision. Revolutionary subordination is not a matter of cultural capitulation to oppressive structures, but a way of following Christ who, being free, freely humbled himself and gave himself for us, in order to demonstrate the way of love.

The *Haustafeln* do not, however, simply call the subject party to be subordinate. Instead, they turn things around, "calling the *dominant* partner in the relationship to a kind of subordination in turn . . . that the call to subordination is *reciprocal* is once again a revolutionary trait."[139] In other words, this ethic of power is mutually empowering. For husbands, fathers, and masters to follow this code of ethics would have been even more revolutionary than for wives, children, and slaves. The power of Jesus, according to Yoder, is not about attaining a status or maintaining a status quo. Just as wives, children, and slaves can recognize the malleable rather than static nature of the Powers, so husbands, fathers, and masters should recognize that there is no reality to which they must conform more basic than the reign of Christ.[140] Although Yoder does not engage the epistle to Philemon extensively, this text provides a prime example of revolutionary subordination.

When Paul writes to Philemon, he could have appealed to his apostleship and his authority in the church to command Philemon to receive his runaway slave Onesimus with love rather than with vengeance. Paul does not do this. Instead, he appeals to something more basic: he, Philemon, and Onesimus are all on the same level, brothers in Christ bound by love and mutual service (Philem 7, 20). Providentially, Onesimus serves Paul on Philemon's behalf, as

---

138. Both 1 Corinthians 7:16 and 1 Peter 3:1 point to the goal of winning over a non-Christian spouse.

139. Yoder, *Politics*, 177 (original emphasis).

140. Ibid., 178.

it were (v. 13), and Paul sends Onesimus back precisely because he affirms that service in the body of Christ springs from the fount of freely given love (v. 14). Must Philemon punish Onesimus? Although that would have been perfectly normal within that context, Paul calls on Philemon to treat Onesimus not simply as a brother, but as he would the apostle himself, as a fellow-worker in the gospel (v. 17).

Paul's points in Philemon fit very well with Yoder's contention that, because the Powers are conquered by Christ and because they are our servants (not vice versa), we are free to do otherwise than our current power configuration might lead us to believe. Paul wants Philemon to recognize that the master-slave relationship does not have an eternal, Platonic essence that must be lived up to by each party. Philemon is free to recognize that his most basic relationship to Onesimus is as his brother in Christ, just as Paul sets aside his apostolic authority in order to relate to Onesimus in the most basic way, as his brother in Christ.

Despite these points, some might still worry that Yoder legitimizes an oppressive status quo. Yoder's ultimate concern must be clarified: perverted power breeds perverted power. Said proverbially, the key to overturning the oppression of the Powers is not to fight fire with fire. Because Yoder worries that the power of resentment defines how we think about liberation from patriarchy or oppression, he is both sympathetic to and cautious about certain forms of feminist and liberation theology.[141] If feminism is merely a call to let women participate in the same domineering practices created by a largely patriarchal society, it is not really revolutionary. For example, Margaret Thatcher can be prime minister, but that may say less about the power of feminism and more about how power politics can inscribe women as well as men into its system.[142] If the role of pastor or priest is conceived in terms of "lording it over," then allowing women to abuse authority in the same way that men do is hardly a sign of true freedom. If liberation theology affirms that oppressed peoples have the same right as superpowers to be violent and bear arms in a just cause, then

---

141. On *ressentiment*, see Nietzsche, *On the Genealogy of Morality*, 19–21.

142. Yoder, *Body Politics*, 60.

it still partakes of the Eurocentric model of missionary colonial-ism that it purportedly rejects.[143] The poet W. B. Yeats expresses Yoder's concern well in his poem "The Great Day": "Hurrah for revolution and more cannon-shot! / A beggar upon horseback lashes a beggar on foot / Hurrah for revolution and cannon come again! / The beggars have changed places but the lash goes on." Yoder's concerns is that what often goes under the name "libera-tion" or "revolution" is not in fact the deep revolution enabled by Jesus, but simply a mirror image of the oppression that it pur-ports to be overturning. So, echoing Augustine, Yoder asks which is worse: oppression, or the oppressed having their desires shaped in conformity with their oppressors?[144]

For Yoder, the latter is more to be feared, so he calls for a change that gets beyond seeing both the oppressed and oppressor as defined by the *oppressive* flow of power. Instead, revolutionary subordination taps into the power of creation and the politics of Jesus to reopen the floodgates of charity, which enables us to see a whole new world, a world turned topsy-turvy by the way we are set free to bear witness to Christ's rule. This revolutionary witness is radical in the way it takes the mundane shape of leaven slowly taking over the flour bin.[145] Although perverted power breeds per-verted power, the *Haustafeln* calls Christians to receive the gift of true power and then pass it on so that Christian relationships might be mutually empowering rather than selfishly oppressive.

This naturally raises the question: how does this doctrine of creation and emphasis on power affect Yoder's view of the state? Does Jesus rule over the state as well? If so, how? Does Yoder speak so negatively of the state that he sets aside at least one part of God's creation as inherently unredeemable? Despite Yoder's affirmation of creation, does this amount to an evil that goes so

---

143. Yoder, *Politics*, 200.

144. Cf. Augustine, *City of God*, 19.15: "It is a happier lot to be the slave of a man than of a lust: indeed, the lust for mastery, to say nothing of any other, is itself the harshest kind of mastery, which lays waste the hearts of mortal men." See also 15.7.

145. Yoder cites this image from Matt 13:33 in "Discerning the Kingdom of God in the World," in *For the Nations*, 244.

deep it overtakes the goodness of creation and withstands the power of redemption? Yoder's view of the state must be examined in light of his view of the Powers.

6

"From the Beginning It Was Not So": The Sword-Bearing State

When Yoder denies that the state is rooted in creation, this leads some to declare that he has a deficient doctrine of creation, which in turn reveals problematic views of redemption and the Trinity.[1] If the state is evil but is part of the orders of creation, then Yoder's doctrine of creation seemingly conflates creation and fall. If the state is creational but is not redeemed, then Yoder appears to concede some realm of creation to sin and the fall, thus limiting the scope of Christ's redemptive activity. In either case, the apparent disjunction between creation and redemption causes problems. Upon closer examination, Yoder shows from Scripture that the sword-bearing state is not rooted in God's original creational intent but in God's postfall preservation of the world.[2]

---

1. Budziszewski, "Four Shapers of Evangelical Political Thought," in *Evangelicals in the Public Square*, 116, 120; Haas, "The Effects of the Fall on Creational Social Structures," 108–29; Wright, *Disavowing Constantine*, 163–66.

2. Two of Yoder's short books deal directly with the question of the state. Cf. *The Christian Witness to the State*; and *Discipleship as Political Responsibility*, (originally published as *Nachfolge Christi also Gestalt politischer Verantwortung*, [Basel: Agape Verlag, 1964]). Yoder recognizes that the modern nation-state is a contingent way that political power can be configured. Because the state is common in our day, however, Yoder sometimes uses this term as a gloss for political power per se (even when it would technically be an anachronism).

God's providential allowance for the sword must not be confused with God's creative and redemptive will, nor should it be confused with the disproportionate, Lamech-like violence of war.

The biblical basis for Yoder's view

For Yoder, any Christian view of the origins of the sword and state must be compatible with Scripture. Yoder finds several texts instructive when discussing the origins of the sword and state, including the narrative of Abel, Cain, and Lamech; God's words to Noah in Genesis 9; and Romans 13.[3]

Abel, Cain, and Lamech. In the beginning, there was harmony between brother and brother, shepherd and farmer. This harmony was torn asunder when Cain killed his brother Abel, for reasons not explicated in the biblical text. This is not only a particular but a paradigmatic story for human history: brother against brother. Notably, the first homicide victim is not the strange and foreign other but the similar and familiar.[4] For Yoder, both Cain's response and God's response to this murder help us better understand retaliation and the sword.

Upon hearing God's declaration of the consequences of his sin—estrangement from the ground and a life of wandering—Cain expresses fear: "Whoever finds me will kill me" (Gen 4:14). Humans outside the immediate family of Adam first appear in the biblical text not as a source of community or procreation but as a threat.[5] Cain knows that the instinctive reaction of humans to a wrong done is to react in kind. Yoder notes that God does not need to instruct humans that retaliation is called for; sinful humans reflexively retaliate in order to exact revenge for wrongs done.[6] Thus, the first word said about human society at large is

---

3. What follows draws upon four of Yoder's essays, "The Voice of Your Brother's Blood," in *He Came Preaching Peace*; "Against the Death Penalty," in *The End of Sacrifice*, 77–152; "On Generating Alternative Paradigms," in *Human Values and the Environment*, 56–62; and "A Theological Critique of Violence," in *The War of the Lamb*, 27–41.

4. Yoder, "Generating Alternative Paradigms," 58.

5. Yoder, "Theological Critique of Violence," in *War of the Lamb*, 28.

6. Yoder, "Against the Death Penalty," in *The End of Sacrifice*, 92.

that of mimetic (or imitational) violence, a gut reaction to the offense of Cain. For Yoder, this reaction precedes any theorizing about why it might be valid: "It will seem self-evident to them that that is what he has asked for by what he did."[7] Any moral, legal, political, or cultic explanation arrives only after the sheer facticity of the vengeance exacted against the offender.[8] The violence of Cain against Abel is mirrored in the violence of other humans against Cain, a violence that is reactive and that leaves no place for Cain's redemption. Crucially, this retaliatory dynamic is the basic impulse inscribed in the sword-bearing state. The text of Scripture is clear that it originates not in God's prescriptive will but in fallen humanity.[9]

God's response is quite different from that of sinful humans, for God brings Cain's sin to light and also displays his own grace. The first time in the biblical narrative we are confronted with the terrible and irreversible act of murder, God's response is forgiveness and preservation of the murderer, a response that sets the tone for the rest of Scripture.[10] God affirms the sacredness of human life not by demanding the life of the murderer (as fallen humans do) but by preserving it. Guilt is superseded by a grace that enables life to go on, a pattern established already in God's response to Adam and Eve.[11] Sin and death are the enemies of God's creatures. God's response to sin is not swift retribution but a patient willingness to continue working with his creatures. Moreover, in marking Cain, God shows grace to the wider society ready to kill Cain, inasmuch as he turns the vengeful reflex of society against itself by the threat of sevenfold vengeance. As a result of human sin, society now occupies a middle space as it embodies neither God's creational

---

7. Yoder, "Theological Critique of Violence," in *War of the Lamb*, 28.

8. Ibid., 29. Cf. "Against the Death Penalty," 156–61.

9. One could draw an analogy to Davidic kingship and the temple in Israel's history. Neither were God's ideas, but God accommodated himself to fallen humans. Notably, both Davidic kingship and the temple get dropped as Israel's history continues and their meaning radically revamped by Jesus: the true king is the suffering servant and he (and his people) is the place where God dwells.

10. Yoder, "Against the Death Penalty," in *The End of Sacrifice*, 93.

11. Yoder, "Generating Alternative Paradigms," 59.

intentions for harmonious humanity nor absolute chaos.[12] Society holds together as much by mutual fear as mutual trust.

In the text of Genesis 4, the retaliatory reflex quickly escalates into disproportionate vengeance, as seen in Lamech's boast: "I have killed a man for wounding me, a young man for injuring me. If Cain is avenged seven times, then Lamech seventy-seven times" (Gen 4:23-24). The retaliatory reflex does not stay purely symmetrical but, given human sinfulness, goes well beyond the original violation. Since the retaliatory reflex was not based on rational calculation to begin with, it easily transforms into machismo, bloodlust, and destruction for its own sake. Rather than operating within the symmetry of "eye for an eye," Lamech's boast makes revenge an absolute value. Sinful humans perpetuate and escalate the cycle of violence by seeking "justice" according to self-centered rationality, which, in the end, only incites further escalating responses as recompense for the previous injustice.[13]

Noah. The problem of Lamech's boast stands in the background of God's words to Noah about the shedding of human blood. The context of Genesis 9, Yoder notes, is that of ritual sacrifice.[14] Until the flood, God had not given permission for humans to eat animals. After the flood, God allows this, with the stipulation that humans should not eat the blood of the animals. The life is in the blood and therefore represents the sacredness of animal life to God. Consequently, a secular slaughter of animals does not exist. Every life of an animal taken is in some respects a ritual sacrifice. This sacrificial worldview is the context for what God says about the taking of human life in Genesis 9:5-6, which states, "For your lifeblood I will surely demand an accounting. I will demand an accounting from every animal. And from each human being, too, I will demand an accounting for the life of another human being. Whoever sheds human blood, by humans shall their blood be shed; for in the image of God has God made mankind."

---

12. Yoder, "Voice of Your Brother's Blood," in *He Came Preaching Peace*, 60.

13. Yoder, "Against the Death Penalty," in *The End of Sacrifice*, 94.

14. Ibid., 95–98.

Yoder makes several observations about this text. He points out that God is not here introducing a new demand that killers be put to death, for that has been humanity's default impulse toward killers since the time of Cain (and remember that the direct cause of the flood was humanity's violence, as Genesis 6:13 notes). Instead, God harnesses the retaliatory reflex of fallen humans by placing it within the context of this sacrificial worldview.[15] If the blood of animals is precious to God, how much more is the blood of humans who were made in God's image.

Given the sacrificial worldview of this text, Yoder rejects three possible interpretations of this text. First, God is not making a moral demand that, for every pain inflicted, there must be an equal pain inflicted that balances the scales of justice. Second, this text is not an educational demand to teach the offender (or other observers) that crime does not pay. Third, God is not prescribing a political order. Instead, we should understand Genesis 9 as a fundamentally ritual, religious, and cultic text. Killing another human does not just offend civil society but destroys one who is the image of God; killing is the murder of God in effigy. Because of this, Yoder argues that killing can only be properly described in specifically religious and cultic terms: "The killing of a killer is not a civil, nonreligious matter. It is a sacrificial act. The blood—i.e., the life—of every man and beast belongs to God. To respect this divine ownership means, in the case of animals, that the blood of a sacrificed victim is not to be consumed. For humans, it means that there shall be no killing. If there is killing, the offense is a cosmic, ritual, religious evil, demanding ceremonial compensation."[16] In describing the taking of a killer's life as ritual sacrifice, Yoder moves beyond both the vengeful violence of Lamech and the purely political/civil description of this act as "capital punishment." It may seem counterintuitive to claim that human sacrifice actually affirms the sacredness of life. Yoder points out, however, that this restrains the human tendency to take disproportionate revenge and demonstrates the utter seriousness that accompanies any taking of human life, even that of a killer.

---

15. Ibid., 96–97.

16. Ibid., 101.

So, as with Cain, God shows grace by restraining the tendency to move from retaliation to revenge. Humans are already, from the beginning, responding to killers with the *lex talionis*: "life for life." God does not need to step in and instruct humans to do this. Rather, he limits the reach of this vengeance by affirming the sacredness of human life and allowing human sacrifice only on the grounds that one has taken the life of another. This puts the brakes on the trajectory established by Lamech, in which human life is discarded with ease and disdain. Even if one were to concede that this text institutes some kind of sword-bearing civil government, Yoder notes that we are no longer in Genesis 1–2 but in Genesis 9. Hence, we are no longer under the rubric of creation but of fall. God's providential grace continues to restrain human sin, but that is neither God's original creational intent nor God's ultimate redemption will. Rather, God's preservation keeps things from falling apart until the coming of the One in whom all things hold together.

Romans 13. Although Yoder addresses Romans 13 in *Politics of Jesus*, he notes that the Bible's teaching about the state does not stand or fall with this one text.[17] Yoder does not develop a theory of the state based on seven verses (Rom 13:1-7), but rather challenges the claim that "by virtue of the divine institution of government as a part of God's *good creation*, its mandate to wield the sword and the Christian's duty to obey the state combine to place upon the Christian a moral obligation to support and participate in the state's legal killing (death penalty, war), despite contrary duties which otherwise would seem to follow from Jesus' teaching and example."[18] Importantly, Yoder focuses on separating the sword (not society or order) from creation.

In discussing the origin of the state, Yoder makes the following claim: "The subordination that is called for recognizes whatever power exists, accepts whatever structure of sovereignty happens to prevail. The text does not affirm, as the tradition has it, a divine act

---

17. Yoder, *Politics*, 194. His chapter "Let Every Soul Be Subject: Romans 13 and the Authority of the State," deals most fully with this text (193–209). Cf. Yoder, *Christian Witness*, 74–83.

18. Yoder, *Politics*, 194 (emphasis added).

of institution or ordination of a particular government."[19] Yoder outlines and rejects two traditional interpretations. First, the positivistic view, a more Lutheran view, holds that whatever government exists expresses the revealed will of God. Yoder points out that the text does not support this kind of blanket sanction upon any and all governments. Second, the normative view, popular in the Calvinist tradition, holds that this text simply presents the concept of proper government and norms for proper governments. Yoder, however, contends that the text provides no concept of the "proper state" by which we could both accredit and disqualify particular states.[20]

Yoder's rejection of these two positions does not lead to anarchy, as some might suppose, for the text of Romans 13 teaches that God is sovereign: "God is not said to *create* or *institute* or *ordain* the powers that be, but only to *order* them, to put them in order, sovereignly to tell them where they belong, what is their place."[21] Yoder contrasts the concept of God ordering the sword-bearing state with the idea of God ordaining it.[22] By "ordain," Yoder means the idea that God creates or institutes either the sword-bearing state as such or a particular state. God gave humanity power in the beginning, and we see certain Powers established already in the garden, including the family and caretaking of the earth. God did not, however, set up the sword-bearing state as a creational institution. Instead, God harnesses a perverted power that fallen humans are already exercising (vengeance) and orders or restrains this retaliatory reflex to preserve rather than destroy life. This explains why one does not find "moral support or religious approval of the state" in Romans 13, but instead a call "for subordination to whatever powers that be."[23] Consequently, Christians should neither deify the state nor overthrow it in the name of a more perfect union that more closely approximates the ideal state.[24]

19. Ibid., 198–99.

20. Ibid., 200–1.

21. Ibid., 201.

22. Ibid., 199.

23. Ibid., 201.

24. Although Yoder does not specifically refer to the American Revolution, I use the phrase "a more perfect union" as an example of justifying a revolution in the name of an ideal.

Preserving power: the place of the sword-bearing state

Cain's mark: preservation. Taken together, Yoder's exegesis and his view of human power and the Powers provide crucial keys to his view of the sword-bearing state. Yoder's view of the sword-bearing state operates from a basic principle of continuity and coherence between creation and redemption. So Yoder states the following about God's kingdom:

> One of the original axioms in this new arrangement [the kingdom] is that it parallels God's original intent. This is most striking in Matthew 19 when the Pharisees are discussing whether divorce is permissible. Jesus conceded that there seems to be room made for divorce in Deuteronomy, but he says that was a concession—a concession made for the sake of the hardness of human hearts. "But from the beginning it was not so." In other words, *"from the beginning"* is the original standard Jesus has now come to restore. One of the things Jesus says about his kingdom, one of the axioms of the new order or relations among people that his kingship establishes, is that things will be as they were meant to be. Things will fulfill the creative intent of God.[25]

Yoder's words on divorce are equally applicable to the sword-bearing state. God makes concessions to work with fallen humanity, but those concessions represent a temporary forbearance rather than a creational or redemptive norm for human life.

We must be clear that Yoder explicitly states that human society, organization, and order are rooted in creation: "An unfallen earthly society would certainly need a civil order to make decisions and to apportion tasks and resources. But it would not need a sword."[26] Because the original creation was good (though not yet perfected), the sword had no proper place. So Yoder states, "What we do deny is that the order of creation can explain to us why and how the *sword*, i.e., the calculated measuring out of evil,

---

25. Yoder, *Preface to Theology*, 246.

26. Yoder, "Reformed versus Anabaptist Social Strategies," 5. See also *Christian Witness*, 34.

can be necessary."[27] Yoder's position on this score is not unique in the Christian tradition being held by Augustine, Bonaventure, Abraham Kuyper, and the Reformed Belgic Confession, among others. Yoder's thought certainly allows other thinkers to entertain the hypothesis that there could be a kind of swordless social order as God's normative intention in creation, operating out of cooperative shalom rather than competitive strife. The problem arises when thinkers see the sword as the essence of social order and politics rather than a postfall phenomenon.[28] When Christians see the sword as *essential* to social order, Yoder contends, creation and fall have been fused.[29]

On this point, Yoder is clear that not all aspects of the Powers can be deemed creational. As both the Powers and human power develop throughout history, institutions and practices bear the marks of sin. Yoder therefore argues for discernment with respect to different Powers. Two examples that elucidate this point are the family and the state: "What we take to be typical of some realms of creatureliness may be farther from the divine purpose than what we take to be definitional for others. It may be that when we define the state as quintessentially the sword, and define the family as a covenant of permanent monogamy, the latter definition is closer to God's original purpose for human sociality than the former."[30] Because the sword (even the sword that limits and restrains evil) ultimately stems from the retaliatory reflex of fallen humanity, we should not construe it as originating in God's good creation. Instead, the sword has a very particular, postfall function: to *preserve*.

If we are to make sense of the sword, Yoder argues that we need categories such as preservation and providence in addition to creation, fall, and redemption. Even in its fallen state, God's world is a cosmos, not chaos.[31] When God places his protection on Cain

---

27. Yoder, *Christian Witness*, 34. Cf. *Discipleship as Political Responsibility*, 19.

28. Yoder, *Christian Witness*, 82.

29. Yoder, "Reformed versus Anabaptist Social Strategies," 5.

30. Yoder, "Behold My Servant Shall Prosper," in *Karl Barth*, 165.

31. Yoder, "The Power Equation, Jesus, and the Politics of King," in *For the Nations*, 138.

and promises vengeance on Cain's potential killers, he desires to *preserve* Cain.[32] The focus is not on taking human life, but preserving it. The mandate of the state is similar: it ought to have a preserving effect on society. This mandate, however, is tangled up in sin, insofar as it uses "evil means [i.e., the sword] to keep evil from getting out of hand."[33] Even if it preserves, the retaliatory reflex is a response and reaction to sin, so that *sin* rather than creative and redemptive grace determines the way the sword operates. The sword also cannot bring about redemption or the fullness of God's kingdom. The preserving effect of the sword is thus *relatively* necessary: it is neither necessary nor able to bring about the peace of the kingdom of God, but it is relatively necessary among fallen people to maintain temporal peace. The sword-bearing state is thus not an end in itself but an instrument that God uses to preserve the postfall social order for the ultimate purposes of redemption.

Because of this preserving work, Yoder can affirm that the state is an "order of grace."[34] This does not mean that the state can be equated with the church or that it is part of redemption, but simply that God's grace works to restrain the effects of sin on all humanity, and one way that he does this is through political power.[35] God's grace operates even in a political situation with a quite tyrannical ruler. For example, the years immediately following Saddam Hussein's 2003 defeat demonstrated that the chaos produced by a vacuum of power may in fact be worse than the rule of a dictatorial state. Importantly, Yoder's affirmation of God's preservation and providence does not condone either the general appeal to the sword or particular states. Rather, we should praise our providential God, who works through what humans mean for evil and turns it for good.

Furthermore, God's preservation manifests itself in what Yoder calls an "order of providence," in which Christ rules over the Powers,

---

32. Yoder, *Discipleship as Political Responsibility*, 18.

33. Ibid.

34. Yoder, *Christian Witness*, 12.

35. At this point, Yoder sounds very similar to the Kuyperian doctrine of common grace. Cf. Abraham Kuyper, *Lectures on Calvinism* (Grand Rapids: Eerdmans, 1931), 83.

including the state, in contrast to the "orders of redemption," in which Christ rules in and through obedient disciples.[36] According to Yoder, the idea of God's sovereignty or providence can be used rightly or wrongly. A faulty notion of providence concludes that, because God is sovereign over every sphere, the Christian can validly participate in every sphere, institution, or practice.[37] But God's sovereignty, Yoder notes, is not a stamp of approval. For example, God can use Assyria as an instrument to judge Israel, but this does not exempt God from immediately judging Assyria for its own wickedness, expressed precisely in what they were doing to Israel. God thus providentially uses Assyria while simultaneously pronouncing woes upon them (Isa 10).[38] Likewise, although God can providentially use the evil of Joseph's brothers (Gen 50:20), providence cannot be claimed as justification for selling a sibling into slavery. Yoder employs this same logic when he affirms both that God is sovereign over the sword-bearing state and that Christians ought to confess faith in God's sovereignty rather than actively wield the sword.[39] In other words, when Christ cries, "Mine!" over certain institutions, practices, and Powers, that cry may be a "no trespassing" sign to the Christian rather than a welcome mat.[40] Some things are usable by God and not by his people precisely because God is God and we are not.[41]

Because the sword is not rooted in creation, it will not persist into the eschaton. Because redemption is the redemption of creation, sinful manifestations of human power and the Powers

---

36. Yoder, *Christian Witness*, 12.

37. Yoder, *Discipleship as Christian Responsibility*, 62. Cf. "The Power Equation," in *For the Nations*, 138.

38. Yoder, *Christian Witness*, 11. See also *Politics*, 198, 202.

39. With respect to sovereignty, Yoder might be accused of "out-Calvinisting" the Calvinists. Cf. Mouw and Yoder, "Evangelical Ethics and the Anabaptist-Reformed Dialogue," 131. On sovereignty, see also Yoder, *Preface*, 246.

40. I refer here to Abraham Kuyper's well-known statement that "There is not a square inch in the whole domain of our existence over which Christ, who is Sovereign over all, does not cry 'Mine!'" (Kuyper, "Sphere Sovereignty," in *Abraham Kuyper: A Centennial Reader*, 488.)

41. Yoder, *Politics*, 198.

will not persist into the fullness of the kingdom. Importantly, for Yoder, the time of the sword-bearing state is limited not because the sword is too powerful, but because it is too weak. This is why Paul states that "the weapons of our warfare are not carnal, but mighty" (2 Cor 10:4 KJV).[42] The opposite of sinful power is not weakness, but true power. The sword serves a purpose within a fallen world, but it is weak because it is always *reactive*, a response to some prior violation. The only way beyond the sword, to a new beginning and new creation, is through Christ's cross and resurrection. As such, the good news of this gospel is "not about delegitimizing violence so much as about overcoming it."[43] The cross and resurrection are more powerful than the sword because they do not allow sin and injustice the final word. Instead, they offer hope that reconciliation and new creation is possible to both offender and offended. In the cross and resurrection, the Word that brought creation into being *ex nihilo* speaks again into the void of human sin, evil, and violence, creating the possibility of a life rooted not in reaction but in creation.

Because the sword-bearing state is neither rooted in creation nor part of redemption, Yoder denies the need to define the ideal sword-bearing state "as such."[44] For Yoder, just as wider society responded to Cain not based on theory but on mimetic reflex, so the sword-bearing state does not exist first and foremost *because of* theoretical justification (although that can be given after the fact), but because of the force behind it.[45] Yoder concludes that no sword-bearing state is ever really "proper" in the sense that it is creationally rooted.[46]

Interestingly, Yoder and Reinhold Niebuhr converge here. Niebuhr describes well how politics works in a sinful world. He and Yoder would agree that *if* justice is defined as primarily retributive justice and the attempt to balance conflicting, selfish interests,

---

42. Yoder, "The Lordship of Christ and the Power Struggle," in *The Lordship of Christ*, 1963).

43. Yoder, "Theological Critique of Violence," in *War of the Lamb*, 41.

44. Yoder, *Christian Witness*, 77.

45. Ibid., 12.

46. Ibid., 32.

then all that can ever be done is a kind of approximation to the ideal which can never be reached. Whereas Niebuhr accepts this as the nature of things, Yoder sees this as the *fallen* nature of things. In the midst of this organized chaos, Yoder argues that we do not need more theories about the ideal state, but we do need increased attention to the practices of our particular state so the state can be called to use its power in accordance with the politics of Jesus and the power of creation, one concrete practice at a time.[47] This is not a call to an impossible possibility, but to real, viable options. For Yoder, an ideal sword-bearing state does not exist, only servant power or the lust for domination.

Lamech's boast: war. Although the sword-bearing state is not rooted in creation, Yoder sees a marked difference between the sword that limits itself to the function of Cain's mark and the sword that degenerates into Lamech's boast. For him, neither the internally-focused police function of the state nor the externally-focused war-waging of the state can be creational.[48] Though the *lex talionis* has been superseded for the Christian, the internal police function better represents God's harnessing of the retaliatory reflex, whereas war does not. War is Lamech's boast writ large.

In *Politics of Jesus,* Yoder argues that the function of police and acts of war must be distinguished: this "is not simply a matter of degree to which the appeal to force goes, the number of persons killed or killing. It is a structural and profound difference in the sociological meaning of the appeal to force."[49] Police force is different from war in the following ways:[50]

> 1. The violence or threat thereof is applied only to the offending party.

---

47. Nicholas Wolterstorff makes a similar point: "We must ask what *this* institution in *this* institutional array ought to be doing . . . We do not owe it to God to realize the inner nature of the State; rather, we owe it to God that our own institutional array, including our state, serves humanity." Cf. *Until Justice and Peace Embrace*, 63.

48. On the issue of Yoder and police force, see Alexis-Baker, "Unbinding Yoder from Just Policing," in *Power and Practices*,147–66.

49. Yoder, *Politics*, 204.

50. The following is quoted verbatim from Yoder, *Politics*, 204.

2. The use of violence by the agent of the police is subject to review by higher authorities.
3. The police officer applies power within the limits of a state whose legislation even the criminal knows to be applicable to him.
4. There are serious safeguards to keep the violence of the police from being applied in a wholesale way against the innocent.
5. The police power generally is great enough to overwhelm that of the individual offender so that any resistance on the offender's part is pointless.

In its limited and retributive nature, police force thus bears similarities to the retaliatory reflex that Cain feared. Given humanity's fallenness, however, that reflex quickly jumps to war without bounds.

When Lamech takes what God meant as a preservative and uses it as an authorization to destroy life on the basis of an insult, we have the paradigm of the sword-bearing state gone awry. For Yoder, the fall of humanity means that this will be the rule, not the exception, for the sword-bearing state. So Yoder contends, "There is no ground in the biblical doctrine of the fall to argue that the hand that bears the sword or the order that defends itself by the sword is any less fallen than the offender against whom the sword is used."[51] Hence, the problem throughout human history is not too little application of the sword, but too much: "What is destroying nature and destroying the possibility of social peace is not anarchy, but government gone beyond bounds. What is killing us is not savagery, but civilization . . . When we fight a war to end war, or to make the world safe for democracy . . . it is obvious that what is explained as a corrective or defensive measure has become itself the problem."[52]

A prime example of Lamech's boast, for Yoder, is nuclear deterrence. The accumulation and threat of nuclear weapons is inconsistent with just war theory, Yoder argues, and therefore partakes of the wildly disproportionate bloodlust of Lamech. In conversation with just war theorists, Yoder notes both similarities

---

51. Yoder, "Reformed versus Anabaptist Social Strategies," 5.

52. Yoder, "Voice of Your Brother's Blood," in *He Came Preaching Peace*, 60, 62.

and dissimilarities with previous notions of deterrence.[53] Although some element of threat has always existed in the posturing of different nations toward one another, the nuclear threat differs because its actual execution would clearly violate central standards of just war theory, including discrimination, proportionality, and noncombatant immunity.[54] Therefore, the possession of a nuclear arsenal must be for purposes either of bluff or revenge. Yoder's central point is that, in both cases, nuclear weapons reveal that Lamech's boast has not gone away but has only intensified. So Yoder points out the contradictions inherent in nuclear deterrence.

Yoder first notes the peculiar moral stance of the supposed bluff in which a nation develops and institutionalizes nuclear weapons and the processes and procedures for their deployment. By their very nature, these weapons are immoral because they destroy without discriminating civilians from soldiers. Further, no just war theorist has explained how these objectively immoral goals can fit with a subjective intention for good. In other words, a person or state cannot do an evil deed for the sake of good.[55] Furthermore, the readiness to carry out the threat after it has failed to deter another state does not fit in the just war framework either, for several reasons:[56]

1. Carrying out the threat after it has failed to deter can no longer be justified as deterring. Now it must be thought of as retaliation. Yet this can no longer be justified by any of the reasons whereby just-war thinking in the past has made the case for reprisal.

2. It can be revenge; yet revenge is not morally justified in any framework except that of a theocratic holy war, and then on the grounds of special revelation. It has no place in modern Western just-war thinking, and no consequentially justifiable social effect.

---

53. Yoder, "Bluff or Revenge," in *Ethics in the Nuclear Age*, 79–92.

54. Yoder, "Bluff or Revenge," 80. Yoder elsewhere outlines the criteria of the just war tradition. Cf. Yoder, *When War Is Unjust*, 147–61.

55. Yoder, "Bluff or Revenge," 83.

56. The following is quoted verbatim from Yoder, "Bluff or Revenge," 80–81.

3. Going through with the counterattack can be intended to prove that the bluff was no bluff, but that proof no longer has the function which was supposed to justify it in the first place. The additional destruction is henceforth gratuitous.

4. It cannot be justified on any consequential grounds that begin by taking stock of the shape of the universe after undergoing the massive first attack which the threat failed to deter. The counterattack will not bring the victim of the massive first strike closer to anything that could be called "winning." It will bring the world, including one's own civilization, closer to destruction either through permanent nuclear winter or through radiation diseases, even where the bombs themselves did not destroy.

For Yoder, when we carefully apply the tools of just war theory to the logic of nuclear deterrence, we see that the forces at play are not rational, but tend toward the machismo, bloodlust, and revenge of Lamech.[57] In this way, war continues to bear the mark of the boast. Although the potential consequences of nuclear deployment are new in human history, what it reveals about war is not: in the hands of sinful humanity, the sword destroys what it is supposed to preserve, namely, life and peace.

The Christian witness to the state

Because of his view of the sword-bearing state, critics sometimes think that Yoder does not allow for (1) Christians speaking to non-Christians and Christians who do not hold Yoder's view of the sword-bearing state, and (2) Christians contributing to the common good. However, a close examination of Yoder reveals otherwise. In outlining Yoder's view, we see that no one can give a final word on this topic, precisely because the shape of actually existing states is always shifting: "There can be no one timeless right way to relate church and state—or for that matter church and university, church and banking, church and the arts—for that other member of the comparison—the state, the economy—has no

---

57. Yoder, "A Theological Critique of Violence," in *War of the Lamb*, 30.

one firm meaning . . . So let us set aside definitions in the abstract, essences, and the idea of the state as such, and look at particular communities, regimes, and rulers, in light of the concrete content of the kingdom."[58] Yoder is not concerned with finding an abstract way to relate to the state (e.g., against, above, or transforming culture) but with articulating the criteria called for by God's kingdom and seeing how Christians might bring that to bear on their particular situations, with all the historical and cultural embeddedness that implies.

Speaking to Caesar: rules of engagement. What is the basis for Christians speaking to non-Christians in positions of governmental authority? Yoder argues that political rulers are as free as anyone else to go with, rather than against, the grain of the universe. Yoder notes that some Christians, including some Anabaptists and Reinhold Niebuhr, have held that what it means to be a Caesar or political leader of any kind is both implanted in the nature of things and goes against the gospel.[59] Yoder rejects this notion. There is no "nature" that is contradictory to Jesus; there is only the cosmos created by the Word. Furthermore, theologians should not invoke the notion of two kingdoms or two norms: "What holds down the performance and the standards that apply in the world is the weight of sin, not a divinely revealed lower order for secular society."[60] The sovereignty of Christ over every sphere means that no sphere can command one to do something contradictory to Christ. So, rather than say that Caesar cannot follow Christ, Yoder questions the underlying logic.

What makes Caesar act contrary to Christ is not "nature" or his office, but his sin and the fallenness of the Powers, which have been disarmed by Christ. Constantine can become a Christian. That does not baptize and sanction the office of emperor but should radically reconfigure how the man Constantine exercises power. Thus, for Yoder, Caesar is as free as anyone else to take the risk of faith: "We will not give in to the view that human autonomy is given up when a person becomes part of the state machinery. We will address government officials just as we do

58. Yoder, "The Spirit of God and the Politics of Men," in *For the Nations*, 234.

59. Yoder, "Constantinian Sources of Western Social Ethics," in *Priestly Kingdom*, 146.

60. Yoder, *Christian Witness*, 72.

other citizens, not treating them as mere cogs in a machine, but rather as persons who are free to oppose the machine's gears when a responsible decision requires them to do so."[61] If Christians do address rulers, what language do they use to do so? How can the confessionally-based language of Christians communicate with a world and with rulers who often do not confess Christ as Lord?

Communication is possible because the Christian, as missionary, always seeks the "interworld transformational grammar" that can make sense to the audience.[62] In his early work, Yoder referred to this language as "middle axioms": "These concepts will translate into meaningful and concrete terms the general relevance of the lordship of Christ for a given social ethical issue. They mediate between the general principles of christological ethics and the concrete problems of political application. They claim no metaphysical status, but serve usefully as rules of thumb to make meaningful the impact of Christian social thought."[63] Yoder later disavows any special attachment to the term "middle axioms" and clarifies that "what matters is to face the challenge of stating good news in pertinent form," which means that "the moral call must be local, occasional, rendered comprehensible and credible by the presence of God's people within the problem setting to which they speak."[64] Given the examples he uses from his day, Yoder might suggest in our post-9/11 world that this could be something as straightforward as asking American intelligence officers to treat prisoners of war according to the principles of the Geneva Convention or not to torture suspects.[65] The call issued to these individuals is based on the ultimate norm of God's love in Christ, but is perfectly comprehensible because it is aimed at the hearer's specific situation.[66]

---

61. Yoder, *Discipleship as Political Responsibility*, 45. Cf. "Constantinian Sources of Western Social Ethics," in *Priestly Kingdom*, 146.

62. Yoder, "'But We Do See Jesus,'" in *Priestly Kingdom*, 56.

63. Yoder, *Christian Witness*, 32–33.

64. Yoder, "Creation and Gospel," 9.

65. Yoder, *Christian Witness*, 25.

66. Yoder lists *liberty, equality, fraternity, education, democracy,* and *human rights* as terms that are particularly important in the Western world (*Christian Witness*, 73).

Admittedly, this call to take a leap of faith might look like personal or professional suicide to the political leader.[67] Yoder argues that following Christ in concrete ways might get political leaders in trouble, but he astutely observes that politics is generally risky business: "It might happen that the result would be that his [Caesar's] enemies would triumph over him, but that often happens to rulers anyway. It might happen that he would have to suffer, or not stay in office all his life, but that too often happens to rulers anyway, and it is something that Christians are supposed to be ready for. It might happen that he would be killed: but most Caesars are killed anyway. It might happen that some of his followers would have to suffer. But emperors and kings are accustomed to asking people to suffer for them."[68] If political leaders were to take the gospel seriously, Yoder argues, we would not be surprised to see them doing justice, loving their enemies, seeking creative social alternatives, and solving the particular problems of their constituents.[69] No inherent impossibility prevents these things from taking place in particular times and places.

Precisely because the Christian and the church are *not* committed ahead of time to one particular theoretical view of the state "as such," they can more readily and easily speak to all actually existing states.[70] Yoder does not demand some kind of theoretical common ground regarding political theory from which to begin, such as agreement on constitutional republicanism. Instead, he argues that the missionary church goes to the ground of the receptor culture, learns the political language of that time and place, and uses that language in conversation with political rulers and representatives to address problems on a case-by-case basis, one step at a time.[71] This position refuses to either deify or demonize any existing state

---

67. Yoder, *Christian Witness*, 73.

68. Yoder, "Constantinian Sources of Western Social Ethics," in *Priestly Kingdom*, 146.

69. Ibid.

70. Yoder, "The Christian Case for Democracy," in *Priestly Kingdom*, 158.

71. Yoder spells this out fully in "Christian Case for Democracy," in *Priestly Kingdom*, 151–71.

188 / Things Hold Together

or political configuration, but instead focuses on the ways in which specific problems, some large and some small, can be addressed. Simply speaking to those within political structures, however, is only one component of the church's relationship to the powers that be.

The common good: conscientious participation. Throughout his works, Yoder persistently denies Reinhold Niebuhr's presumption that to be a faithful Christian entails a refusal to contribute to the common good. Moreover, in the last decade of his life, Yoder seems to have worried that Stanley Hauerwas risked reinforcing Niebuhr's faithfulness-effectiveness dichotomy. Yoder's concern is manifested most clearly in Yoder's titling a book *For the Nations*, a clear and direct rejoinder to Hauerwas's *Against the Nations: Essays Public and Evangelical*.[72] For Yoder, the church's worship of the one true God enables it to recognize the reality of the common good. When used uncritically, the term *common good* too often refers to the particular good of a particular people, and the good is conceived as a finite quantity for which humans must compete.[73] By contrast, the church, as a particular people, seeks the peace of the entire city in which it finds itself.[74] Hence, for Yoder, faithfulness to the gospel and effective contribution to the common good are not opposites, but two sides of the same coin.

Thus, when addressing the question of whether and how Christians can participate in present governmental and societal structures, Yoder refuses the legalistic question: "Is this or that action forbidden for the Christian?"[75] Instead, the real question is this: Where is the greatest opportunity for me to serve? In what vocations and positions will I have the greatest freedom for such service?[76] Yoder

---

72. The essays were not new essays, but Yoder's intentional compilation of these essays together and naming of this collection is significant.

73. On this mistaken notion, see Augustine, *City of God*, 15.5.

74. Yoder frequently references Jeremiah's injunction to the Babylonian exiles to "seek the peace . . . of the city" (Jer 29:7). For Yoder's succinct summary of this theme, cf. "See How They Go with Their Face to the Sun," in *For the Nations*, 51–78.

75. Yoder, *Discipleship as Political Responsibility*, 45. Cf. *Christian Witness*, 56.

76. Ibid.

states this point very clearly in conversation with his Notre Dame colleague Thomas Shaffer: "It is epistemologically backward to put the question thus: 'The state is defined as xxx [*sic*]; can a Christian have to do with it?' Proper epistemology would say: 'The Kingdom of God is like . . . ; what does that tell me to share with my neighbor, who has not joined me in following Jesus, but whose human dignity I am pledged to affirm, in our common life?' Often there will be things to do that are of higher priority for the disciple to do than running the jails; but if so the reason for that is the stewardship of creativity, not a legalism which writes off certain territories."[77]

In other words, the shape of the Christian's obedience is not simply adherence to "Thou shalt nots." Instead, freedom in Christ enables us to fully and truly serve other humans and the wider society. Christians should be reticent to seek power in civil government, according to Yoder, not because they want to stay untainted from the world but because they can more productively serve the common good by pioneering culture in ways that do not depend on the approval or structure of the present powers that be.[78] Thus, to prevent the audacity of hope morphing into Niebuhrian "realism," Yoder would counsel the hopeful kingdom citizen that the structures of the sword-bearing state are often least effective in producing the real and lasting change we need. The Christian should know that more possibilities for human life and power exist than the governing authorities can see. The alleged "realism" that closes down these possibilities ought to remind us that "realism is not reality but an ism. Realism is the opiate of the elites."[79]

Although Yoder rules out the Christian wielding the sword on Christological grounds, he points out that the modern state has many more functions than bearing the sword: it builds roads, leads schools, provides medical services, cares for the elderly,

---

77. Yoder, in Shaffer, *Moral Memoranda*, 108.

78. Cf. Yoder, "How H. Richard Niebuhr Reasoned," in *Authentic Transformation*, 69. See also Yoder's illustration in *Discipleship as Political Responsibility*, 45.

79. Yoder, "Creation and Gospel," 9.

delivers the mail, has forestry departments, and makes laws.[80] Because these general functions are qualitatively different from wielding the sword, Yoder sees nothing inherently problematic in them. Christians should, however, continually engage and discern their approach to these functions, since they may easily get pulled into the vortex of a sword-bearing state that escalates from Cain's mark to Lamech's boast.[81]

The state always risks becoming a master rather than a servant of the common good. Because this possibility always exists, Christians need to exercise constant discernment. The need for discernment never stops because the flow of power never ceases, and we cannot say ahead of time where it is going to go. Rather than calling for consistency to a typological relationship between Christ and culture or the church and state, Yoder calls for something else: "The consistency which counts is the concrete community process of discernment, as that community converses, in the light of the confession 'Christ is Lord,' about particular hard choices."[82] God calls Christians to inhabit institutions and vocations in a way that bends the power given therein to flow with "the arc from creation to apocalypse," created in and through Christ.[83] Whereas the fall threatens to undo the very fabric of creation, redemption entails being incorporated into Christ, the thread that weaves and holds all things together.

We must ask: is Yoder primarily negative, outlining what he rejects, namely, the sword-bearing state? He connects Christ and creation, but does this merely underscore the necessity of nonviolence and suffering love, which are good ideas but quite abstract? Does Yoder give us clear and concrete ideas about the shape of

---

80. For this list, see Yoder, *Discipleship as Political Responsibility*, 19, 40; and *Christian Witness*, 56. Yoder also clarifies that even for the early Anabaptists, renouncing the sword did not mean withdrawal from public life. Cf. "The Forms of a Possible Obedience," in *The Jewish-Christian Schism Revisited*, 128.

81. For example, Yoder notes that the school system can get turned into a "propaganda machine" rather than truly serving the people it is meant to serve. Cf. *Discipleship as Political Responsibility*, 41.

82. Yoder, "How H. Richard Niebuhr Reasoned," 74.

83. Yoder, "That Household We Are," 7.

redeemed and renewed culture? Moreover, if he provides a trinitarian theology of culture, where does the Holy Spirit fit in? If the Spirit empowers us to follow Jesus, what exactly does this following entail? We have seen his emphasis on the power of creation and the politics of Jesus but not how those emphases come to fruition in his pneumatology. Thus, Yoder's doctrine of the Spirit must be explored to fully grasp his trinitarian theology of culture.

7

The Spirit Pioneering Culture

B ecause Yoder criticizes the sword-bearing state and Christians' willingness to participate in wielding the sword, critics often charge him with being "against culture" or pitting nature against grace.[1] When Yoder rejects the sword, however, he intends to disavow fallen culture, not culture as God intends it. In fact, Yoder makes explicit that he is not against but *for* the nations.[2] To that end, he spent the last decade of his life more intentionally connecting his account of the social processes of the Christian community with his view of the sacraments and the Holy Spirit. Furthermore, he showed how the Spirit and the sacraments relate directly to a theology of culture. Indeed, the subtitle of his essay "Sacrament as Social Process" is "Christ the Transformer of Culture," showing that the sacraments are a key facet of his alternative to H. Richard Niebuhr's account of how Christ transforms culture.[3]

---

1. For example, see Charles, "Protestants and Natural Law," 33–38; and Haas, "The Effects of the Fall," 108–29.

2. This was the title of Yoder's last book of collected essays before he died. The title is, of course, a rejoinder to Hauerwas's *Against the Nations: War and Survival in a Liberal Society*. (Notre Dame: University of Notre Dame Press, 1992). Although some presume that Hauerwas and Yoder are synonymous on all important issues, Yoder's own attempt to differentiate and distance himself from both the content and tone of Hauerwas's work is important.

3. Yoder, "Sacrament as Social Process," in *The Royal Priesthood*, 359–73. Yoder expands this article into *Body Politics: Five Practices of*

For Yoder, culture is transformed through the pioneering work of God's Spirit and the in-breaking of God's kingdom. This is centered in the life of the church but also flows into the surrounding world as well. In redemption, grace restores nature. The work of the Spirit has to do with renewing all aspects of life, including culture. Redemption does not add a new supernatural or religious realm to the life of humanity, but reorients us to God so that we may carry out the mundane tasks of life and culture in conformity with God's desires for human flourishing. Thus understood, redemption is not escapist or dualistic. Grace also perfects nature, in the sense that the Spirit orients culture toward its proper end: the fullness of God's kingdom. As the "already" of God's kingdom commences in the here and now, that kingdom is centered in the church's life together. This life together is not sectarian or private but public, carried on in the midst of and for the sake of the nations, who can see and be transformed through the practices pioneered by the church in the power of the Spirit. When the power of creation and the politics of Jesus are unleashed by the person of the Spirit, the public practices of the church cannot help but overflow and exert a transformative effect, not only in the church but in all human culture. There is thus a twofold meaning to transformation: in the church the culture of God's kingdom takes root empowered by the Spirit, and in the world transformation of culture leads to a sort of humanization that flows from but is not identical with the redemption of culture that takes place in the church.

The church as sacrament of the kingdom

A recent document growing out of Reformed-Roman Catholic dialogue summarizes the idea of church as a sacrament of the kingdom: "The kingdom of God is a symbol of a universal community ordered according to the will of God so that fullness of life and right relationships abound for all. In Christian theology, the

---

the Christian Community before the Watching World. He also addresses the sacraments in "Firstfruits: The Paradigmatic Public Role of God's People," and "The New Humanity as Pulpit and Paradigm," in *For the Nations.* He focuses on one of the practices in "Binding and Loosing," in *The Royal Priesthood.*

church is a sacrament of the kingdom in so far as it represents the inauguration of such fullness and such right relations in the community of believers gathered together in faith, hope and love."[4] Likewise, for Yoder, the church now embodies and points to the fullness of God's ultimate intentions for creation. As practices that are simultaneously religious and cultural, the sacraments both participate in and point to the eschatological fullness of the kingdom. So although Yoder does not use the exact language of "church as sacrament of the kingdom," close examination reveals that this is precisely his line of thought. Moreover, Yoder's position helpfully clarifies how the church, kingdom, and sacraments directly inform a theology of culture.[5] To properly understand Yoder's view of the redemption of culture, we must examine three related facets of his thought: eschatology, pneumatology, and ecclesiology. These topics are generally interconnected in systematic theology because they are closely interconnected in the Bible and the third article of the Apostles' Creed. Similarly, these topics are interwoven in Yoder as well.

Eschatology. Yoder's eschatology begins by affirming that the kingdom has already begun in the person and work of Jesus.[6] He draws on Oscar Cullman's well-known analogy of D-Day and V-Day, contending that the New Testament both proclaims Christ's lordship but also recognizes that evil forces resist God's kingdom coming.[7] D-Day was the decisive battle of World War II, yet the war continued. Between the decisive battle and the final surrender

---

4. International Roman Catholic-Reformed Dialogue, "The Church as Community of Common Witness to the Kingdom of God."

5. It also holds ecumenical promise. On his notion of the sacraments as a way beyond traditional Protestant and Roman Catholic divisions, see Yoder, "Sacrament as Social Process," in *Royal Priesthood*, 372. The idea of the church as a sacrament of the kingdom has been promoted by, among others, the International Roman Catholic-Reformed Dialogue, "The Church as Community of Common Witness to the Kingdom of God."

6. The following is a summary of Yoder, *The Christian Witness to the State*, 8–10. Cf. also Carter, *The Politics of the Cross*, 145–50.

7. See Cullman, *Christ and Time*, 84. Yoder references Cullman's D-Day and V-Day analogy in "Peace Without Eschatology," in *Royal Priesthood*, 150.

on V-Day, the Axis powers were defeated if not finally so and the Allies were realizing a victory whose final culmination was still to come. Yoder, drawing on Cullman, likens this time to the present age of the church. At the culmination of all things, the Son will hand all things over to the Father, and God will be all in all. Even if this is not fully realized in the present, the life, death, resurrection, and ascension of Jesus enables us to proclaim that God's new reign has broken into the midst of the old age, with all that it entails for human culture.

The central proclamation of the church is that Jesus is Lord. Drawing on Psalm 110, Yoder focuses on Jesus' life, death, resurrection, ascension, and his pouring out of the Spirit as the turning point in human history. In the present, two overlapping ages coexist alongside each other, the old and the new. For Yoder, the essential difference between the old and new *aeons* is directional: the kingdom of God orients the new age whereas the refusal of Christ's lordship guides the old age. By virtue of Christ's work and the advent of the Spirit, the presence of the future kingdom is already here. When Spirit-empowered people do God's will, we are not only in tune with God, but the well-being of all humans is promoted. Yoder notes that this kingdom has its roots not in human potential but divine grace: "The seal of the possibility of His will's being done is the presence of the Holy Spirit, given to the church as a foretaste of the eventual consummation of God's kingdom."[8] The church serves as the beachhead where God, by his Spirit, has established his kingdom.

Pneumatology. In his essay "The Spirit of God and the Politics of Men," Yoder charts the connection between the Spirit and the kingdom.[9] He first points beyond a dualism that locates the Spirit in a sacred realm and politics in a secular one. For Yoder, politics

---

8. Yoder, *Christian Witness*, 9.

9. Yoder, "The Spirit of God and the Politics of Men," in *For the Nations*, 221–36. The following section is a summary of that essay. This essay was first presented in 1979 and Yoder notes, "Out of respect for the historical datedness of the text, the generic language of the assigned and published title has not been changed, but the term 'men' is sometimes put in quotes to signal that I recognize that datedness." Yoder, "Spirit of God and Politics of Men," in *For the Nations*, 221, n. 1.

involves "anything to do with how people live together in organized ways."[10] Yoder deconstructs the binary opposition of Spirit and politics or Spirit and culture by pointing out that in Scripture the real duality is between faithfulness and rebellion, true and false politics, true and false spirits. Drawing on the Servant Songs of Isaiah, he notes that the Spirit's empowerment of God's servant has to do with bringing justice to the nations (Isa 42:1) and being a light to the nations in doing so (Isa 49:6). When God calls his servant to a life of trust and obedience, those are eminently political virtues as well as alternatives to Israel's trust in horses, chariots, and military alliances.

This same Spirit empowers Jesus when he takes up Isaiah 61 as his platform for ministry. This message, Yoder notes, is inherently social, political, and cultural. The oppressed are set free, the hungry receive food, the mighty are humbled, and God's shalom is proclaimed on earth. What Jesus and his followers refer to as the kingdom, Yoder notes, is "the shape of the working of the Spirit of God in the politics of men and women."[11] The Spirit thus empowers followers of Jesus to live in the new order of the kingdom as they serve and patiently wait for God to bring justice to the nations.

Although Yoder does not draw upon the promise of the Spirit in the Old Testament, this only further underscores his point that the Spirit directly relates to questions of culture and politics. In Ezekiel 11:19-20, the prophet declares, "I will give them an undivided heart, and put a new spirit within them; I will remove from them their heart of stone and give them a heart of flesh. Then they will follow my decrees and be careful to keep my laws. They will be my people and I will be their God." God's decrees here are not merely cultic but also cultural. Unlike those who would disregard or downplay the importance of Old Testament law, Yoder notes that Jesus' agenda is as broad as Torah,[12] and that we can extend this agenda by honoring the Spirit's work—not to abolish

---

10. Yoder, "Spirit of God and Politics of Men," in *For the Nations*, 223.

11. Ibid., 228.

12. Yoder, "Jesus: A Model of Radical Political Action," in *The War of the Lamb*, 78.

the central commands of Torah—but to write them on the hearts of God's people (Jer 31:33) in such a way that Torah no longer divides but unites Jew and Gentile. Just as Torah directly connects to the cultural life of Israel, so the Spirit enables Christians to live a life of cultural discipleship, following the One in whom the Torah was fulfilled.

Because the Spirit is the source of cultural transformation, Yoder soundly rejects any notion that the coming of the kingdom ultimately depends on us:

> As a servant people we are relaxed. The weight of the world has been lifted from our shoulders; we are not the managers of society—nor would we be if we thought we were. We don't have to save democracy and the free world; we don't even have to save ourselves . . . Should we be ineffective, our cause is not lost; should our efforts bear fruit, this will not be their justification. Our living in the present reality of the kingdom and the triumphant coming of the kingdom are not connected like the links in a causal chain, but like promise and fulfillment, as the artesian well to the distant mountain lake. We serve not in order that the kingdom might come, but because it is coming; the certainty of victory is the beginning not the end of our course.[13]

God's empowering presence, made manifest in the Spirit, enables humans to live the way God intended—an empowerment that pertains to all realms of life.

When we see the Spirit and the kingdom in this light, the political-nonpolitical dualism collapses. We see further that redemption inherently entails questions of culture, politics, economics, and so on. The pressing need, according to Yoder, is to choose between different ways of being political and cultural, some that stand in line with the kingdom and others that do not:

1. Vengeance or forgiveness?
2. Domination or servanthood?
3. Rigidity or concession?
4. Misinformation or truth?

---

13. Yoder, "The Lordship of Christ and the Power Struggle," in *The Lordship of Christ*, 511.

5. Determination or hope?
6. Manipulation or dialogue?
7. Hierarchy or equality?
8. Ideology or objectivity?[14]

Yoder contends that these issues are inherent in human sociality. So the real question is therefore not *whether* the people of God will address such matters, but which ones have priority and what methods should be used to accomplish God's purposes. Empowered by God's Spirit, the Christian community will have a singular contribution to make: to make God's reign seen and known.[15]

Ecclesiology. Yoder's eschatology emphasizes the "already/not yet" nature of the kingdom, and his pneumatology connects the Spirit to the kingdom, with all that entails for the redemption of culture. Because of this, he sees the church as a firstfruits, foretaste, testing ground, and model of the Spirit's sociopolitical work of redemption.[16] We must underscore that, for Yoder, the life of the church is inherently cultural. The modern world often thinks of "religion" and "culture" or "religion" and "politics" as separate realms pertaining to church and world or church and state. As I have argued elsewhere, Yoder resists this and instead sees the social existence of the church as cultural and political.[17] For him, politics is always already doxology, and ethics is always already theology and liturgy. Rather than divorce these things, as modernity is prone to do, Yoder highlights that they all hold together. What we worship as ultimate will always shape and form the mundane questions of how we live with other human beings. For him, "God's politics" is not first God's agenda for what American

---

14. The following list is from Yoder, "Kingdom of God and Politics of Men," in *For the Nations*, 234. For more elaboration of these points, see 228–33.

15. See Yoder, "Kingdom of God and Politics of Men," in *For the Nations*, 235.

16. These images are taken from Yoder, "Firstfruits," and "Kingdom of God and Politics of Men," both in *For the Nations*.

17. See my "Spinning the Liturgical Turn," in *Radical Ecumenicity*, 173–92; and *The Forest and the Trees: Engaging Paul Martens'* The Heterodox Yoder.

government should do but what the church should do, regardless of what nation they find themselves in. So when we talk about how Christ redeems culture, we must remember that this has first to do with the very life of the church itself. For Yoder, there are not two sets of norms or two kingdoms, religious and secular, but two communities, one which recognizes the true *telos* of human life and lives toward it and another which does not. As such, the church's life is both paradigmatic and public. Yoder explains this by both criticizing and building on the thought of Karl Barth.

Yoder finds Barth's "Christian Community and Civil Community" unsatisfactory in large part because Barth conceives the two communities as having a distinct essence, one public and accessible, the other private and esoteric.[18] As a result, Barth tries to bridge the gap between the two by making comparisons and analogies between the two communities, most of which do not bear up under close scrutiny. In Barth's *Church Dogmatics* IV/2, however, Yoder contends that Barth overcomes this problematic dualism and therefore depicts the gospel order as paradigmatic. Yoder approvingly quotes Barth, stating, "Church law is exemplary law. For all its particularity, it is a pattern for the formation and administration of human law generally, and therefore the law of other political, economic, cultural and other human societies."[19] Yoder then glosses Barth's point, saying, "The calling of the people of God is thus no different from the calling of all humanity. The difference between the human community as a whole ("*Bürgergemeinde*") and the faith community ("*Christengemeinde*") is a matter of awareness or knowledge or commitment or celebration, but not of ultimate destiny. What believers are called to is not different from what all humanity is called to. That Jesus Christ is Lord is a statement not about my inner piety or my intellect or ideas but about the cosmos."[20] More concisely, there are not two kingdoms, two different sets of norms for human life, but one.[21]

---

18. See Barth, "Christian Community and Civil Community," in *Community, State, and Church*, esp. 171–89.

19. Barth, *Church Dogmatics* IV/2, 719.

20. Yoder, "Firstfruits," in *For the Nations*, 24.

21. Cf. Yoder, "The Two Kingdoms," *Christus Victor* 106 (Sept. 1959): 3–7.

This can be seen by looking at Israel in the Old Testament.[22] When God sets Israel apart, he calls them to live an exemplary life, a life not confined to the cultic aspect. As a priestly kingdom (Exod 19:6), every aspect of Israel's life was meant to exemplify God's ways in God's world. Although Yoder does not draw on specific examples, many are readily available. Whether in tilling the fields, making provision for the poor, lending without usury, honoring a neighbor's marriage, or trading with just weights, Israel is called to do God's will. In this sense, all life is religion. The liturgy or service offered by God's priestly people takes place not only in the tabernacle, but in the fields, the marketplace, and the home. Although Yoder is speaking of the church, he could just as well speak of Old Testament Israel when he says that "the faith community and the human community are connatural; each is human, historical, social . . . The order of the faith community constitutes a public offer to the entire society."[23] God's offer to the world in and through his people is not to join a mystery cult but to properly orient us to God so that our whole life may be lived more abundantly. As Paul puts it, "whether you eat or drink or what-ever you do, do it all for the glory of God" (1 Cor 10:31). So how is the church a sacrament of the kingdom, a pioneering people? According to Yoder, "It tells the world what is the world's own calling and destiny, not by announcing either a utopia or a realis-tic goal to be imposed on the whole society, but by pioneering a paradigmatic demonstration of both the power and the practices that define the shape of restored humanity. The confessing people of God is the new world on the way."[24]

The sacraments as pioneering power and practices

Yoder's metaphor of the church as a pioneer people is particularly apt because it conveys the missionary posture of the church as fun-damentally *for*, not against, the nations. That is, God intends to

---

22. Yoder discusses this point in "A Light to the Nations," 15. My comments about Israel go beyond Yoder in that essay but they make the same point.

23. Yoder, "Firstfruits," in *For the Nations*, 27.

24. Yoder, "Sacrament as Social Process," in *Royal Priesthood*, 373.

bring the world further along the cultural trail blazed by his people, for pioneers may be the first to arrive at a place, but they are not the last.[25] Indeed, Spirit-empowered pioneers go forth precisely with the task and intent of forging the proper way ahead for the sake of those who follow in their train, as they themselves follow in the victory train of the pioneer and perfector of their faith. The sacraments, as social processes, are not simply the means to an end, but the end (or fullness of the kingdom) that is made present already in these means. When Christians participate in these processes, they show the way to the ultimate transformation of culture and they celebrate the way that the end, Jesus Christ, has already transformed culture in the present.

The observable nature of the sacraments. Yoder's use of the term *sacrament* is atypical. Most Mennonites do not use this terminology, referring instead to baptism and the Lord's Supper as *signs*, *ordinances*, or *symbols*. The term *sacrament* is often looked at suspiciously because it is thought to carry a quasi-magical meaning that is based on extraneous medieval metaphysics or problematic post-New Testament developments.[26] Yoder, however, finds this term useful, in part because the term *sacrament* points to a transcendent source of meaning and power (God) and also to the way the church presently participates in the fullness of the glory to come. This term thus enables both low and high church traditions to see these practices with fresh eyes.

Yoder lists five pioneering practices of the church: binding and loosing, the Lord's Supper, baptism, the universality of giftedness, and the open meeting.[27] Although only baptism and the Lord's Supper are generally labeled as ordinances or sacraments, Yoder highlights nine characteristics that these practices share in common:[28]

---

25. Cf. Yoder, "How H. Richard Niebuhr Reasoned," in *Authentic Transformation*, 69.

26. See Yoder, "The Mandate to Share," in *Revolutionary Christianity*, 26.

27. One need not agree with labeling all five of these practices as sacraments to see the value in Yoder's creative work here.

28. The following list is summarized from Yoder, "Sacrament as Social Process," in *Royal Priesthood*, 369–72. One need not agree to

1. These practices are wholly human, not esoteric, but also an act of God "in, with, and under the human practice."
2. These practices are social, such that the language of sociology (not philosophy or semantics) is most appropriate.
3. These practices can be paradigmatic for other social groups.
4. These practices are not "religious" or "ritual" activities, but "public" phenomena.
5. These practices are "enabled and illuminated by Jesus of Nazareth, who is confessed as Messiah and Lord."
6. These practices focus on the believing community as the primary agent of change, rather than isolated individuals.
7. These practices were new in and of themselves in the first century, but each was taken up by Jesus and the early church, such that their meaning and source of power was new.
8. These practices do not depend on one specific meta-ethical discourse (e.g., deontological, consequentialist, or virtue ethics).
9. These practices transcend traditional dichotomies, including "Protestant/Catholic," "radical/liberal," and "revelation/reason."

For our purposes, Yoder's first and fourth entries are most relevant. With respect to the first, Yoder clearly underscores that the Spirit is the empowering source behind these practices. This is especially important, because it reminds Christians of both their source of strength and their uniqueness with respect to the world. We can do what we do not because of some generic optimism about human

---

every detail of Yoder's view of the sacraments to see its usefulness for others within the Christian tradition. Indeed, Yoder's own pioneering project has been followed by others making similar points from within the Roman Catholic, Anglican, Methodist, Presbyterian, Reformed, Mennonite, and Pentecostal traditions. For example, see the essays in Hauerwas and Wells, *The Blackwell Companion to Ethics*, and Smith, *Desiring the Kingdom*.

nature but because of the power of the Spirit. With respect to the fourth, Yoder risks being misunderstood. His rhetorical point is that the sacraments are not unintelligible rituals in a mystery cult. He thinks that a "sacramentalistic" approach separates the liturgy of the church from everyday life so that we cannot see, for example, what celebrating the Lord's Supper might have to do with economic provision for a brother or sister in Christ.[29] A properly sacramental approach recognizes the multiple levels of meaning in the church practices, and therefore can chart how, in the book of Acts, table fellowship led directly to economic sharing and how, in 1 Corinthians 11, the shared meal of the Lord's Supper failed to properly embody the breakdown of socioeconomic stratification. The sacraments should be seen as mundane mysteries: the Spirit works in and through these sacraments to enable the church to be a pioneer people, charting a new way of being cultural. These practices are not "religious" *over against* "cultural," but religious inasmuch as they are cultural processes directed toward their proper *telos*.[30]

This explains why Yoder repeatedly refers to the sacraments as "social," "public," or "secular." In labeling the sacraments in this way, he does not mean that they are *merely* social processes devoid of any special activity of the Spirit.[31] Instead, he is attempting to underscore that these are activities of the church that can be seen and observed by the watching world, just as Israel's life was meant to be a light to the nations. As a social scientist ought to be able to observe and describe the difference between Israel and the social-political life of Egypt, Assyria, or Babylon, so Yoder thinks a social scientist ought to be able to observe and describe differences between how the church and the wider world deal with issues such as decision making, power, money, and forgiveness. Although the world may not use the church's language to account for the church's life together, the world can see a difference in the church's life together.[32]

---

29. Yoder, "The Mandate to Share," in *Revolutionary Christianity*, 26.

30. This point is developed further in Smith, *Desiring the Kingdom*.

31. Against those who might presume that Yoder's sacramentology is reductionistic, see my response, "Spinning the Liturgical Turn."

32. If this were not so, it would falsify numerous biblical texts about the visible difference between God's people and the watching world and the world's awareness of that difference.

The creational foundation of the sacraments. Yoder's discussion of the sacraments raises a conundrum, particularly in how he sees the relationship between the church and the world. Paul Martens's recent book *The Heterodox Yoder* captures this conundrum well. Martens's line of thought proceeds as follows. We know that Yoder repeatedly emphasizes things like the particularity of the church, that Christian ethics is for Christians (not for the nonbelieving world), and that the church is the unique people of God. If, however, in Yoder's later years, he asserts that the sacraments—as social processes of the church—are paradigms that the world can imitate, what does this say about the uniqueness of the church, even the uniqueness of Jesus?[33] If the world can basically follow suit by doing what the church does, then it appears that Yoder elides the difference between church and world, a move that Martens is right to see as highly problematic, if that is in fact what Yoder is doing.

Yoder's Christ-centered doctrine of creation must be brought to the fore here. If we do not recognize this facet of Yoder's thought and how it intersects with his view of the sacraments, we will end up precisely with Martens's conundrum. But once it has been established that Jesus is the one by whom all things were created and in whom all things hold together, it naturally follows that what happens in the church will have what Yoder calls "reflections" and "spin-offs" in the world.[34] In other words, if sin is a parasite on our created nature, and if we were created to go with the grain of a universe whose *logos* is Jesus, then we should expect that what works in the Spirit-empowered church may still work, albeit to a lesser extent, outside the church. Imagine two non-Christian marriages. Is it any wonder that a non-Christian marriage in which the partners have some sense of servanthood would be relatively healthier than a marriage in which neither partner has any sense of servanthood? Is it any wonder that a non-Christian who forgives would be able to maintain healthier relationships than a vengeful person? Yoder is simply saying that if you see something relatively good happening outside the church, it is ultimately explainable by

33. Martens, *The Heterodox Yoder*, 2, 140.
34. Yoder, *Body Politics*, 58.

reference to Jesus. If you do not account for Yoder's doctrine of creation and how Jesus relates to it, then I can see why Martens might think Yoder is abandoning Christian particularity. Once we understand Yoder's doctrine of creation, as argued in chapter 5, we can see how Jesus enables his Spirit-filled people to pioneer practices that strike a chord even with non-Christians. Why do these practices strike a chord? Not at the expense of Christian particularity, as Martens contends, but because sin and the fall distort but do not eradicate human nature, which finds its apex in Jesus, the *logos* who became flesh.

A doctrine of creation is necessary to avoid two equally bad mistakes. One is an emphasis on social justice that *does* in fact elide the church/world difference in its optimism (and perhaps neo-Constantinianism) about the possibility of making the entire society operate by Christian norms. Yoder speaks strongly against collapsing the church/world distinction. In fact, far from sacrificing the particularity of Jesus or the church, Yoder continues to emphasize the slogan, "Let the church be the church." Do you care about the world's shalom as well as that of the church? If so, Yoder tells you (in 1996, a year before he died) that your first step should not be the neo-Constantinianism of Jim Wallis or James Dobson, but a focus on the life of the church:

> "Seek first the righteousness of the kingdom, and the rest will be thrown in," is a recipe not for poverty but for plenty. It may be similar when we ask how the value-laden sub-community goes about caring about justice in the wider society. It may be the case not only by happenstance but by a deep inner logic, if God is God, that the sub-community's fidelity to its own vocation will "contribute to state policy" more strongly—and certainly more authentically—than if they worried about just how and why to go about compromising their principles in order to be effective.[35]

The more Christians forgive one another, the more forgiveness will be seen as a viable path for human flourishing. The more Christians share material goods with one another, the more economic sharing will be seen as viable economics.

---

35. Yoder, "On Not Being in Charge," in *Jewish-Christian Schism*, 175.

Does this encourage Christians to abandon the church for involvement in more generic attempts at social justice? By no means. At the end of *Body Politics*, a text in which Martens thinks that Yoder has elided the difference between church and world, Yoder closes by noting the sharp *contrast* between church and world: "A church that is not 'against the world' in fundamental ways has nothing worth saying to and for the world."[36] Moreover, Yoder states that, while Christians and non-Christians alike may agree with various points he has made, he sees his unique contribution as "the conception that the Christian social ethical witness must be defined not by independence from the witness of the faith community but by its derivation therefrom."[37] In other words, the particularity and uniqueness of the church is essential to the church's social witness. That is why the subtitle of *Body Politics* is not "generic ways that any human can behave" but "practices *of the Christian community* before the watching world." The church's message and life together is central, from beginning to end in Yoder's thought, because it is the church who is equipped by the Spirit to pioneer the way into the new age, living from Christ's victory. The way that Christians truly contribute to the world is not by living on the world's terms, but by going "about the business of being Christian, proclaiming the Gospel, modeling an exemplary community life, and praying for all people,"[38] knowing that there is nothing more real or more foundational to reality than the good news that Christ died, was buried, rose again on the third day, and is now seated at the right hand of the Father.[39] So the church must remember its distinct identity and mission and not conflate the church and world.

But a doctrine of creation also prevents an opposite mistake: a communitarian approach that focuses solely on the church and the church's antithetical relationship to the world. For Yoder, this approach risks backhandedly limiting the reign and work of Jesus.[40]

---

36. Yoder, *Body Politics*, 78.

37. Ibid.

38. Yoder, *Discipleship as Political Responsibility*, 44.

39. See Yoder, *Body Politics*, 74.

40. Yoder clearly seems to have Stanley Hauerwas in mind here. See "Sacrament as Social Process: Christ the Transformer of Culture," in *The Royal Priesthood*, 370.

This approach unwittingly mirrors the position of those who draw a sharp dualism between creation and redemption by saying, "I can live in light of redemption in the church, but I am constrained (by something like necessity, the orders of creation, etc.) to operate in a different way in my vocation outside the church, either because that's just the way it is or because non-Christians wouldn't understand it if I called them to live as I live." This makes no sense to Yoder because Jesus is Word and Lord, which means that following him goes *with* the grain of the universe, no matter where you are in said universe. The "wider world" cannot dictate how to run a factory, a university, or a town, because there is no wider world than the world ruled by the Crucified Lamb.

So should a Christian in the workplace assume that "forgiveness, enemy love, and servanthood" do not apply in this sphere?[41] Should Christians avoid calling non-Christians to forgiveness, enemy love, and servanthood? Yoder answers no and affirms that non-Christians may approximate forgiveness, enemy love, and servanthood, even if they cannot fully do these things or have true grounds for doing them without the regenerating work of the Spirit. There is no hint of two kingdoms or two sets of norms: one derived from fallen necessity and the other from God's redemptive work. Yoder is not here compromising Christian particularity, but affirming the scandal of a particularity that absorbs all other claims to universality. As Yoder puts it in describing Jews in Jeremiah's day, "Jews knew that there was no larger world than the one their Lord had made and their prophets knew the most about. Its compatibility with kinds of 'wisdom' that the Gentiles could understand seemed to them to validate their holy history rather than to relativize it. When Hellenism penetrated their world, they did not hesitate to affirm that whatever truth there was in Plato or Aristotle was derived from Moses."[42] Yoder's does not want to deny that the world can see or live out any shred of truth but to give a Christological account of whatever good there is in the universe. Yoder powerfully summarizes this point:

---

41. Yoder, "New Humanity," in *For the Nations*, 48.

42. Yoder, "See How They Go With Their Face to the Sun," in *For the Nations*, 73.

As a servant people we are humanists. We cannot love our neighbor without loving his joys, his virtues, his vision. As bearers of the gospel we proclaim not judgment but fulfillment-through-judgment, not gloom but joy, not condemnation but restoration. It is not our business to deny that a communist can be unselfish or a Hindu happy, but to gather every fiber of goodness, whatever the source, every insight, every good intention, just as God wove such pagans as the priest Melchizedek and the harlot Rahab into the fabric of the salvation story. Jesus' words, "apart from me you can do nothing" do not mean that non-Christians can do nothing; if they deal with this subject at all they mean that whatever good any man does, it is not apart from Christ. Who, if not the servant we should be, can afford to give the neighbor the benefit of the doubt? Who, if not we, can run the risk of believing all things, hoping all things, enduring all things?[43]

Yoder is not here sacrificing Christian particularity but doing something that virtually all theologians and Christian traditions have found it necessary to do: account for the relative goodness that persists even beyond the church.

Through a Christ-centered doctrine of creation, Yoder is able to explain how and why the world is reducible neither to the church nor to pure evil. A mistake in either direction is prevented by a proper doctrine of creation. This doctrine of creation also undergirds Yoder's account of the social practices in the world that reflect the life-giving sacraments in the church.

The transformative power of the sacraments. Having laid this groundwork, we can now turn to consider the sacraments in detail. In doing so, three framing points regarding Yoder's view of the sacraments must be remembered. First, Yoder distinguishes between the reality of the sacrament in the church and its "reflection" or "spin-off" in the social processes of the world.[44] This distinction is key to retaining a proper church/world distinction. In other words, the sacraments as practiced in the church and the social processes undertaken outside the church are not simple equivalents. So, as we walk through the sacraments, I highlight both the continuity and discontinuity between the church's

43. Yoder, "The Lordship of Christ and the Power Struggle," 512.
44. Yoder, *Body Politics*, 58.

210/ *Things Hold Together*

sacraments and the world's social practices. We must carefully balance both continuity and discontinuity to get Yoder right. If we overemphasize continuity, we risk losing his unflinching contrast between church and world. If we overemphasize discontinuity, we risk losing his insistence that the world has no other norm than the grain of the universe revealed in Jesus.

A second framing point is that since Jesus is both creative Word and Messiah, there is only one set of norms for both church and world. There is no "proper" norm for unbelief and thus no "proper" way for the world to be the world. The church is therefore called to reveal to the world what the world is called to be: those who worship the Crucified Lamb and live with the grain of the universe. To refuse to call the world to do this would be, in some sense, to grant that there is a proper way to be in rebellion and unbelief toward the Creator of the universe. For Yoder, this should not be done.

A third framing point is that we must properly distinguish between the transformation of culture inside the church and outside the church. The church is God's new culture, God's new people. This new creation inevitably affects the broader culture, often humanizing it in ways not previously thought possible. What is the precise status of this transformation and humanization beyond the church? In a section of *The End of Sacrifice* entitled "Christ Transforming Culture," Yoder argues that we should not simplistically equate such humanization with the gospel, but neither should we pretend that the new creation has not entered history and affected the thoughts, practices, and institutions of unbelievers. For Yoder, the humanization of culture that happens in the wake of the church "is not the same as the salvation of individual souls, nor is it the same as the praise of God in gatherings for worship, nor is it the same as the coming of the ultimate kingdom of God, but it is a fruit of the gospel for which we should be grateful, and for whose furtherance we are responsible. The fact that persons believing in other value systems share in the humanization process, and that some of them may overvalue it as if it could do away with evil, is no reason for followers of Jesus to disavow it or leave it to unbelievers to carry out."[45]

---

45. Yoder, "Against the Death Penalty," in *End of Sacrifice*, 126.

Although Yoder underscores Christian participation in these extraecclesial processes, we would do well to note that the Scripture-guided church remains the center of what God is doing and the center for knowing how God is doing it. This fits with Yoder's persistent claim that Christians are called to be a priestly kingdom. The priestly metaphor is an apt one because priests are both *set apart from* the broader community and *set apart for* the broader community. The way to be *for* the nations is by being purposefully and distinctively Christian, as Yoder forcefully states at the end of *Body Politics*: "A church that is not 'against the world' in fundamental ways has nothing worth saying to and for the world. Conversion and separation are not the way to become otherworldly; they are the only way to be present, relevantly and redemptively, in the midst of things."[46] Yoder argues that it is precisely the particularity and faithfulness of the church that enables it to be relevant and transformative with respect to the world. Why? Because the church lives from the vision of the Crucified Lamb in Revelation 5. The Christian can be unashamed of the gospel, recognizing that the real world is the world of Revelation 5—a world in which the suffering servant is proclaimed the King of kings— not some "wider world" that determines ahead of time what does or does not count as intelligible, relevant, or public.[47] With this framework, Yoder's account of these practices can be spelled out.

Binding and loosing. A key aspect of the first practice, binding and loosing, is the process of confrontation, forgiveness, and reconciliation.[48] Yoder draws on a variety of biblical texts, including Matthew 18:15-18: "If your brother or sister sins, go and point out their fault, just between the two of you. If they listen to you, you have won them over. But if they will not listen, take one or two others along, so that 'every matter may be established by the testimony of two or three witnesses.' If they still refuse to listen, tell it to the church; and if they refuse to listen even to the church, treat them as you would a pagan or a tax collector. Truly I

---

46. Yoder, *Body Politics*, 78.

47. Ibid., 74.

48. Yoder also discusses communal moral discernment under this heading, but it is less relevant for my purposes.

tell you, whatever you bind on earth will be bound in heaven, and whatever you loose on earth will be loosed in heaven."

Yoder makes several observations about the reconciliation called for in this text.[49] All individuals can and should confront and address problems, not just the clergy. Second, the goal of the confrontation is to restore relationships and bring about reconciliation, not to punish the offender. Third, Jesus does not outline a distinction between major and minor offenses. All offenses can be forgiven, but none are negligible. Finally, the goal of this process is not to protect the church's reputation but to serve the offender's own well-being by walking through this process of restoration. If this text is taken to heart, the members of the church should reject both legalism and indifference, and they should embrace loving confrontation and forgiveness. What gives the disciples the right and the power to forgive? Jesus empowers his disciples for this task by giving them the Spirit (John 20:22-23).

Beyond the church, Yoder sees the "reflection" of this biblical prescription in the growing social science of conflict resolution.[50] Without using specifically religious language, this process aims to avoid both civil litigation and, sometimes, criminal prosecution.[51] This process begins with a concrete offense and seeks to resolve the problem created by the offense. The ultimate goal is not simply to punish the offender but to have the offender acknowledge the reality and human face of their offense. In addition, the victim's welfare is the central concern of the entire process, unlike the punitive process of the criminal courts. Often, mediators enable both victim and offender to recognize that the process of reconciliation is not a zero-sum game. Rather, parties enter this process assuming there can be a solution that brings healing and progress for all involved. As a result, the threat of publicity and shame are kept to a minimum.[52] Those who serve as mediators should be competent and

---

49. The following summarizes Yoder, *Body Politics*, 2–3.

50. On conflict resolution, see Yoder, "The Science of Conflict," in *War of the Lamb*, 125–134.

51. The following summarizes Yoder, *Body Politics*, 12.

52. This is not to say that public knowledge of the offense is necessarily excluded. One could imagine scenarios where a key part of repentance

caring, and they are often accredited by colleagues and validated by their experience. If the negotiations or reconciliation process fails, the party refusing to reconcile is publicly disavowed and the only course of action is to either let the injustice remain or call for the civil powers to carry out their version of due process.

Although the presence of the Spirit is crucial to the church's binding and loosing,[53] those beyond the church can also see the importance of forgiveness even if they do not know the *logos* who created the grain of the universe. Although forgiveness might be explained so as to make sense in a variety of worldviews, Yoder is clear that Hannah Arendt, Rene Girard, and others can emphasize forgiveness, ultimately, because of Jesus, who is the ontological and epistemological key to reality. Yoder does not deny that forgiveness can take place outside the church. Rather, he argues that because "is true in the gospel; it is also true, *mutatis mutandis*, in the world."[54] The *mutatis mutandis* in the sentence is important, because this Latin phrase means "changing the things needing to be changed." It indicates that two things are analogous, but not identical. This means that Yoder recognizes that conflict resolution will be practiced differently in the church and the world. Precisely because forgiveness is not understood or practiced in the world the same way as in the church, Yoder points out that forgiveness generally remains scandalous and impossible for the world, especially for those who hold the most power.[55] Whereas Yoder sees the social practices of the church as open for the world to "observe, imitate, and extrapolate,"[56] he equally sees that they will always do this *as*

---

and reconciliation would be the public acknowledgement of the wrongs done. Yoder's concern is that publicity not be used as a weapon turned back against the offender. In that case, what happens is not restoration and reconciliation, but publicity used as a tool of shame or scandal for its own sake. By the same token, a truly repentant offender should not object too strenuously to a certain level of publicity. For example, there can and should be publicity in cases where the nature of the offense requires a broader accountability than can be provided in a person-to-person context.

53. Yoder, "Firstfruits," in *For the Nations*, 30; *Body Politics*, 8–9.

54. Yoder, *Body Politics*, 13.

55. Yoder, "Firstfruits," in *For the Nations*, 31.

56. Yoder, *Body Politics*, 75.

the world, i.e., without the regenerating power of the Holy Spirit, without Scripture, and so on. But this does not mean that any talk of forgiveness is *absurd* or *unintelligible* to the broader world or that social scientists might not pick up on the idea. This is not an all-or-nothing game, not least of all because Jesus instructed his followers to act as a salt-like preservative in the broader world. When the world sees an Amish community forgive a murderous gunman, they see that something strange is going on and can recognize the power of God at work, even if they lack the language or framework to fully grasp it. The world can even approximate these practices, but this provides no grounds for thinking that this somehow displaces the particularity of the church, at least not for Yoder.

Lord's Supper. A second practice, the Lord's Supper, connects directly to the practice of sharing meals and breaking bread, a central practice of Jesus and the early church. Note that Yoder does not reduce this meal to *nothing more than* a common meal or economic sharing. As I have pointed out elsewhere, Yoder highlights at least eleven layers of meaning to this meal,[57] including remembrance of Christ's death and hope for his triumphant return.[58] In his lecture on "The Eucharist and Economics" at Holden Village in 1988, Yoder again insists that his point is not to reject what is understood as the traditional Mennonite view of the Lord's Supper, but to focus on the Supper as a meal, with all that meals entailed in the life of the early church.[59] He also rightly notes that the basic act of sharing a meal is a practice that says something about the worldview of the table participants, namely, that they are called to economic solidarity in Christ.

This practice directly flows into other forms of economic sharing.[60] By breaking bread together, Yoder contends, the church embodies an ordinary, day-to-day economic sharing that is suffused

---

57. See Parler, "Spinning the Liturgical Turn," 182–83.

58. Yoder, "New Humanity," in *For the Nations*, 44; *Body Politics*, 20.

59. http://www.hvsvc.net/audio/01_Yo%20J%201988-07.mp3 (accessed Feb. 29, 2012). For this point, listen especially from 56 minutes onward.

60. References to these practices and questions that arose surrounding it include Acts 2:42, 46; 4:32-37; 6:1-4; 15:1-35. See also 1 Corinthians chapters 8, 10, and 11.

with a new understanding of what it means to partake together of the goods that God has provided for his people. This should not be seen as a religious ritual disconnected from economics. Rather, "bread *is* daily sustenance. Bread eaten together *is* economic sharing. Not merely symbolically but also in fact, eating together extends to a wider circle the economic solidarity normally obtained in the family. When in most of his postresurrection appearances Jesus took up again his wonted role of the family head distributing bread (and fish) around the table, he projected into the post-Passion world the common table of the pre-Passion wandering disciple band, whose members had left their prior economic bases to join his movement."[61] Jesus transforms who we consider part of our household and therefore changes the way we think about economics. Just as true members of a household work together as one unit, each responsibly doing what they can and each graciously receiving what they need, so God calls the church to practice this type of economics.[62]

This vision of being householders rather than competitors has "reflections" in the wider world in a variety of ways. Although Yoder does not use the term "common good" in this context, the policies and principles he references all in some way recognize that reality. Those policies and practices include forgiveness of debts (e.g., bankruptcy); low-interest and no-interest loans; public funding of roads, schools, and welfare support; international debt amnesty; equal opportunity; economic cooperation; and certain forms of socialism.[63] Human community, properly understood, involves being bound together as a household, in which the good of each is tied to the good of all.

So what can the church say to the world about economic justice? Yoder notes that Christians use a variety of terms, including "the epistemological privilege of the oppressed or cooperation or

---

61. Yoder, *Body Politics*, 20. Cf. Yoder, "Sacrament as Social Process," in *Royal Priesthood*, 365.

62. Yoder notes that the church's broader use of goods stems from the practice of sharing meals, not from speculation about "ideal economic relations" (Yoder, *Body Politics*, 17).

63. Yoder, *Body Politics*, 25, and "Firstfruits," in *For the Nations*, 32.

equal opportunity or socialism."[64] Is Yoder saying that all of these translate without remainder the meaning of the Lord's Supper? No. In fact, he references his discussion of this in *Body Politics* where he clarifies that, without a biblical foundation, these translations of "economic justice" fail to capture what the Bible means. Instead, he insists that terms such as *economic democracy, socialism, taking the side of the poor, social justice, rights,* or *responsibility for human needs* are all insufficient as self-enclosed or self-describing realities and cannot operate independently of the Eucharist or Lord's Supper, which Yoder calls the "center" for any vision of economic solidarity.[65] In other words, the Lord's Supper is not simply a paradigm, it is *the* irreplaceable paradigm. In arguing that the non-Christian world might "observe, imitate, and extrapolate" from Christian practices, Yoder is not somehow suggesting that these sub-Christian practices are equal to the Lord's Supper and can somehow replace it; he is suggesting that the Lord's Supper is the indispensable foundation for these imitative practices. Far from diminishing Christian particularity, he is saying that Christians who try to make sense of economic justice *apart from the church's particular practice of the Lord's Supper,* including its economic aspect, will ultimately fall short. Why? Because a generic vision of economic justice lacks its transcendent anchor and source, namely, the Crucified Lamb who gave himself for us that we might freely give to one another.

Baptism. Baptism, a third practice, underscores the social unity of the church. According to Paul, the mystery of the gospel he preached was the unity of Jews and Gentiles in one new body.[66] Two texts are particularly significant for Yoder. First, he translates 2 Corinthians 5:17 as follows: "If anyone is united to Christ, there is a new world; everything old has passed away; see, everything has become new!"[67] Second, he translates Galatians 3:27-28:

64. Yoder, "Firstfruits," in *For the Nations*, 32.

65. Yoder, *Body Politics*, 22.

66. See 2 Cor 5:14-17; Gal 3:27-29; Eph 2:11–3:13.

67. Yoder, *Body Politics*, 28. For more thorough exegetical work on the text of 2 Cor 5:17, see Yoder, "'There Is a Whole New World,'" in *To Hear the Word*, 1–24. The New Century Version translates this verse in a similar way.

"Baptized in Christ, you are clothed in Christ, and there is neither slave nor free, neither male nor female; you are all one in Christ Jesus."[68] When a person is baptized, they become part of a body where prior definitions of identity are transcended.[69] Paul has seen the evidence of this in his own ministry, and he speaks of the mystery only lately revealed, namely, that Gentiles have been included in God's covenant purposes and promises. Baptism merges the Jewish and Gentile peoples and stories, in which the inheritance of Abraham is open to all, by faith rather than birth. The Spirit of Jesus not only relativizes the Jew-Gentile barrier but other barriers as well, including those of gender and socioeconomic class. For Yoder, baptism into Christ does not erase identities, such as Jew, Gentile, male, or female. Rather than ignoring differences between these identities, the unity of baptism maintains and transforms them through Christ. Instead of suppressing identity to maintain a feigned unity, Yoder argues that the body of Christ gains baptismal unity only in and through acknowledging difference.[70]

Yoder identifies three transforming effects or "reflections" of baptism in the broader world. The first transformative effect is an emphasis on the dignity and equality of all persons. The Enlightenment preached the equality of all humans, drawing partly on a Stoic affirmation of the dignity of all and partly on the Reformed appeal to the equality of all as creatures of God. Modern notions of liberty, equality, and rights can be traced to these sources, including the opening lines of the Declaration of Independence, which Yoder sees as a secular version of the unity proclaimed by Scripture. Moreover, in the messages proclaimed by abolitionists, Abraham Lincoln, and Martin Luther King Jr., we hear a message of judgment on sin and selfishness and a proclamation that all have dignity because of God's grace.[71]

Importantly, we must notice that Yoder does not claim that one can just simplistically translate the meaning of baptism into what the non-Christian means by "egalitarianism," "democracy,"

---

68. Ibid., 29.

69. Yoder, "Sacrament as Social Process," in *Royal Priesthood*, 367.

70. Yoder, *Body Politics*, 30.

71. Yoder, *Body Politics*, 35.

or respect for "cultural diversity."[72] *True respect, equality,* and *dignity* are terms that, ultimately, cannot be sustained in a world-view cut free from the specificity of Christian baptism. As Yoder notes, "the equality of all people as they are created certainly is not self-evident."[73] In other words, only Christians know the basis for equality, fraternity, and democracy, and it is not a generic respect for people or human dignity; it is a recognition of who God is and what he has done in Jesus. Yet, this baptismal reality overflows and affects cultural practices and institutions beyond the church and the church has no reason to decry this when it happens.

A second transformative effect of baptism is that repentance and change are possible. Against strictly behaviorist understandings of humanity, baptism affirms that sinners are not doomed to repeat their past. Thus, the possibility of repentance can be communicated in the world at large. One example of this is the nonviolence of Gandhi and King.[74] The goal of nonviolence is not the destruction of the enemy but conversion. By appealing to the conscience of the oppressor and by refusing to let past or present guilt determine the oppressor's identity, the nonviolent resistor holds out hope that the oppressor can change. Importantly, the ultimate ground of this change is the power of God proclaimed in baptism, not a generic belief in the goodness of humanity. Repentant reconciliation "is possible for all because it has already been celebrated in Christian baptism by some of us."[75] Thus, even when non-Christians do not explicitly proclaim Jesus, we can see and know that the Spirit is working beyond the church because we know how the Spirit works within the church.

A third transformative effect of baptism is religious liberty.[76] In the early church, baptism entailed the joining of (at least) two different cultures and peoples. The church did not, however, force baptism upon the city or the nation at large, but allowed non-Christians the

---

72. Yoder, "Firstfruits," in *For the Nations*, 30. See also "Sacrament as Social Process," in *Royal Priesthood*, 370.

73. Yoder, *Body Politics*, 35.

74. Ibid., 41.

75. Ibid., 42.

76. Ibid., 42–43.

freedom to reject the gospel. The corollary of this, Yoder argues, is a civil order that grants its citizens true religious freedom. Paradoxically, Yoder thus recognizes that at least some political institutions and traditions that value religious freedom spring directly from *religious* (rather than nonreligious or antireligious) sources.

Universality of giftedness. The fourth sacrament is the universality of giftedness for the edification of the body.[77] These gifts originate in the work of the Spirit and therefore leave no room for spiritual pride. Moreover, the Spirit gives these gifts for the common good, not just for personal aggrandizement. Consequently, we must eschew any notion that just one role in the church deserves the title of "minister." Every member is a minister gifted by the Spirit. Therefore, all are priests in the sense that all are Spirit-empowered to serve fellow members of the body.[78] As a result, Christians should not see power as the prerogative of a high office to be hoarded and used to rule over the rest of the body. Instead, it is diffuse and service-oriented, reorienting the notion of ministry so "there would be no one ungifted, no one not called, no one not empowered, and no one dominated."[79] For Yoder, the power of creation and politics of Jesus come through in a Spirit-empowered life for the common good.

Yoder argues that the universality of giftedness transforms how we think about human community and culture in general. The plurality of gifts holds true for any complex task that requires a multitude of functions. Yoder gives examples such as the city, the university, the research team, and the division of labor.[80] He contends that, given the Pauline vision, businesses based on teamwork and mutual feedback will function better than those based on entrenched hierarchical models.[81] Importantly for Yoder, collaborative and deliberative business models are not simply true because they work, but they work because, unbeknownst to many who practice them, they

---

77. Relevant texts include 1 Cor 12:7; 14:1-40; and Eph 4:8-13. Yoder discusses this topic further in *The Fullness of Christ*.

78. Yoder, *Body Politics*, 56.

79. Ibid., 60.

80. Ibid., 58.

81. Yoder, "Sacrament as Social Process," in *Royal Priesthood*, 370.

are grounded in new possibilities of being human afforded by the humanity and lordship of Christ and the power of the Spirit.

In addition, just as all are ministers in the body of Christ, within the larger society all have a role to play in contributing to the common good. As some Christians overemphasize the role of priest or pastor in the church, Christians and non-Christians alike have overemphasized statecraft as the primary way to contribute to the common good.[82] Yoder's vision of the common good stresses the importance of faithfulness in mundane things. In 1979, he stressed that

> who is in high office or what laws are written will make less difference for many indices of where things will have gone by the year 2000 than the cumulation of an infinity of tiny deeds: mothers who feed their children, children who learn their lessons, craftsmen who finish a job, doctors who get the dosage right, drivers who stay on the road, and policemen who hold their fire . . . The predilection to see one's own small deed as significant or as right when and because it can be shown to contribute to some overall victory scenario overburdens punctual responsibility in decision and undervalues the continuities of character and covenant. The kingdom is like the grain growing while no one watches (Mark 4:26f.), like the hidden leaven silently taking over the flour bin (Matt 13:33).[83]

Because all members are respected as an integral part of the whole no matter what their role, the Spirit empowers them to embrace their responsibility and the meaning it gives as a vital part of contributing to the good of the whole.

Is this focus on the multiplicity of gifts simply a first-century, Pauline view of the modern idea of teamwork and division of labor? Yoder disagrees. The universality of giftedness in the church depends on the ascension of Christ, as Paul argues in Ephesians 4.[84] The theological ground for this practice is the ascended Jesus pouring out the power and presence of his Spirit, who gifts and equips each

---

82. For a reiteration of this point, see Hunter, *To Change the World*, 167–75.

83. Yoder, "Discerning the Kingdom of God," in *For the Nations*, 244.

84. Yoder, *Body Politics*, 48.

member of the body for the building up of the whole.[85] As a result, this practice must not be equated with modern notions of teamwork or Western individualism. Without Jesus' ascension, there is no sacrament. Further, Paul's vision of organic interdependence is not reducible to nonbiblical terms like *individualism* or *collectivism*.[86] Again, Yoder argues that there is an analogy but not a simplistic equivalency between the Christian sacrament and its *extra ecclesiam* analogs.

With this sacrament in particular, Yoder explains quite clearly how practices in the church and world relate in analogous, *not identical* ways. As Yoder states, "The modern notions of teamwork, which I argued above are not the source of Paul's vision, are in fact reflections or spin-offs from it . . . It enables the factory system, the research team, the university, and the city. It explains why factories and businesses where every worker participates in policy making and quality control can make better automobiles or sell more software than those whose organization is vertical."[87] Again, Yoder underscores that there are not two norms, one for the church and one for the autonomous world, and that the church's practices are foundational and anchored in Christ. Yoder later adds that dialogue in the Spirit is the "ground floor" of democracy and that binding and loosing is the "foundation" for any conflict resolution.[88] Yet one is not free to reverse the order and deduce that the "rule of Paul" and "democracy" are equivalent. Yoder is clear about that. This comports with his view of the church as "pioneering" culture.[89] It may surprise those who focus only on his critique of Constantinianism to learn that Yoder claimed that the church has been doing this pioneering work for a long time and has produced many "reflections" and "spin-offs" throughout the centuries, including institutions like hospitals, public education, and social work. Because the church lives in and into the new creation, this affects the world as well as the church.

---

85. Ibid., 48–49.

86. Ibid., 49.

87. Ibid., 58.

88. Ibid., 72.

89. Yoder, "Sacrament as Social Process," in *Royal Priesthood*, 373.

222 / *Things Hold Together*

Open meeting. The fifth and final sacrament that Yoder discusses is the open meeting. Drawing upon Paul's instructions for an orderly meeting in 1 Corinthians 14, Yoder terms this "the Rule of Paul," namely, that everyone be allowed the opportunity to speak. Yoder sees this as applicable to both the regular meetings of the church body and to occasions that address specific issues or questions for deliberations. Just as the universality of giftedness means that all members must contribute to the life of the body, so the Spirit's presence in each member means that all can speak and contribute to the edification and deliberation of the congregation. This process overlaps with binding and loosing, and Yoder again references Acts 15 as a model, with participants sharing experiences of the Spirit's work and drawing upon Scripture to inform deliberation. Yoder notes that the open meeting has been emphasized at various points throughout church history, including early synods in Cappadocia and later emphases in Luther, Zwingli, and the Swiss Anabaptists.[90] For Yoder, until there has been open dialogue with all interested parties enabled to speak, the church should not go forward. Only when there is trust that the Spirit will speak in and through the conversation of the gathered deliberative body will a willingness to listen to other members of the body arise, with trust that God is using each one to bring wisdom before the group as a whole. Yoder expects that the results will be like those proclaimed in Acts 15:28: "It seemed good to the Holy Spirit and to us." Because God is not a God of disorder, the Spirit does not operate apart from roles, structures, and proper procedure, but precisely in, with, and under those roles, structures, and proper procedure.[91]

According to Yoder, this practice of open meeting transforms culture and leads to democratic forms in the civil order. Yoder lists three factors that, broadly considered, contributed to the development of democracy.[92] First, John Calvin's vision of society and its

---

90. Yoder, *Body Politics*, 63–64.

91. Yoder lists four roles in particular: agents of direction, agents of memory, agents of linguistic self-consciousness, and agents of order and due process. Yoder, "The Hermeneutics of Peoplehood," in *Priestly Kingdom*, 29–34.

92. Yoder, "Sacrament as Social Process," 368, n. 12.

connection with a council (rather than a solitary leader) shaped thinking about the broader civil order. Second, Yoder, citing A. D. Lindsay, puts forth the idea that Anglo-Saxon democracy (different from the Enlightenment democracy of the Continent) extends the experience and practice of the Puritan meeting to democracy as practiced in England and New England.[93] Third, as time went by, many Reformed communities found themselves in positions of dissent rather than government, a position that contributed to their emphasis on civil rights. This direct influence of gospel order on civil order explains why Yoder is more positive toward democracy than other forms of governance.

In "The Christian Case for Democracy," Yoder first argues that democracy is not qualitatively different from all other configurations of political power and, as such, it should not be deified as *the* political structure. The *demos* can be as tyrannical and demonic as any dictator.[94] Nevertheless, Yoder argues for democracy, understood not as the rule of the majority but as the practice of granting a voice to all within society, including the underdog and oppressed: "The irreducible bulwark of social freedom is the dignity of dissent; the ability of the outsider, the other, the critic to speak and be heard. This is not majority rule; it is minority leverage . . . The crucial need is not to believe that 'we, the people' are ruling ourselves. It is to commit ourselves to defending *their* right to be heard."[95] The irony and strength of the experiments pioneered by Roger Williams and William Penn is that they applied gospel order to civil order, thereby grounding religious freedom in

---

93. See also Yoder, *Body Politics*, 67; and "The Christian Case for Democracy," in *Priestly Kingdom*, 168.

94. For a similar point regarding democracy, see Koyzis, *Political Visions and Illusions*, 124–51.

95. Yoder, "The Christian Case for Democracy," in *Priestly Kingdom*, 167 (emphasis original). Jeffrey Stout offers an account of "thick" conversation that, he argues, should characterize a health democracy. There are certain affinities between Stout and Yoder on this score. Cf. Stout, *Democracy and Tradition*, especially chapter 12, "Ethics as a Social Practice." Romand Coles also draws upon Yoder's thought to inform his own view of democracy in "The Wild Patience of John Howard Yoder: 'Outsiders' and the 'Otherness of the Church,'" 305–31.

a robustly religious reason, namely, the willingness to learn from any and every member of the assembly.[96] Although Yoder does not deify democracy, when the democratic process entails a willingness to listen and grant respect to the weak and the oppressed, we can say that the transformative wind of the Spirit has been blowing.

For Yoder, it should be clear then that democracy as practiced by non-Christians is the simple equivalent to the Spirit-led dialogue of the church. Nevertheless, the Christian can promote dialogue outside the church because of the conviction that "in the age of Jesus the Messiah, the healing resources of his ministry can by the nature of things reach" beyond the Christian community.[97] This move does not break down the church/world distinction, but reinforces it. Inside the church, we know what we do and we know why we do it: because the Messiah has come and poured out his Spirit. Outside the church, we can encourage dialogue even for those who do not confess Jesus as Lord precisely because we know Jesus is both Word and Lord. Do they have the same resources of the Christian community? Of course not, but that does not mean there is some other norm or *telos* for how humans should function. The only norm is God's kingdom as presented in Scripture and embodied (albeit imperfectly) in the life of the church. So Christians should call non-Christians to greater dialogue with their enemies, even if they initially do so in "thinner" terms that are not specifically Christian.[98]

When Yoder summarizes the work of the Spirit through the sacraments, he asks "Have we happened onto a deep logic of things?"[99] Although he initially backs away from affirming any overconfident proclamation of a discovery of a new "system," he nevertheless contends that "it should not be surprising if there were such a deep structure that, once discerned in the five places where we have touched it, would then illuminate more broadly

96. Yoder, "Civil Religion in America," in *Priestly Kingdom*, 180–81.

97. Yoder, *Body Politics*, 69.

98. Ibid.

99. Ibid., 79.

the shape of all God's saving purposes."[100] That is, Yoder points to continuity and coherence in the cultural practices that God calls for throughout human history. The way God was leading his people in the Old Testament brought them to the fulfillment of the covenant through the Messiah and the promised Spirit. And the ultimate destiny of the world is expressed already in the life of the church, which in turn shapes the larger culture by its witness. The purposes of the trinitarian God have a reliable rhythm and coherence in the power of creation, the politics of Jesus, and the pioneering public practices produced by the Spirit-empowered pilgrim people.

---

100. Ibid., 80.

8

Conclusion

Theologies of culture often focus on either Christ or creation to the exclusion of the other. Yoder offers a way beyond this impasse and offers an alternative in his trinitarian theology of culture, which upholds the continuity and coherence between creation and redemption. Moreover, far from being sectarian, Yoder's work is irenic and ecumenical insofar as the continuity between creation and redemption outlines the way to true transformation of culture. That is, Yoder shows how to get what Reinhold Niebuhr and H. Richard Niebuhr wanted all along: true effectiveness in engaging the wider world; a responsible and proactive approach to the pressing social issues of our day; a trinitarian emphasis; a creation-affirming approach to culture; and authentic transformation of culture.

Being trinitarian: Yoder's theology of culture

Many scholars either focus on creation to the detriment of Christ or on Christ to the detriment of creation. Several commentators on Yoder's work place him in the latter camp. However, we best understand Yoder's work when we see that it presents a trinitarian theology of culture. That is, proper trinitarian thought posits a unity between Father, Son, and Holy Spirit, and therefore a unity to what God desires in the cultural life of humanity. Chapter 2 demonstrates that Reinhold Niebuhr's social ethics and H. Richard Niebuhr's theology of culture are interwoven with their broader theology. Thus, Yoder does not simply disagree with Reinhold's antipacifism or with H. Richard's characterization of Mennonites. Rather, his disagreement with them has to do with core doctrinal issues, including doctrines of the Trinity, Christology, pneumatology, creation, and resurrection. Chapter 3 argues that Yoder's thought is compatible with the Christological and trinitarian content of Nicea and Chalcedon. If Yoder was antitrinitarian and denounced the substance of these creeds, it would be questionable to characterize his thought as presenting a trinitarian theology of culture. By placing Yoder's understanding of the creeds within the larger context of his theology, one can see that he does not disagree with the substance of Nicea and Chalcedon nor does he deny the ongoing and ever-present need to adequately translate the truth of the gospel in new contexts and thought worlds.

Chapter 4 demonstrates that, for Yoder, the biblical affirmation of the humanity and divinity of Jesus are central to a theology of culture. As a fully human person and as Israel's Messiah, Jesus is directly relevant to culture, politics, economics, and other questions of social ethics. As fully divine, Jesus creates, sustains, and directs all things and, in him, all things hold together. Chapter 5 contends that, for Yoder, the power of Jesus reestablishes the politics of creation. By moving through Yoder's account of creation, fall, and redemption, one can see that he presents an ontology of peaceful power in which humans were created to exercise Christlike power and in which the Powers were created to be dynamic servants of peace and flourishing. Careful scrutiny of Yoder's corpus as a whole therefore reveals a doctrine of creation that coheres with redemption. For many scholars, however, his rejection of the sword reveals a deficient doctrine of creation. Chapter 6 demonstrates that, for Yoder, the sword-bearing state is not rooted in prelapsarian creation but in postlapsarian preservation. This being the case, God's providential allowance of the sword must not be confused or conflated with God's creative and redemptive will. Finally, chapter 7 shows that Yoder's view of the Holy Spirit and sacraments connects directly to the authentic transformation of culture. This transformation is dependent on the pioneering work of the Spirit and the in-breaking kingdom of God. When the person of the Spirit unleashes the power of creation and the politics of Jesus, the public practices of the church inevitably overflow and exert transformative effects not only in the church but in all human culture.

Being cultural: creation and redemption

Yoder contends that across the ages there is but one trinitarian God—Father, Son, and Spirit—working out his plan for the world. There is unity and continuity to this trinitarian God and there is unity and continuity to the drama of Scripture. By emphasizing the continuity and coherence between creation and redemption, we can build on Yoder's thought to extrapolate and articulate more thoroughly what it means to consistently hold to a trinitarian theology of culture.

Yoder's position clearly entails a rejection of any Gnostic view of culture and life in this world. God created the world good. A key aspect of this goodness is the inherent goodness of human social life, ordered to both the glory of God and the flourishing of all creation. God created the Powers as good servants of human shalom, meant to provide order, stability, and coherence to human life. He created humans to exercise and participate in the peaceful power of love, servanthood, truth-telling, creativity, and trust in God alone. Indeed, as God's royal image, humanity was created to be a channel of God's power, caring for and ministering to all creation. This includes the development of culture in a manner that goes with the grain of the universe.

As Yoder repeatedly emphasizes, redemption should be seen as the redemption of creation. Jesus, as the true *imago Dei* and second Adam, exercises power by imitating the Father: he loves his enemies and serves his friends. When the Word, the agent of creation, assumes our flesh for our redemption, we see in him the grain of the universe and the politics of creation fully unveiled. This revelation takes place not in a pristine Eden but in the midst of a hurting, fallen, and rebellious world. The power of creation is therefore manifest in Jesus' following the path of cross and resurrection on the way to ascension and glorification. When worked out as a concrete social strategy, Jesus' approach is what Yoder terms revolutionary subordination. Importantly, this emulates God's strategy throughout Scripture of avoiding total annihilation of his creation and instead seeking to redeem it. Revolutionary subordination does not entail the destruction of creation, but the in-breaking of God's kingdom in the midst of other kingdoms. This leaven-like kingdom releases humans from the grip of sin. In doing so, the power of creation is unleashed from the shackles of sin and reworked into the ties that bind all things together through redemptive and suffering love.

Being coherent: implications of continuity between creation and redemption

Several implications follow from the coherence and continuity of creation and redemption. Since creation and redemption cohere, then true natural law cannot be opposed to Christ.[1] If Jesus tells his followers to live a certain way or calls them to certain practices, those things cannot contradict God's ultimate intentions in creation. If human sin had never entered God's world, some of these practices would not be needed. For example, cross-bearing would be unnecessary if there was no sin. God's design for life, however, always included self-giving love and mutuality, two qualities that are manifested in the postfall practice of cross-bearing. But inasmuch as cross-bearing represents a *refusal* of a fallen response to evil, it is a creational-messianic practice. The one who bears a cross does not allow sin, death, or the devil to have a final say about how power ought to be exercised but instead follows Jesus in entrusting oneself to God.

Since creation and redemption cohere, the first Adam cannot be normative in a way that supersedes or trumps Jesus, the second Adam. In the language of Hebrews 8:5, we ought to be suspicious of approaches to culture that do not adequately emphasize that Adam is but a "type" and "shadow" of Jesus, and this includes matters of culture. In the language of Ephesians 5:31-32, the union between Adam and Eve points to the deeper reality of Christ and the church, and this includes matters of culture. In the language of Colossians 1:15, Jesus, not Adam, is the true image of the invisible God and the preeminent one in all creation. This focus on Christ does not eclipse creation; rather, properly understood, it underscores that because Christ is both Creator and *true* Adam, we see God's creational intent for human life and culture *best* when we look to Jesus and the activity of his Spirit.

---

1. For an excellent exposition of this point, see Matthew Levering, *Biblical Natural Law*.

Since creation and redemption cohere, faithfulness cannot be set against effectiveness or responsibility, properly defined and understood. We see this consummately in Jesus. Indeed, Jesus refuses to follow Cain's path of irresponsibility for his brother and instead bears his brothers' sins upon himself. Although faithfulness unto death, even death on a cross, might appear ineffective on the world's register, the resurrection confirms that God is not dead, a reality that opens up unforeseen cruciform possibilities for effective action. Because the second Adam is also the divine Word, we have the ultimate grounds for knowing what action is most effective, namely, that which conforms to the Crucified Lamb. So the way of Jesus is right precisely because "it goes with the grain of the universe, and that is why *in the long run* nothing else will work."[2] For those who have eyes to see the doxological vision of Revelation 5, the way of faithfulness is, ultimately, the way of effectiveness.

Since creation and redemption cohere, the distinctiveness and transformative effect of God's people are not two different options but two sides of the same coin. Because they live in a fallen world, God calls his people to be attentive to ways in which they can live out their creational-messianic distinctiveness. Just as God called Abraham out of Babylon in order to form a people who would bless the nations, so the church must distance itself from Babylon. God's people must always keep in mind, however, that he set them apart *from* the nations so that they can be *for* the nations. If the church deems its set-apartness as an end in itself, it does not account for God's work of redemption. Just as God sent his people back to Babylon with Jeremiah's injunction to "seek the peace of the city where you dwell," so the church must be *in* Babylon, *with* Babylon, and *for* Babylon. Of course, the church can do this only inasmuch as it is not *of* Babylon, recognizing that its citizenship is in a city whose foundations cannot be shaken and whose builder and maker is God.

Finally, since creation and redemption cohere, the great commission of Matthew 28:18-20 ought to be seen as the continuation of the creation mandate of Genesis 1:26-28. When Jesus

---

2. Yoder, "The Political Meaning of Hope," in *The War of the Lamb*, 62.

tells his disciples to go forth and make disciples, he is not simply telling them to spread a message that will enable individuals to attain a particular postmortem destination. As rightful Lord of the cosmos, Jesus is commanding his disciples to proclaim verbally the good news of Jesus' lordship and work out in the power of the Spirit what that lordship means for all facets of human life. Christianity, then, should be seen not as a "religion" in the compartmentalized modern sense, but as a new way of being social, cultural, political, and economic, a new way that springs to life as God's people live in community with one another. In other words, to be ecclesial and to be public are not two different realms or spheres. Redemption is as broad as creation, and so to follow the great commission will entail working out new Spirit-empowered ways of dealing with questions relating to matters such as conflict, money, forgiveness, community order and roles, technology, and justice. Christians receive guidance on these matters not merely by a broad and sometimes epistemologically vague appeal to creation, but by the specific life and Spirit of the Lord of creation. So, cultural practices and institutions that operate against the way of Jesus also go against the grain of the universe. The redemption of culture must therefore entail a whole host of strategies for engagement, including rejection, adaptation, transformation, and, most crucially, pioneering new forms of culture that enable a hurting world to envision cultural possibilities not perceived or even imagined without a pioneering community that blazes the trail.

Under the forces of human sin and evil, things fall apart. Oftentimes, this disintegration appears to be the most real thing about our world. Yet, while we do not yet see all things in subjection to him, we do see Jesus, the pioneer of our faith who, for the joy set before him, endured the cross, despising its shame, and sat down at the right hand of God as Lord of an unshakeable kingdom, of which we are the heirs. In the power of creation, the politics of Jesus, and the Spirit-empowered practices of God's people, God is binding his creation back together—this time bound by the healing power of love rather than the destructive force of sin. Thus we confess that by the grace of the Father, the power of the Son, and the presence of the Spirit, all things hold together.

Bibliography

Alexis-Baker, Andy. "Unbinding Yoder from Just Policing." In *Power and Practices: Engaging the Work of John Howard Yoder*, edited by Jeremy M. Bergen and Anthony S. Siegrist, 147–66. Scottdale, PA: Herald Press, 2009.

Arendt, Hannah. *The Human Condition*. Chicago: University of Chicago Press, 1958.

Augustine. *The City of God against the Pagans*. Edited and translated by R. W. Dyson. Cambridge, UK: Cambridge University Press, 1998.

_____. *The Enchiridion on Faith, Hope, and Love*. Edited by John E. Rotelle. Translated by Bruce Harbert. Hyde Park, NY: New City Press, 1999.

Barth, Karl. "Christ and Adam: Man and Humanity in Romans 5." *Scottish Journal of Theology Occasional Papers No. 5*. Translated by T. A. Smail. Edinburgh: Oliver and Boyd, 1956.

_____. *Church Dogmatics* III/1. Edinburgh: T&T Clark, 1958.

_____. *Church Dogmatics* IV/2. Edinburgh: T&T Clark, 1958.

_____. *Community, State and Church*. Edited by Will Herberg. Garden City, NY: Doubleday, 1960.

_____. *The Humanity of God*. John Knox Press, 1960.

Barth, Markus. *The Broken Wall: A Study of the Epistle to the Ephesians*. Valley Forge, PA: Judson Press, 1959.

Bartholomew, Craig, and Michael Goheen. *The Drama of Scripture: Finding Our Place in the Biblical Story*. Grand Rapids, MI: Baker, 2004.

Begbie, Jeremy. "Creation, Christ, and Culture in Dutch Neo-Calvinism." In *Christ in Our Place: The Humanity of God in Christ for the Reconciliation of the World*, edited by Trevor A. Hart and Daniel P. Thimell, 113–32. Exeter, UK: Paternoster, 1989.

Berkhof, Hendrikus. *Christ and the Powers*. 2nd ed. Translated by John H. Yoder. Scottdale, PA: Herald Press, 1977.

Biesecker-Mast, Gerald. "The Radical Christological Rhetoric of John Howard Yoder." In *A Mind Patient and Untamed: Assessing John Howard Yoder's Contributions to Theology, Ethics, and Peacemaking*, edited by Ben C. Ollenburger and Gayle Gerber Koontz. Telford, PA: Cascadia Publishing House / Scottdale, PA: Herald Press, 2004.

Bonhoeffer, Dietrich. *Ethics*. Translated by Neville Horton Smith. Edited by Eberhard Bethge. London: SCM Press, 1955.

Brown, Robert McAfee. *Introduction to The Essential Reinhold Niebuhr: Selected Essays and Addresses*, edited by Robert McAfee Brown. New Haven, CT: Yale University Press, 1986.

Brunner, Emil. *The Divine Imperative: A Study in Christian Ethics*. Translated by Olive Wyon. New York: Macmillan, 1937.

_____. "Nature and Grace." In *Natural Theology*, translated by Peter Fraenkel, 15–64. 1946. Reprint, Eugene, OR: Wipf and Stock, 2002.

Budziszewski, J. "Four Shapers of Evangelical Political Thought." In *Evangelicals in the Public Square: Four Formative Voices on Political Thought and Action*, 39–121. Grand Rapids, MI: Baker, 2006.

_____. *What We Can't Not Know: A Guide*. Dallas, TX: Spence Publishing, 2003.

_____. *Written on the Heart: The Case for Natural Law*. Downers Grove, IL: InterVarsity Press, 1997.

Caird, G. B. *Principalities and Powers*. Oxford, UK: Clarendon Press, 1956.

Calvin, John. *Institutes of the Christian Religion*. 2 vols. Translated by Ford Lewis Battles. Edited by John T. McNeill. Philadelphia, PA: Westminster John Knox Press, 1960.

Carson, D. A. *Christ and Culture Revisited*. Grand Rapids, MI: Eerdmans, 2008.

Carter, Craig A. "The Legacy of an Inadequate Christology: Yoder's Critique of Niebuhr's Christ and Culture." *Mennonite Quarterly Review* 77, no. 3 (2003): 387–401.

————. *The Politics of the Cross: The Theology and Social Ethics of John Howard Yoder.* Grand Rapids, MI: Brazos Press, 2001.

————. *Rethinking Christ and Culture: A Post-Christendom Perspective.* Grand Rapids, MI: Brazos Press, 2006.

Cartwright, Michael. "Introduction: Radical Reform, Radical Catholicity: John Howard Yoder's Vision of the Faithful Church." In *The Royal Priesthood: Essays Ecclesiological and Ecumenical,* by John Howard Yoder, 1–49. Grand Rapids, MI: Eerdmans, 1994.

Charles, J. Daryl. "Protestants and Natural Law." *First Things* 168 (Dec. 2006): 33–38.

————. *Retrieving the Natural Law: A Return to Moral First Things.* Grand Rapids, MI: Eerdmans, 2008.

Coles, Romand. "The Wild Patience of John Howard Yoder: 'Outsiders' and the 'Otherness of the Church.'" *Modern Theology* 18, no. 3 (2002): 305–31.

Cullman, Oscar. *Christ and Time: The Primitive Christian Conception of Time and History.* Translated by Floyd V. Filson. London: SCM Press, 1951.

de Gruchy, John W. *The Church Struggle in South Africa.* Grand Rapids, MI: Eerdmans, 1979.

Dooyeweerd, Herman. *Roots of Western Culture: Pagan, Secular, and Christian Options.* Translated by John Kraay. Edited by Mark Vander Vennen and Bernard Zylstra. Toronto: Wedge Publishing, 1979.

Finger, Thomas. *A Contemporary Anabaptist Theology: Biblical, Historical, Constructive.* Downers Grove, IL: InterVarsity Press, 2004.

————. "Did Yoder Reduce Theology to Ethics?" In *A Mind Patient and Untamed: Assessing John Howard Yoder's Contributions to Theology, Ethics, and Peacemaking,* edited by Ben C. Ollenburger and Gayle Gerber Koontz, 318–39. Telford, PA: Cascadia Publishing House / Scottdale, PA: Herald Press, 2004.

Friesen, Duane K. *Artists, Citizens, Philosophers Seeking the Peace of the City: An Anabaptist Theology of Culture.* Scottdale, PA: Herald Press, 2000.

Gardner, Edward Clinton. "Ethical Issues for the 1970's: A Critique of Christocentric Models of Ethical Analysis." *Religion in Life* 39 (1970): 205–20.

Gilkey, Langdon. *On Niebuhr: A Theological Study.* Chicago: University of Chicago Press, 2001.

Goudzwaard, Bob, Mark Vander Vennen, and David Van Heemst. *Hope in Troubled Times: A New Vision for Confronting Global Crises.* Grand Rapids, MI: Baker, 2007.

Gregory of Nazianzus. "Epistle 130." In *Creeds, Councils and Controversies: Documents Illustrating the History of the Church, AD 337–461,* edited by J. Stevenson, 118–19. Revised edition edited by W. H. C. Frend. Cambridge, UK: SPCK, 1989.

Haas, Guenther. "Creational Ethics Is Public Ethics." *Journal for Christian Theological Research* 12 (2007): 1–36.

————. "The Effects of the Fall on Creational Social Structures: A Comparison of Anabaptist and Reformed Perspectives." *Calvin Theological Journal* 30 (1995): 108–29.

Hauerwas, Stanley. *Against the Nations: War and Survival in a Liberal Society.* Notre Dame, IN: University of Notre Dame Press, 1992.

————. "Introduction: Lingering with Yoder's Wild Work." In *A Mind Patient and Untamed: Assessing John Howard Yoder's Contributions to Theology, Ethics, and Peacemaking,* edited by Ben C. Ollenburger and Gayle Gerber Koontz, 11–22. Telford, PA: Cascadia Publishing House / Scottdale, PA: Herald Press, 2004.

————. *The Peaceable Kingdom: A Primer in Christian Ethics.* Notre Dame, IN: University of Notre Dame Press, 1983.

————. *With the Grain of the Universe: The Church's Witness and Natural Theology.* Grand Rapids, MI: Brazos, 2001.

Hauerwas, Stanley, and Alex Sider. *Introduction to Preface to Theology: Christology and Theological Method,* by John Howard Yoder. Grand Rapids, MI: Brazos, 2002.

Hauerwas, Stanley, and Samuel Wells, ed. *The Blackwell Companion to Christian Ethics.* Oxford, UK: Blackwell, 2004.

Huebner, Chris K. "Globalization, Theory, and Dialogical Vulnerability: John Howard Yoder and the Possibility of a Pacifist Epistemology." *Mennonite Quarterly Review* 76, no. 1 (2002): 49–62.

Huebner, Harry. "The Christian Life as Gift and Patience: Why Yoder Has Trouble with Method." In *A Mind Patient and Untamed: Assessing John Howard Yoder's Contributions to Theology, Ethics, and Peacemaking*, edited by Ben C. Ollenburger and Gayle Gerber Koontz, 23–38. Telford, PA: Cascadia Publishing House / Scottdale, PA: Herald Press, 2004.

Hicks, Douglas A. "Self-Interest, Agency, and Deprivation." *Journal of the Society of Christian Ethics* 25, no. 1 (2005): 147–67.

Hunter, James Davidson. *To Change the World: The Irony, Tragedy, and Possibility of Christianity in the Late Modern World*. Oxford, UK: Oxford University Press, 2010.

International Roman Catholic-Reformed Dialogue. "The Church as Community of Common Witness to the Kingdom of God." 2007. http://www.prounione.urbe.it/dia-int/r-rc/doc/e_r-rc_3-printable.html. Accessed May 29, 2012.

Irish, Jerry A. *The Religious Thought of H. Richard Niebuhr* (Atlanta: John Knox Press, 1983).

Jones, Joe. "Yoder and Stone-Campbellites: Sorting the Grammar of Radical Orthodoxy and Radical Discipleship." In *Radical Ecumenicity: Pursuing Unity and Continuity after John Howard Yoder*, edited by John C. Nugent, 107–28. Abilene, TX: Abilene Christian University Press, 2010.

Kaethler, Andrew Brubacher, "The Practice of Reading the Other: John Howard Yoder's Critical and Caricatured Portrayal of Scholasticism." In *Power and Practices: Engaging the Work of John Howard Yoder*, edited by Jeremy M. Bergen and Anthony S. Siegrist, 47–64. Scottdale, PA: Herald Press, 2009.

Kant, Immanuel. *Groundwork of the Metaphysics of Morals*. Translated by H. J. Paton. London: Hutchinson & Co., 1961.

King, Rachel Hadley. *The Omission of the Holy Spirit from Reinhold Niebuhr's Theology*. New York: Philosophical Library, 1964.

Klapwijk, J. "Antithesis, Synthesis, and the Idea of Transformational Philosophy." *Philosophia Reformata* 51 (1986): 138–54.

Kliever, Lonnie D. "The Christology of H. Richard Niebuhr," *The Journal of Religion* 50:1 (1970): 33–57.

Kooi, Cornelis van der. "A Theology of Culture: A Critical Appraisal of Kuyper's Doctrine of Common Grace." In *Kuyper Reconsidered: Aspects of his Life and Work*, edited by Cornelis van der Kooi and Jan de Bruijn, 95–101. Amsterdam: VU Uitgeverij, 1999.

Koyzis, David P. *Political Visions and Illusions: A Survey and Christian Critique of Contemporary Ideologies*. Downers Grove, IL: InterVarsity Press, 2003.

Kuyper, Abraham. *Lectures on Calvinism*. Grand Rapids, MI: Eerdmans, 1931.

————. "Sphere Sovereignty." In *Abraham Kuyper: A Centennial Reader*, edited by James Bratt, 461–90. Grand Rapids, MI: Eerdmans, 1998.

Levering, Matthew. *Biblical Natural Law: A Theocentric and Teleological Approach*. Oxford, UK: Oxford University Press, 2008.

Long, D. Stephen. *The Goodness of God: Theology, the Church, and Social Order*. Grand Rapids, MI: Brazos, 2001.

————. *Theology and Culture: A Guide to the Discussion*. Eugene, OR: Cascade Books, 2008.

MacGregor, G. H. C. "Principalities and Powers: The Cosmic Background of Paul's Thought." *New Testament Studies* 1, no. 1 (1954): 17–28.

Marsden, George. "Christianity and Cultures: Transforming Niebuhr's Categories." *Insights: The Faculty Journal of Austin Seminary* (Fall 1999). http://www.religion-online.org/showarticle. asp?title=517. Accessed June 20, 2008.

Martens, Paul. *The Heterodox Yoder*. Eugene, OR: Cascade, 2012.

McClendon, James. *Systematic Theology*. Vols. 1–3. Nashville, TN: Abingdon Press, 1986-1994.

Middleton, J. Richard. *The Liberating Image: The Imago Dei in Genesis 1*. Grand Rapids, MI: Brazos, 2005.

————. "The Liberating Image? Interpreting the Imago Dei in Context." *Christian Scholar's Review* 24, no. 1 (1994).

Milbank, John. "The Ethics of Self-Sacrifice." *First Things* 91:1 (1999): 33–38.

_____. "The Midwinter Sacrifice: A Sequel to 'Can Morality Be Christian?'" Studies in *Christian Ethics* 10, no. 2 (1997): 13–38.

_____. *The Word Made Strange: Theology, Language, Culture.* Oxford, UK: Blackwell, 1997.

Miller, John W. "In the Footsteps of Marcion: Notes toward an Understanding of John Yoder's Theology." *Conrad Grebel Review* 16, no. 2 (1998).

Minnema, Theodore. *The Social Ethics of Reinhold Niebuhr.* Kampen, Neth.: J. H. Kok, 1958.

Moltmann, Jürgen. "Creation and Redemption." In *Creation, Christ, and Culture: Studies in Honour of T. F. Torrance,* edited by Richard W. A. McKinney, 119–34. Edinburgh: T&T Clark, 1976.

_____. *The Future of Creation.* Translated by Margaret Kohl. Philadelphia, PA: Fortress, 1979.

_____. "Religion, Revolution, and the Future." In *Religion, Revolution, and the Future,* translated by M. Douglas Meeks, 19–41. New York: Charles Scribner's Sons, 1969.

Morrison, Clinton. *The Powers That Be.* London: SCM Press, 1960.

Mouw, Richard J. "Abandoning the Typology: A Reformed Assist." *Theological Students Fellowship Bulletin* (May–June 1985): 7–10.

_____. "Creational Politics: Some Calvinist Amendments." *Christian Scholar's Review* 23, no. 2 (1993): 181–93.

_____. "Jesus and Political Authority." In *Perspectives on Christology: Essays in Honor of Paul K. Jewett,* edited by Marguerite Shuster and Richard Muller, 253–67. Grand Rapids, MI: Zondervan, 1991.

_____. *Politics and the Biblical Drama.* Grand Rapids, MI: Eerdmans, 1976.

_____. "Providence and Politics." In *Life Is Religion: Essays in Honor of H. Evan Runner,* edited by Henry Vander Goot, 207–20. St. Catharines, ON: Paideia Press, 1981.

Mouw, Richard J., and John Howard Yoder. "Evangelical Ethics and the Anabaptist-Reformed Dialogue." *The Journal of Religious Ethics* 17 (Fall 1989): 121–37.

Nation, Mark Thiessen. *John Howard Yoder: Mennonite Patience, Evangelical Witness, Catholic Convictions.* Grand Rapids, MI: Eerdmans, 2006.

_____. "Mending Fences and Finding Grace: Regarding Christology and Divine Agency in Yoder's Thought." Presented at the conference "Inheriting John Howard Yoder." Toronto Mennonite Theological Centre, May 25–26, 2007. http://www.emu.edu/seminary/resources/christologymtn.html. Accessed December 29, 2009.

Niebuhr, H. Richard. *Christ and Culture*. New York: Harper & Row, 1951.

_____. "The Doctrine of the Trinity and the Unity of the Church." *Theology Today* 3, no. 3 (1946): 371–84.

_____. *Radical Monotheism and Western Culture*. New York: Harper & Row, 1970.

_____. *The Responsible Self: An Essay in Christian Moral Philosophy*. San Francisco: Harper & Row, 1963.

_____. "Theological Unitarianisms." *Theology Today* 40, no. 2 (1983): 150–57.

_____. *Theology, History, and Culture: Major Unpublished Writings*. Edited by William Stacy Johnson. New Haven, CT: Yale University Press, 1996.

Niebuhr, Reinhold. *The Essential Reinhold Niebuhr: Selected Essays and Addresses*. Edited and introduced by Robert McAfee Brown. New Haven, CT: Yale University Press, 1986.

_____. *An Interpretation of Christian Ethics*. Cleveland, OH: Meridian Books, 1956.

_____. *Moral Man and Immoral Society*. New York: Charles Scribner's Sons, 1932.

_____. *The Nature and Destiny of Man: A Christian Interpretation*. 2 vols. New York: Charles Scribner's Sons, vol. 1: 1941, vol. 2: 1943. Reprint, 1964.

Nietzsche, Friedrich. *On the Genealogy of Morality*. Translated by Maudemarie Clark and Alan J. Swenson. Indianapolis, IN: Hackett, 1998.

Nugent, John C. *The Politics of Yahweh: John Howard Yoder, the Old Testament, and the People of God*. Eugene, OR: Cascade, 2011.

Nygren, Anders. "Christ and the Forces of Destruction,." *Scottish Journal of Theology* 4, no. 4 (1951): 363–75.

O'Donovan, Oliver. *Resurrection and Moral Order: An Outline for Evangelical Ethics*. 2nd ed. Grand Rapids, MI: Eerdmans, 1994.

Parler, Branson. *The Forest and the Trees: Engaging Paul Martens'*
The Heterodox Yoder. Indianapolis, IN: Englewood Review
of Books, 2012. http://erb.kingdomnow.org/wp-content/
uploads/2012/03/BParler-Forest.pdf. Accessed Apr. 1, 2012.
_____. "Spinning the Liturgical Turn: Why Yoder Is Not
an Ethicist." In *Radical Ecumenicity: Pursuing Unity and
Continuity after John Howard Yoder*, edited by John C.
Nugent, 173–92. Abilene, TX: Abilene Christian University
Press, 2010.

Plantinga, Cornelius Jr. *Engaging God's World: A Reformed
Vision of Faith, Learning, and Living.* Grand Rapids, MI:
Eerdmans, 2002.

Reimer, A. James. "Biblical and Systematic Theology: Two
Parallel but Related Activities." In *Mennonites and Classical
Theology: Dogmatic Foundations for Christian Ethics*, 372–
91. Kitchener, ON: Pandora Press / Scottdale, PA: Herald
Press, 2001.
_____. "'I came not to abolish the law but to fulfill it': A Positive
Theology of Law and Civil Institutions." In *A Mind Patient
and Untamed: Assessing John Howard Yoder's Contributions
to Theology, Ethics, and Peacemaking*, edited by Ben C.
Ollenburger and Gayle Gerber Koontz, 245–73. Telford, PA:
Cascadia Publishing House / Scottdale, PA: Herald Press, 2004.
_____. "Mennonites, Christ, and Culture: The Yoder Legacy."
Conrad Grebel Review 16 (Spring 1998): 5–15.
_____. "Theological Orthodoxy and Jewish Christianity: A
Personal Tribute to John Howard Yoder." In *The Wisdom of
the Cross: Essays in Honor of John Howard Yoder*, edited
by Stanley Hauerwas, Chris K. Huebner, Harry J. Huebner,
and Mark Thiessen Nation, 430–48. Grand Rapids, MI:
Eerdmans, 1999.

Rice, Daniel F., ed. *Reinhold Niebuhr Revisited: Engagements with
an American Original.* Grand Rapids, MI: Eerdmans, 2009.

Ringe, Sharon. *Jesus, Liberation, and the Biblical Jubilee: Images for
Ethics and Christology.* Philadelphia, PA: Fortress Press, 1985.

Rohls, Jan. *Reformed Confessions: Theology from Zurich to
Barmen.* Louisville, KY: Westminster John Knox Press, 1998.

Saiving, Valerie C. "The Human Situation: A Feminine View."
Journal of Religion 40, no. 2 (1960): 100–12.

Schlabach, Gerald W. "The Christian Witness in the Earthly City: John Howard Yoder as Augustinian Interlocutor." In *A Mind Patient and Untamed: Assessing John Howard Yoder's Contributions to Theology, Ethics, and Peacemaking*, edited by Ben C. Ollenburger and Gayle Gerber Koontz, 221–44. Telford, PA: Cascadia Publishing House / Scottdale, PA: Herald Press, 2004.

_____. *For the Joy Set Before Us: Augustine and Self-Denying Love*. Notre Dame, IN: Notre Dame University Press, 2001.

Shaffer, Thomas L. *Moral Memoranda from John Howard Yoder: Conversations on Law, Ethics and the Church between a Mennonite Theologian and a Hoosier Lawyer*. Eugene, OR: Wipf and Stock, 2002.

Slater, Jonathan. "Does Yoder throw the Christological baby out with the Constantinian bathwater?" Presented at the conference "Inheriting John Howard Yoder." Toronto Mennonite Theological Centre, May 25-26, 2007. http://grebel.uwaterloo.ca/tmtc/Slater-YoderProject.pdf. Accessed August 17, 2009.

Smith, James K. A. *Desiring the Kingdom: Worship, Worldview, and Cultural Formation*. Grand Rapids, MI: Baker, 2009.

Stassen, Glen H. "Concrete Christological Norms for Transformation." In *Authentic Transformation: A New Vision of Christ and Culture*. Nashville, TN: Abingdon, 1996.

Stassen, Glen H., and David P. Gushee. *Kingdom Ethics: Following Jesus in Everyday Context*. Downers Grove, IL: InterVarsity Press, 2003.

Stewart, James S. "On a Neglected Emphasis in New Testament Theology." *Scottish Journal of Theology* 4, no. 3 (1951): 292–301.

Stone, Ronald H. *Professor Reinhold Niebuhr: Mentor to the Twentieth Century*. Louisville, KY: Westminster/John Knox Press, 1992.

Stott, John. *God's New Society: The Message of Ephesians*. Downers Grove, IL: InterVarsity, 1979.

_____. "Letter to John H. Yoder." Oct. 27, 1976.

_____. "Letter to John H. Yoder." June 28, 1978.

_____. "Letter to John H. Yoder." Oct. 27, 1978.

Stout, Jeffrey. *Democracy and Tradition*. Princeton, NJ: Princeton University Press, 2004.

Thielicke, Helmut. *Theological Ethics. Vol. 1.* Edited by William H. Lazareth. Grand Rapids, MI: Eerdmans, 1979.

Trocmé, André. *Jesus and the Nonviolent Revolution.* Scottdale, PA: Herald Press, 1973.

Troeltsch, Ernst. *The Social Teaching of the Christian Churches.* 2 vols. 1931. Reprint, Louisville, KY: Westminster/John Knox Press, 1992.

Visser't Hooft, Willem A. *The Kingship of Christ.* New York: Harper, 1948.

Volf, Miroslav. "Creation, Eschaton, and Social Ethics." *Calvin Theological Journal* 30, no. 1 (1995): 130–43.

Walsh, Brian J., and J. Richard Middleton. *The Transforming Vision: Shaping a Christian Worldview.* Downers Grove, IL: InterVarsity Press, 1984.

Weaver, Alain Epp. "Missionary Christology: John Howard Yoder and the Creeds." *Mennonite Quarterly Review* 74, no. 3 (2000): 423–39.

Weaver, J. Denny. "The John Howard Yoder Legacy: Whither the Second Generation?" *Mennonite Quarterly Review* 77, no. 3 (2003): 451–71.

_____. *The Nonviolent Atonement.* Grand Rapids, MI: Eerdmans, 2001.

_____. "The United States Shape of Mennonite Theologizing: Some Preliminary Observations." *Mennonite Quarterly Review* 73, no. 3 (1999): 631–44.

Whiteley, D. E. H. *The Theology of St. Paul.* London: Blackwell, 1964.

Wilson, Stephen B. "Christ and Cult(ure): Some Preliminary Reflections on Liturgy and Life." *Liturgical Ministry* 12 (Fall 2003): 177–87.

Wittmer, Michael. "Analysis and Critique of 'Christ the Transformer of Culture.'" PhD diss., Calvin Theological Seminary, 2000.

_____. *Heaven Is a Place on Earth: Why Everything You Do Matters to God.* Grand Rapids, MI: Zondervan, 2004.

Wolters, Albert M. "Creation Order: A Historical Look at Our Heritage." In *An Ethos of Compassion and the Integrity of Creation*, edited by Brian J. Walsh, Hendrik Hart, and Robert E. VanderVennen, 33–48. Lanham, MD: University Press of America, 1995.

_____. *Creation Regained: Biblical Basics for a Reformational Worldview*. 2nd ed. Grand Rapids, MI: Eerdmans, 2005.

Wolterstorff, Nicholas. *Until Justice and Peace Embrace*. Grand Rapids, MI: Eerdmans, 1983.

Woodiwiss, Ashley. "John Howard Yoder and a Church-Centered Political Theory." In *Evangelicals in the Public Square: Four Formative Voices on Political Thought and Action*, 187–94. Grand Rapids, MI: Baker, 2006.

Wright, Nigel Goring. *Disavowing Constantine: Mission, Church, and Social Order in the Theologies of John Howard Yoder and Jürgen Moltmann*. Milton Keynes, UK: Paternoster Press, 2000.

Yoder, John Howard. "Armaments and Eschatology." *Studies in Christian Ethics* 1 (1988): 43–61.

_____. "As You Go: The Old Mission in a New Day." *Focal Pamphlet No. 5*. Scottdale, PA: Herald Press, 1961.

_____. "Biblical Roots of Liberation Theology." *Grail* (Sept 1985): 55–74.

_____. "Bluff or Revenge: The Watershed in Democratic Deterrence Awareness." In *Ethics in the Nuclear Age: Strategy, Religious Studies, and the Churches*, edited by Todd Whitmore, 79–92. Dallas, TX: Southern Methodist University Press, 1989.

_____. *Body Politics*. Nashville, TN: Discipleship Resources, 1992. Reprint, Scottdale, PA: Herald Press, 2001.

_____. "The Challenge of Peace: A Historic Peace Church Perspective." In *Peace in a Nuclear Age: The Bishops' Pastoral Letter in Perspective*, edited by Charles J. Reid, Jr., 273–90. Washington, D.C.: Catholic University of America Press, 1986.

_____. *Christian Attitudes to War, Peace, and Revolution*. Edited by Theodore J. Koontz and Andy Alexis-Baker. Grand Rapids, MI: Brazos Press, 2009.

_____. *The Christian Witness to the State*. Newton, KS: Faith and Life Press, 1964.

_____. "A Consistent Alternative View within the Just War Family." *Faith and Philosophy* 2, no. 2 (1985): 112–20.

_____. "Creation and Gospel." *Perspectives: A Journal of Reformed Thought* 3, no. 8 (1988): 8–10.

————. "The Credibility of Ecclesiastical Teaching on the Morality of War." In *Celebrating Peace*, edited by Leroy S. Rouner, 33–51. Notre Dame, IN: University of Notre Dame Press, 1990.

————. *Discipleship as Political Responsibility*. Translated by Timothy J. Geddert. Scottdale, PA: Herald Press, 2003.

————. *The End of Sacrifice: The Capital Punishment Writings of John Howard Yoder*, edited by John C. Nugent. Harrisonburg, VA: Herald Press, 2011.

————. "Ethics and Eschatology." *Ex Auditu* 6 (1990): 119–28.

————. "Exodus and Exile: The Two Faces of Liberation." *Cross Currents* (Fall 1973): 297–309.

————. "Exodus: Probing the Meaning of Liberation." *Sojourners* 5 (S 1976): 26–29.

————. "Feminist Theology Miscellany #1: Salvation through Mothering?" General Papers, Associated Mennonite Biblical Seminary Library, Elkhart, IN, 1988.

————. *For the Nations: Essays Public & Evangelical*. Grand Rapids, MI: Eerdmans, 1997.

————. *The Fullness of Christ: Paul's Revolutionary Vision of Universal Ministry*. Elgin, IL: Brethren Press, 1987.

————. *He Came Preaching Peace: Bible Lectures on Peacemaking*. Scottdale, PA: Herald Press, 1985.

————. "How H. Richard Niebuhr Reasoned: A Critique of Christ and Culture." In *Authentic Transformation: A New Vision of Christ and Culture*, 31–90. Nashville, TN: Abingdon, 1996.

————. "How Many Ways Are There to Think Morally about War?" *Journal of Law & Religion* 11, no. 1 (1994): 83–107.

————. Introduction to *Yahweh is a Warrior: The Theology of Warfare in Ancient Israel*, by Millard C. Lind. Scottdale, PA: Herald Press, 1980.

————. "Jesus and Power." *The Ecumenical Review* 25 (Oct. 1973): 447–54.

————. *The Jewish-Christian Schism Revisited*. Edited by Michael G. Cartwright & Peter Ochs. Grand Rapids, MI: Eerdmans, 2003.

————. "Just War Tradition: Is It Credible?" *Christian Century* (Mar. 13, 1991): 295–98.

_____. *Karl Barth and the Problem of War and Other Essays on Barth*. Edited by Mark Thiessen Nation. Eugene, OR: Cascade Books, 2003.

_____. "Letter to John Stott." Oct. 27, 1976. From the personal collection of Mark Thiessen Nation.

_____. "Letter to John Stott." June 28, 1978. From the personal collection of Mark Thiessen Nation.

_____. "Letter to John Stott." Dec. 7, 1978. From the personal collection of Mark Thiessen Nation.

_____. "A Light to the Nations." *Concern* 9 (Mar. 1961): 14–18.

_____. "The Lordship of Christ and the Power Struggle." In *The Lordship of Christ: Proceedings of the Seventh Mennonite World Conference*. Edited by Cornelius J. Dyck. Scottdale, PA: Mennonite Publishing House, 1963.

_____. "The Lord's Supper in Historical Perspective." Lecture presented at Assembly Mennonite Church, Goshen, IN. General Papers, Associated Mennonite Biblical Seminary Library, November 26, 1978.

_____. "Military Realities and Teaching the Laws of War." In *Theology, Politics, and Peace*, edited by Theodore Runyon, 176–80. Maryknoll, NY: Orbis Books, 1989.

_____. *Nevertheless: The Varieties and Shortcoming of Religious Pacifism*. Scottdale, PA: Herald Press, 1971.

_____. "Nuclear Arms in Christian Pacifist Perspective." In *War No More? Options in Nuclear Ethics*, edited by James W. Walters, 17–31. Minneapolis, MN: Fortress Press, 1989.

_____. "On Generating Alternative Paradigms." *Human Values and the Environment: Conference Proceedings 140* (Madison, WI: Wisconsin Academy of Sciences, Arts and Letters, 1992): 56–62.

_____. "On Not Being in Charge." In *War and Its Discontents: Pacifism and Quietism in the Abrahamic Traditions*, edited by J. Patout Burns, 74–90. Washington, D.C.: Georgetown University Press, 1996.

_____. *The Original Revolution*. Scottdale, PA: Herald Press, 1971.

_____. *The Politics of Jesus: Vicit Agnus Noster*, 2nd edition. Grand Rapids, MI: Eerdmans, 1994.

_____. *Preface to Theology: Christology and Theological Method.* Grand Rapids, MI: Brazos Press, 2002.

_____. *The Priestly Kingdom: Social Ethics as Gospel.* Notre Dame, IN: University of Notre Dame Press, 1984.

_____. "Primitivism in the Radical Reformation: Strengths and Weaknesses." In *The Primitive Church in the Modern World,* edited by Richard T. Hughes, 74–97. Urbana/Chicago: University of Illinois Press, 1995.

_____. "The Reception of the Just War Tradition by the Magisterial Reformers." *History of European Ideas* 9, no. 1 (1988): 1–23.

_____. "Regarding Nature." In *The Teachings of Modern Protestantism on Law, Politics, and Human Nature,* edited by John Witte Jr. and Frank S. Alexander, 427–30. New York: Columbia University Press, 2007.

_____. "Reformed versus Anabaptist Social Strategies: An Inadequate Typology." *Theological Students Fellowship Bulletin* (May–June 1985): 2–7.

_____. "Reinhold Niebuhr and Christian Pacifism." *Mennonite Quarterly Review* 29 (Apr. 1955): 101–17.

_____. *Reinhold Niebuhr and Christian Pacifism.* Church Peace Mission Pamphlet No. 6. Washington, D.C.: Church Peace Mission, 1966.

_____. *The Royal Priesthood: Essays Ecclesiological and Ecumenical.* Edited by Michael G. Cartwright. Scottdale, PA: Herald Press, 1998.

_____. *Revolutionary Christianity: The 1966 South American Lectures.* Edited by Paul Martens, Mark Thiessen Nation, and Myles Werntz. Eugene, OR: Cascade, 2012.

_____. "Surrender: A Moral Imperative." *The Review of Politics* 48 (Fall 1986): 576–95.

_____. "Texts That Serve or Texts That Summon? A Response to Michael Walzer." *Journal of Religious Ethics* 20 (Fall 1992): 229–34.

_____. "That Household We Are." Unpublished address at Believers' Church Conference, "Is There a Believers' Church Christology?" Bluffton College, Bluffton, Ohio, Oct. 1980.

_____. "Thinking Theologically from a Free-Church Perspective." In *Doing Theology in Today's World: Essays in*

Honor of Kenneth S. Kantzer, edited by John D. Woodbridge and Thomas Edward McComiskey, 251–66. Grand Rapids, MI: Zondervan, 1991.

————. *To Hear the Word.* 2nd ed. Eugene, OR: Cascade Books, 2010.

————. "'To Your Tents, O Israel': The Legacy of Israel's Experience with Holy War." *Studies in Religion* 18, no. 3 (1989): 345–62.

————. "The Two Kingdoms." *Christus Victor* 106 (Sept. 1959): 3–7.

————. "Walk and Word: The Alternatives to Methodologism." In *Theology Without Foundations: Religious Practice and the Future of Theological Truth*, edited by Stanley Hauerwas, Nancey Murphey, and Mark Nation. Nashville, TN: Abingdon Press, 1994.

————. "War as a Moral Problem in the Early Church: The Historian's Hermeneutical Assumptions." In *The Pacifist Impulse in Historical Perspective*, edited by Harvey L. Dyck, 90–110. Toronto: University of Toronto Press, 1996.

————. *The War of the Lamb: The Ethics of Nonviolence and Peacemaking.* Edited by Glen Stassen, Mark Thiessen Nation, and Matt Hamsher. Grand Rapids, MI: Brazos, 2009.

————. *What Would You Do?* Scottdale, PA: Herald Press, 1983.

————. *When War is Unjust: Being Honest in Just-War Thinking.* 2nd ed. Maryknoll, NY: Orbis Books, 1996.

Zimmerman, Earl. *Practicing the Politics of Jesus: The Origin and Significance of John Howard Yoder's Social Ethics.* Telford, PA: Cascadia Publishing House / Scottdale,PA: Herald Press, 2007.

Subject Index

Abel, 149–50, 170
Abimelech, 110
Abraham, 104–5, 110, 129, 140, 217, 231
Adam, 44, 54n, 120, 146, 148–50, 155, 170–71
agape, 55, 94, 95
Alexis-Baker, Andy, 181n
American Revolution, 175n
anxiety, 44–45, 47
Apostles' Creed, 75n, 126, 195
Arendt, Hannah, 213
Arianism/Arians, 32, 90, 98–99
Aristotle, 208
Arius, 31, 33, 90, 124
Artaxerxes, 110
Asa, 110
ascension, 50, 116–17, 196, 220
Augustine, 23, 45, 46, 47, 51–52, 58n, 60n, 66, 142n, 158n, 162n, 166, 177, 188n
and Reinhold Niebuhr 54–59

baptism, 216–19
Barth, Karl, 20n, 47, 65, 66, 134nn, 200
Barth, Markus, 134n, 137

Bartholomew, Craig, 40n
Basil the Great. *See* Cappadocians.
Begbie, Jeremy, 19
Belgic Confession, 52n, 177
Berkhof, Hendrik, 134nn, 137, 148
Bible,
and transformation of culture, 160
and tradition, 85–86
faithfulness to, 87–88
Biesecker-Mast, Gerald, 75n
binding and loosing, 211–14
bloodshed, 172
Bonaventure, 177
Bonhoeffer, Dietrich, 20n
Botha, P. W., 158
Brown, Robert McAfee, 149
Brunner, Emil, 18n, 19n, 27, 118
Budziszewski, J., 18n, 23–24, 133n, 162n, 169n

Cain, 54, 149–51, 170–71, 173, 177, 182, 190, 231
Caird, G. B., 134n
Calvin, John, 45, 46, 51–52, 66, 222

Scripture Index

The Author

Branson Parler is associate professor of theological studies at Kuyper College in Grand Rapids, Michigan, where he has taught since 2008. He teaches a variety of courses, including Introduction to Biblical Interpretation, Doctrine I and II, Introduction to Philosophy, Christ and Culture, and Creeds and Confessions. He has published articles and presented papers on the thought of several thinkers, including John Howard Yoder, Abraham Kuyper, and Augustine. Along with John Nugent and Jason Vance, he has developed an online searchable index of the works of John Howard Yoder (www.yoderindex.com). This massive undertaking has recently launched and works continue to be added.

Branson earned his BA at Cornerstone University (Grand Rapids), where he majored in pre-seminary studies and minored in ancient languages and English literature. He earned his master of arts from the Institute for Christian Studies in Toronto, Ontario, where he focused on theology and philosophy of religion. He earned his PhD from Calvin Theological Seminary in Grand Rapids. For three years before serving full time at Kuyper College, he taught at Calvin College and Cornerstone University.

Branson was born in Waterloo, Iowa, and raised Baptist. He is currently a member of Fourth Reformed Church in Grand Rapids. There he serves as an elder, helps with adult education and children's worship, and preaches on occasion. He and his wife, Sarah, have two beautiful daughters, Eliana and Ruby, and a son on the way.